DE VALERA'S CONSTITU

De Valera's Constitution and Ours

Edited by Brian Farrell

The Thomas Davis Lecture Series
General Editor: Michael Littleton

Published for Radio Telefís Éireann
by
GILL AND MACMILLAN

Published in Ireland for Radio Telefís Éireann by
Gill and Macmillan Ltd
Goldenbridge
Dublin 8
with associated companies in
Auckland, Delhi, Gaborone, Hamburg, Harare,
Hong Kong, Johannesburg, Kuala Lumpur, Lagos, London,
Manzini, Melbourne, Mexico City, Nairobi,
New York, Singapore, Tokyo

Print origination in Ireland by
Graphic Plan
Printed in England by Camelot Press, Southampton

British Library Cataloguing in Publication Data

De Valera's constitution and Ours. — (Thomas Davis Lectures).
1. Ireland—(Republic). Constitution
1. Farrell, Brian II. Series
342.417'02

ISBN 0—7171—1612—3

The Thomas Davis Lectures
General Editor: Michael Littleton
Every year since September 1953, Radio Telefís Éireann has been broadcasting half-hour lectures, named in honour of Thomas Davis. Inspired by one of his famous sayings, 'Educate that you may be free,' the aim of these lectures has been to provide in popular form what is best in Irish scholarship and the sciences.

Most of the lectures have been in series; many have been single broadcasts; some have been in English, some in Irish. In the time that has passed since they were initiated the lectures have dealt with many aspects and with many centuries of Irish social life, history, science and literature. The lecturers, distinguished for their special learning at home and abroad, have been drawn from many nations but mainly from Ireland.

Contents

Preface

TWO hundred years ago, the men who sat down to frame the American Constitution knew they were embarked on revolution. They sought a new way of understanding and ordering political reality. In place of an unthinking acceptance of traditional authority (so notably expressed in King Louis's phrase, '*L'état c'est moi*') they laboured to create a new kind of political system: 'a government of laws and not of men.' It was a radical experiment. Deliberately it turned its back on the past. It could not know what lay ahead.

There was nothing natural, casual or inevitable about the creation of the modern constitutional state. It was the product of the political equivalent of planned parenthood: a conscious decision to construct a new kind of political life. The original framers were practical men of affairs, in many ways conservative. The first modern constitution—like all the subsequent constitutions it has inspired—still rests on the few central elements they put together two centuries ago: the idea of government as an artefact, a contract; the notion of controlled government, a government that could be defined and therefore contained; the emphasis on the rule of law as security, certainty, guarantee.

The founding fathers summarised and encapsulated the happy certainty of Enlightenment man, the heavenly city of the eighteenth-century philosophers: a commitment to rational solutions for rationally analysed problems. But they were practical enough to warn that it was not enough to create a constitution; they had to construct and maintain a constitutional state, to go beyond solemnly inscribing high-sounding principles on paper and make them work in the disorganised, contrary and contradictory circumstances of everyday life. The Constitution was no more than a recipe, a method for achieving the promise of 'life, liberty and the pursuit of happiness'.

There was no guarantee that the great experiment would work. At one stage in the twentieth century it appeared to have failed. Yet Éamon de Valera chose that moment to frame a new Irish constitution.

In the middle 1930s, constitutional government was under siege throughout Europe. New ideologies, exotic titles, old suspicions had eroded the naïve expectation that the 'war to end all wars' had inaugurated a new era of reasonably free and reasonably effective self-government. De Valera's decision to fashion a new constitution for the fledgling Irish state was controversial and contentious. It was questionable if it could provide a secure basis on which to build a developing democratic state.

Over the next fifty years that Constitution, Bunreacht na hÉireann, has been amended, interpreted, re-shaped by judges, politicians, civil servants and the people. One man's document has become a political community's common charter—a living and effective guarantee of broadly based and expanding liberties. This volume is intended not merely to celebrate that achievement but to scrutinise and elucidate how it came about.

The title *De Valera's Constitution and Ours* was inadvertently, but happily, borrowed from an address by Mr Justice Brian Walsh to the Patrick McGill Summer School in Glenties, Co. Donegal. It is chosen to focus attention on the particular contribution of de Valera himself and on the ways in which his documentary framework has been translated into the living constitution of the Irish people. The essays are wide-ranging: the creation of Bunreacht na hÉireann is placed in its ideological, historical and political context; its major provisions and institutions are examined; the men and forces shaping its religious ethos are re-assessed in the light of the most recent drafting documents released from the de Valera archives in Killiney, Co. Dublin. Three senior judges, two former Attorneys General and a panel of distinguished academic lawyers consider such central themes as the status of Northern Ireland, property, the role of women, judicial review and amendment, the protection of fundamental rights, and the European Communities dimension. The volume is designed to present a multi-faceted but clear lay person's guide to the Constitution as it was created and as it functions today.

The essays in this book were originally delivered, in a shorter form, in a Thomas Davis Lecture series broadcast on RTE between January and April 1988. It is a pleasure to acknowledge once again the commitment, care and patience of Michael Littleton, Head of Features and Current Affairs, RTE Radio, who commissioned and produced this series and has done so much to maintain the proud tradition of the Thomas Davis Lectures. Deirdre Rennison of Gill and Macmillan has been both a spur and encouragement in achieving early publication. Séamas Ó Brógáin has been a meticulous and understanding copy-editor. Colleagues in the Department of Politics, University College, Dublin, have been generous with assistance, conspicuously Geraldine Meyler, without whom this work could not have been accomplished. I am grateful to all the contributors for their ready and cheerful co-operation, and to my family for their continuing tolerance.

Brian Farrell

PROFESSOR NICHOLAS CANNY

1. The Birth of the Modern Constitution

Nicholas Canny is Professor of Modern History at University College, Galway. He is the author of *The Elizabethan Conquest of Ireland: a Pattern Established, 1565-76* (1976), *The Upstart Earl: a Study of the Social and Mental World of Richard Boyle, First Earl of Cork* (1982), *From Reformation to Restoration: Ireland 1534-1660* (1987) and *Kingdom and Colony: Ireland in the Atlantic World, 1560-1800* (1988).

THE birth of the modern constitution can be dated precisely to the closing decades of the eighteenth century. This is so because the Enlightenment in both Europe and America then questioned the nature and origin of political authority, and discredited the notion that power should belong exclusively to hereditary monarchies and aristocracies. Then also political leaders were called upon to translate ideas into action and to provide a framework of government for the various new states that were brought into being through revolutionary action.

The most consequential of the several political revolts that occurred during the turbulent closing decades of the eighteenth century were those that produced the American and the French revolutionary regimes. Those who strove to direct these movements called upon people to reject existing political authority because it had transgressed what they identified as the fundamental rights and liberties of the individual; they sought to establish alternative governments that would have a particular responsibility to preserve these identified rights and liberties; and they attempted to define the powers of these new governments so that subjects would have no reason to fear that their freedom and property would be trespassed upon by the capricious actions of an unreasonable authority.

The initial concern of the early leaders of the movements that became both the American and French revolutions was therefore to curtail the power of government, and they first strove to do this by affirming the inalienable rights of the individual against all external authority. It soon became evident, however, that the existing political regimes would not accept any restraint upon their authority; and those who opposed their untrammelled authority had no choice but to proceed from resistance to revolution. This transition forced them to engage in actions that would effect the destruction of the existing regimes and the establishment in their place of a new political order. The act of destruction could clearly only be effected by force, but the positive aspect of the undertaking prompted certain fundamental questions that required an urgent response. The first of these related to the qualities that were appropriate to those who would be entrusted with executive authority, and this in turn raised the problems of how such rulers should be appointed, who should be involved in the selection process, and what controls were necessary to ensure that they remained answerable to those whose interests they purported to uphold.

This succession of problems pointed to the need for a compact between the rulers and the ruled within the new revolutionary order. No ready-made formula for such a compact was to hand in the eighteenth century, and neither was it evident how any such compact could be devised. What *was* evident however was that any form of government that was specifically brought into being to defend the liberties of the subjects over whom it ruled would only become legitimate once it had received the endorsement of those same subjects. Moreover, if all exigencies were to be provided for, and if a stable and enduring order was to be established, it was clear that nothing less than a constitution would serve as a basis for the democratic republics which, it was hoped, would displace the hereditary monarchies that were generally prevalent throughout the western world at the end of the eighteenth century.

All who then contemplated revolutionary action were aware of this reality. Few among them, however, were prepared to engage in the business of constitution-making, and most would have settled for half measures. This was so because many revolutionary leaders were quickly absorbed into the military effort that was necessary to secure the revolution. Even those who were not so distracted were reluctant to devote themselves to the task, because they were uncertain of how a constitution should be agreed upon, and even more so of what form it should take. Furthermore, all revolutionaries were keenly aware that previous efforts at establishing democratic republics had either proved abortive or been short-lived. Thus, for example, in 1787 as the delegates at the American Federal Convention sat down to business they were cautioned against innovation by Pierce Butler of South Carolina, on the grounds that 'a Cataline or a Cromwell [might] arise in this country as well as in others.'[1]

For these reasons the early revolutionaries in France, as in British North America, first sought to negotiate a constitutional compromise with their existing rulers in preference to striking out for the theoretically more desirable but less certain goal of a democratic republic. This also seemed reasonable as well as practical, because respected authors of the Enlightenment had expounded upon the virtues of the constitutional monarchy that had prevailed in Britain ever since the Glorious Revolution of 1688. French authors, notably Voltaire and Montesquieu, were the most insistent upon this point, but American revolutionary leaders also stood in admiration of the very government whose authority they were called upon to reject. Thus, in 1787, eleven years after the American Declaration of Independence, John Dickenson of Delaware could still praise the virtues of 'limited monarchy', and declared himself 'certain that equal blessings had never yet been derived from any [government] of the republican form.'[2] But however much the leaders of revolution might wish for a negotiated settlement, they were forced to recognise that none was available from their existing monarchs. Therefore they were left with no choice but to seek to establish a completely new political order, and in doing so they set an example that was to be closely studied, if not followed in detail, by all subsequent revolutionary leaders.

The American revolutionaries led the way when in 1776 they declared King George III a tyrant, 'unfit to be the ruler of a free people.' This, they contended, left them with no choice but 'to institute a new government, laying its foundations on such principles, and organising its powers in such form as to them shall seem most likely to effect their safety and happiness.'[3] Such an expression of intent made it incumbent upon those who signed the Declaration of Independence to make good their challenge by force of arms, but it also committed them to giving constitutional form to the new state that had been proclaimed. Little thought was given to this constitutional aspect of the American Revolution in its early stages, and the leaders satisfied themselves with declaring the existing colonial assemblies in each of the thirteen colonies to be the legislative bodies for the now independent thirteen states. These assemblies had traditionally been chosen by a broadly based electorate, which usually included most free adult males, and the delegates were elected from small, intimate constituencies and for short terms of office. This populist aspect of government was continued under the new revolutionary regimes, and the executive and judicial authorities in each of the thirteen states ultimately owed their appointments to the popularly elected assemblies. The governments of each of the thirteen states, except Pennsylvania, did have a second parliamentary chamber, known as the Senate, but these were not truly independent houses and did not enjoy the power of rejecting decisions of the Houses of Representatives. The legislatures of the various states were therefore the dominant element of government in all of the thirteen states, and it was these legislatures that nominated individuals to uphold their interests in the Confederate Congress, which dealt with business of national importance. These nominees were allowed little freedom of action in Congress, because they were required to report back to their state governments for guidance in all controversial matters.

This new form of government proved effective at both state and national levels while the Revolutionary War was in progress, and the Confederate government further enhanced its reputation by negotiating a favourable peace treaty. Thereafter, however, the constitution that had been adopted was subjected to intense criticism from within the United States, and was faulted principally on the grounds that it had been devised in reaction to the perceived corruption of British rule rather than in conformity with any political principles. As a consequence, it was argued, insufficient autonomy had been given to the executive branch of government at both state and national level, while uncritical concern had been shown to restoring power to the people. The result, it was contended, was an executive that was incapable of decisive action or quick decision, because the constitution dictated that those who participated in the Confederate Congress should always be delegates rather than representatives of their local state legislatures. What had emerged, it was argued, was a government which, although democratic, fell short of being republican, because the obligations that were placed upon elected members to uphold the interests of their particular communities did not leave them sufficient scope to advance the common good—the *res publica*.

Those who advanced this critique of the first revolutionary government included spokesmen of the merchant communities on the east coast of the United States, where a deep-seated fear existed of the supposed levelling ambitions of the poorer citizens of the new nation. To these were added some senior statesmen who genuinely believed that the persistent pursuit of local interests would result in the dismemberment of the United States into several sections; while those who had served on diplomatic missions were concerned over the proven indecision of the American government. The lobbying of these disparate elements did much to promote the belief that there was need for a fundamental reform of the United States constitution. Even more persistent on this point were spokesmen for the larger states, who advanced a fundamental objection to the Articles of Confederation, under which the thirteen states were bound together to form a single government, because these articles provided for equal representation in Congress for each of the thirteen states regardless of size, population, or resources. It was patently unjust, asserted a succession of statesmen from Virginia, that their state, which commanded a quarter of the wealth and population of the United States, should be forced to accept equal representation in Congress with such poor states as New Jersey and Delaware. Representation in Congress, they contended, should be in proportion to the free population of the individual states; and it was these Virginians who worked most consistently for the convening in 1787 of a special Federal Convention that was empowered by Congress to make recommendations for a revision of the constitution of the United States.

In the event, this body recommended the adoption of a completely new national constitution rather than a revision of the existing one. But while this was the eventual outcome of the convention, there seemed little hope at the outset that the representatives of the thirteen states who participated in the convention would be able to agree on any set of recommendations. However, while divided over several particular issues, the members of the convention were agreed upon certain general propositions, and the constitution that was eventually devised and recommended to the citizens of the United States for their ratification was organised around these fundamental constitutional principles.

The fundamental proposition that united all members of the Convention was that political power derived from the people, and whatever form of government was eventually agreed among themselves would have to be put before the citizens of the thirteen states for their approval. Recognition of this fact meant that the delegates believed themselves to be limited in their recommendations to those modes of government that were likely to meet with popular approval. This meant that, despite the frequent reservations that were voiced over the populist mode of government that existed at the state level, the delegates at the Convention refrained from any recommendations in relation to state government, because they were fully aware of the popular attachment to existing institutions. But while reconciled to accepting this existing arrangement, the delegates at the Federal Convention—or certainly the radicals among them—were concerned that the national government should be as free as possible from the control of the state governments.

When advancing proposals for a strengthening of government at the national level, the delegates were also conscious of the need for a system of checks and balances that would ensure that the three different elements of the national government—the legislature, the executive, and the judiciary—would each remain independent of the other and that no one element would become corrupted by power. This concern over corruption derived from the second assumption shared by the members of the Convention, that it was a lust for power that induced people to become involved in politics. Such avarice, it was believed, if uncontrolled would lead inevitably either to tyranny or chaos. However, it was also believed that avarice could be harnessed to serve beneficial ends if it was contained within a strict frame of constitutional government.

It was with this purpose in mind that the members of the Constitutional Convention of 1787 set to their task. They differed from their predecessors of 1776 only in believing that the representative element of government was as liable as the executive to become corrupted by power. So convinced were they of this that some members of the Convention recommended that citizenship in a republic should be confined to substantial property-owners, because only they would enjoy the financial independence that would enable them to place the public good above their selfish interests. However, while accepting the validity of this proposition, most members of the Convention did not think it practical to deprive people who were already enfranchised of the vote, and most especially not if they had fought for the achievement of American independence. For this reason it was thought proper to accord citizenship to all free adult males within the United States. This, it was agreed, would not necessarily prove detrimental to the public good, because people of limited means, and even recent immigrants, could advance themselves in a country that provided unparalleled opportunity for the industrious.

Because the drafters of the United States Constitution were liberal in the matter of the franchise, they had to be even more careful when it came to introducing checks and balances into the Constitution. They were particularly concerned to ensure that private property, which was considered essential to human happiness, should not be subverted by the popular will. To this end they saw the need to have a bicameral legislature. In this, the upper house or Senate would have power to amend all legislation and to initiate bills, with the exception of financial bills. These latter were to originate in the House of Representatives, which was to be elected directly by the people of the several states in proportion to their population, and whose members were to hold office for two years. The senators (two from each state) were to be appointed by the legislatures of the several states, rather than directly by the people, and they were to hold office for six years. This longer term of office was intended to make senators more independent from popular pressure than the members of the House of Representatives. For this reason the Senate was the only house of Congress that would have a role in the conduct of foreign policy and in the appointment or dismissal of executive and judicial officers. But while the Senate was given a checking role in such matters, the initiative rested with the executive branch of government.

The principal executive officer was designated President of the United States, and he would owe his appointment neither to the houses of Congress nor to the people but to a group of electors chosen by the legislatures of the several states in proportion to their populations. To this extent the President was to be as independent of the legislative branch of government as ever any monarch had been, except that he could be removed from office by the Senate for serious offence and that he was not empowered to dismiss those he had appointed as judges to the Supreme Court. These judges were to hold office for life 'during good behaviour', and it was the Senate and not the President who would determine their guilt if charges of misdemeanour were brought against any of them. This safeguard provided an assurance that the judiciary would be independent of both executive and legislature, and the Supreme Court was to be the final arbiter in the event of any dispute occurring between the different branches of government.

The most striking feature of the United States Constitution was that it achieved a strict separation of powers between the legislative, executive and judicial branches of government, with a view to preventing any one of the three elements from gaining a monopoly of power. The result was a complex and slow-moving system of government, but the ambition of its designers was to devise a constitution that would be republican as well as democratic.

While the combined delegates made this claim for the constitution they had devised, they decided against putting it directly to the citizens of the United States for their approval. Instead, they suggested that special ratifying conventions should be held in the several states and that the representatives of the people elected to these ratifying conventions should be empowered to accept or reject the Constitution. These conventions were held in each of the thirteen states, and the discussion that took place at them was held in public. Desperate efforts were made in the weeks leading up to these ratifying conventions to influence public opinion for or against the Constitution, and extensive use was made of pamphleteering on both sides. The general contention on the opposition side was that the proposed scheme of government was excessively élitist and would convert what had been a democratic government into a monarchic or an aristocratic form. This was strongly denied by the defenders of the Constitution, but they were forced to concede the necessity of a Bill of Rights as an assurance of the liberties of the individual against aggressive action by the government. Even in this amended form the Constitution won popular approval with only a narrow majority, and the charge that the government provided for under the Constitution was too remote from the people continued to be a live issue during succeeding generations.

But while opinion was divided over the merits of the new Constitution for the United States, the members of the Federal Convention had come forward with a near-unanimous proposal, and the differences that subsequently emerged were resolved without resort to violence. The key to the first of these achievements was that the proceedings of the Federal Convention in Philadelphia were held in strict secrecy; and while some of the fifty-five members who participated in the proceedings saw the need to withdraw, nobody broke the code of silence and divulged what was taking place behind closed doors. This meant that the delegates could enter into compromises that would hasten agreement without encountering an immediate clamour from the groups whose interests they were expected to uphold. Then, when the document was completed, the majority of delegates decided to give it their full support when bringing it before the ratifying conventions in their individual states. And we can take it that the Constitution was ratified and came into effect only because it enjoyed the enthusiastic support of such outstanding statesmen as George Washington, James Madison, and Benjamin Franklin.

While these points are apparent to those of us who have the benefit of hindsight, they were less evident to contemporaries. For them the most impressive aspect of the creation of a new American constitution was the national debate associated with the ratification of the Constitution. It was this aspect of the proceedings that particularly captured the imagination of French politicians, who grappled with the problem of how to improve upon their own constitution just as ratifying conventions were in progress throughout the United States. As a consequence, the expectation was created in France that constitutional debate there should also be conducted in public and with the agreement of a broad spectrum of the population.

This expectation was to make it more difficult for politicians in France to arrive at a consensus over how the country should be governed. Even without this complicating factor, consensus was more difficult to attain in France, because social divisions were altogether more rigid there than in America and the representatives of each social group were so jealous of their privileges and possessions that they would place little trust in those above or below them on the social scale.

This reality had already become evident in May 1789 when the Estates General of France, which had been convened by Louis XVI to consider the financial difficulties of the government, met for the first time. The essential problem of the government was that its tax base was too narrow, because the property of both the church and the nobility in France was exempt from tax. The nobles made it clear from the start of the meeting of the Estates General that they had no intention of surrendering this exemption, and it was the further insistence of the nobility that all votes of the Estates General should be taken by Estates rather than by poll that provoked the representatives of the Third Estate to withdraw completely on 12 June 1789. Then they declared themselves to be a National Assembly, which individual members of the nobility and clergy were welcome to join. This essential act of defiance marks the beginning of the French Revolution, as the 648 elected members of the Third Estate declared themselves to be representatives of the nation and resolved never to disband 'until the Constitution of the kingdom is laid and established on secure foundations.'[4]

From the outset, therefore, the revolutionaries in France, like their counterparts in America, recognised that this revolution would not be complete until a new political order had been defined in constitutional terms. The self-proclaimed National Assembly, which now styled itself a Constituent Assembly, and which continued to meet until it dissolved itself on 30 September 1891, undertook this task. Its most tangible accomplishments were the Declaration of the Rights of Man and the Citizen of 26 August 1789;[5] the effective nationalisation of the personnel and property of the Catholic Church in France; and the creation of a decentralised system of administration. Under this latter arrangement the country was divided into eighty-three *départements*, and it was declared' that popularly elected officials in each of these administrative units would have the responsibility to put the decrees of the Constituent Assembly into effect.

The Assembly experienced no difficulty over deciding on the question of local representation, and the decision to proclaim the civil rights of all Frenchmen was also a unanimous one. Deciding upon who should enjoy political rights at the national level proved to be more contentious, however, because the vast majority of the members of the Constituent Assembly came from relatively prosperous backgrounds and could not countenance a situation whereby all French males, regardless of wealth or education, should enjoy equal political rights at the national level. Neither were they attracted by the solution that had been devised in the United States of providing for a senate that would function as a restraining influence upon a more popularly elected legislative house, because a senate that would enjoy powers of veto was associated in the minds of Frenchmen with the aristocracy whose constitutional role they had just rejected. Instead, the French Constituent Assembly opted for a distinction between 'active' and 'passive' citizens, which would be determined by property qualifications. All citizens were to continue to participate in local elections within the *départements*, but only active citizens would participate in the choice of electors for the purposes of national elections. These electors were to be men of considerable means, and they in turn would elect deputies to a National Assembly from among an even more wealthy group of qualified candidates.[6]

Such restriction based on property qualification was consistent with the clause in the Declaration of the Rights of Man and the Citizen that held that while 'men were born free and equal in rights', distinction could still be founded on 'common utility'. To recommend such a process of filtration for the election of popular representatives to a National Assembly was not, however, politic for a body so large and diverse in representation (648 members, as opposed to 55 members who attended the Federal Convention in the United States) and that conducted its proceedings in public. The suggested limitation of political power at the national level was opposed within the Assembly by Maximilien de Robespierre, who became the advocate of universal male suffrage. His hand was greatly strengthened by the regular intrusions of the Paris mob into the proceedings of the Constituent Assembly, first when it convened at Versailles and later when the Convention had been compelled by the mob to transfer its proceedings to the city of Paris itself.

The issue of restricting political power at the national level was only one of the two major issues that complicated the work of the French Constituent Assembly. The other vexing problem related to the appointment of an executive; and the decision of the Assembly to entrust King Louis XVI with executive authority gave rise to heated debate in the popular press that now emerged in Paris. This lack of unanimity meant that the Legislative Assembly elected in the autumn of 1791 under the terms of this first French revolutionary constitution was controversial from the beginning. Then, in August 1792, when it had become evident that the king was really in alliance with the exiled aristocrats and foreign monarchs who were aiming to end the revolutionary regime through military invasion, this first French experiment at constitutional government was in effect brought to an end by the Paris mob.

At this juncture, when a massive war effort was required to save the revolution, the French monarchy was brought to a summary end with the execution of Louis XVI on a charge of treason. This necessitated a fresh start at constitution-making, and responsibility for this was entrusted to a National Convention that was elected on universal male suffrage. This Convention, or at least that group within it that was led by Robespierre, moved to further democratise French society by enforcing the equal division of inheritances among male heirs, with a view to creating greater equality of wealth. The Convention also created a French national conscript army, the *levée en masse*, that essentially saved the revolution by the defeats it inflicted on the opposing armies of the united monarchies of Europe. The Convention also purported to save the revolution from its enemies within France (and even within the Convention itself) by striking to right and left during the Terror of 1793-4 against those it believed to be opposed to its objectives. All of these very real achievements were, however, attained extraconstitutionally by a self-appointed Committee of Public Safety and under pressure from elements of the Paris mob.

The Convention also devoted itself to devising a fresh national constitution for France. However, the fact that it produced two quite clearly contrasting constitutions, and the further fact that neither one ever came fully into operation, is an indication both of the conflicting views that existed within that assembly of 780 men and of the difference of opinion that existed between the Convention and the various pressure groups in Paris that sought to influence its decisions.

The overwhelming majority of the members of the National Convention were, like the members of two earlier bodies, the Constituent Assembly and the Legislative Assembly, men of property. These were committed to the revolution that had been accomplished in 1789, but they were fearful of the demands of the poor, and they wished to contain the revolution within constitutional limits. However, the crisis that emerged during the years 1792–4 created the situation whereby the Convention became a prisoner of its more radical members, and it devised in 1793 the highly populist constitution known as the Constitution of the Year I.[7] This document included a detailed statement of political rights, it conceded the vote to all adult men, and it devised machinery for the formulation of policy by direct popular initiative and by referendum. Despite the fact that this constitution was ratified by the electorate at large, it was never brought into effect by the National Convention, on the pretext that the time was not appropriate for conducting elections. Instead, as was noted, the members of the Convention had resort to the Committee of Public Safety to conduct the business of government, but they quickly dispensed with the services of this extreme body once the crisis was past and once Robespierre, the dominant personality on the Committee of Public Safety, had been executed on the direction of the Convention on 25 July 1794.

Thereafter the National Convention began work on a new constitution, and eventually in 1795 adopted the Constitution of the Year III.[8] This document, like its predecessors, allowed for universal male suffrage, but the voters were empowered only to select electors who in turn would choose deputies from the more wealthy elements of the population. The legislature under this constitution was to be divided into two chambers and these would in turn elect an executive of five 'directors'. Elections under this new constitution were held in 1795 and again in 1797, and a Directory was duly established. The directors encountered difficulty in steering the moderate course that they preferred, and had to resort increasingly to the generals of the revolutionary army to subdue the excesses of the extremists to both left and right. Their position was rendered even more difficult when the election of 1797 produced a legislature that was strongly royalist in composition. The result was an impasse between legislature and executive, and the paralysis in government was only resolved in

1799 when the Directory decided to abandon constitutional rule and called upon General Napoleon Bonaparte to become the saviour of the revolution.

This development marked the failure of the revolutionaries in France to create a democratic republic in place of the monarchy they had overthrown. But while the members of the Directory failed to provide France with an enduring constitution, they did provide constitutional governments to the series of republics, modelled on revolutionary France, that were then established in northern Italy, in the Rhineland area of Germany, and in Belgium and the Netherlands. This export of the French revolution, while temporary in the short term proved most potent in the long term, because it popularised the idea that each national group in Europe was entitled to separate political status as a constitutional republic. This concept served to challenge and discredit all the existing multinational states, and was one reason why monarchs turned vehemently against the French Revolution and the concepts associated with it.

Another reason why conservatives throughout Europe were opposed to the revolution in France was that it served to politicise the entire adult male population in the country. Even the large bulk of the revolutionary leaders were suspicious of this development, but their repeated efforts to curtail the franchise proved abortive, and the most enduring legacy of the French Revolution was the popular control over local affairs that was established within the newly constituted *départements*. This proved to be irreversible, and can be likened to the populist control over state government that was created by the American Revolution in its early phases.

Such parallels were not lost on contemporaries, and many of them recognised that they had lived through a revolutionary continuum that stretched from 1776 to 1799 and that had produced a sequence of experiments in constitutional government on both sides of the Atlantic. The problem that had confronted all these experiments was how to reconcile broadly based democratic government with a concern for the public good. Only the Americans succeeded in this attempt at reconciliation, while the French provided a practical demonstration of the chaos that could ensue when revolutionary leaders could not arrive at a consensus among themselves. However, while radicals as well as conservatives looked askance at the tumult that was associated with the French Revolution they were also impressed with the powerful appeal that the Declaration of the Rights of Man held for middle-class people, who were previously denied the opportunity to enjoy political influence commensurate with their wealth and service to the community. This meant that the demand for an extension of political rights was not dissipated because of the initial failure of the French Revolution; and the more pragmatic of Europe's conservative leaders saw the need gradually to extend political rights to the disfranchised if they were to prevent revolution within their several jurisdictions. Thus were created constitutional monarchies if not democratic republics.

The more astute of the conservative leaders in nineteenth and twentieth-century Europe also took cognisance of the powerful military force that had been created by the French Revolution. The prodigious military success of the French revolutionary armies brought rulers to realise that they could not hope to enjoy the same commitment from their subjects in time of war unless they too elevated them to the status of citizens. There were therefore positive as well as negative reasons why those who had first opposed the principles of the rights of man came, over the course of time, to see merit in constitutional government. A constitution, after all, established limits to freedom while guaranteeing the freedom of the individual from oppression by the state. To this extent a constitution could be regarded as an instrument of order and stability as much as it was a declaration of revolutionary intent. There was every reason, therefore, why the leaders of all new states in Europe should wish to fashion a constitution to meet their particular needs, and they had plenty of examples available from these first efforts at constitution-making that were attempted at the close of the eighteenth century.

NOTES

1. The remark was made by Pierce Butler to the members of the Federal Convention on 4 June 1787. Adrienne Koch (ed.), *Notes of Debates in the Federal Convention of 1787 Reported by James Madison*, Athens, Ohio, 1984, 63.
2. Remark made by John Dickenson on 2 June 1787. *Notes of Debates*, 56-7.
3. *The American Declaration of Independence*, edition prepared by US Information Service, Washington, DC, 1976, 2, 5.
4. The Tennis Court Oath, 20 June 1789, in John Hall Steward (ed.), *A Documentary Survey of the French Revolution*, New York 1965, 88.
5. Declaration of the Rights of Man and Citizen, 27 August 1789, in *A Documentary Survey*, 113.
6. Decree Establishing Municipalities, 14 December 1789, and Decree Establishing Electoral and Administrative Assemblies, 22 December 1789, in *A Documentary Survey*, 120-41; Decree Relative to the Convocation of the Next Legislature, 28 May 1791, in *A Documentary Survey*, 225-62.
7. The Constitution of 1793 in *A Documentary Survey*, 454-68.
8. The Constitution of the Year III in *A Documentary Survey*, 571-612.

The documentary material relating to the American Federal Convention of 1787 is presented in Max Farrand (ed.), *Records of the Federal Convention of 1787*, 4 vols., New Haven, Conn.: Yale University Press 1937. The most reliable record of events by a contemporary is that of James Madison, in Adrienne Koch (ed.), *Notes of Debates in the Federal Convention of 1787 Reported by James Madison*, paperback edition, Athens, Ohio: Ohio University Press 1984. The debate concerning the ratification of the Constitution can be followed in Clinton Rossiter (ed.), *The Federalist Papers: Hamilton, Madison, Jay*, Mentor paperback edition, New York 1961 and Herbert J. Storing (ed.), *The Anti-Federalist: Writings by the Opponents of the Constitution*, paperback edition, Chicago: University of Chicago Press 1985. The most comprehensive study of this episode of American history is Gordon S. Wood, *The Creation of the American Republic, 1776-1787*, Norton paperback edition, New York 1972.

Most recent work on the French Revolution has concentrated on the social aspects of that movement. The constitutional dimension is best treated in R. R. Palmer, *Age of the Democratic Revolution*, 2 vols., Princeton University Press 1964. See also Denis Woronoff, *The Thermidorean Regime and the Directory, 1794-99*, paperback edition, Cambridge University Press 1984. The documentary record can be pursued in John Hall Steward (ed.), *A Documentary Survey of the French Revolution*, New York: Macmillan 1965. Extracts from a broader range of contemporary documents can be found in John Hardman (ed.), *The French Revolution: the Fall of the Ancien Régime to the Thermidorian Reaction, 1785-95*, paperback edition, London: Arnold, Documents of Modern History, 1981.

PROFESSOR BRIAN FARRELL

2. From First Dáil through Irish Free State

Brian Farrell is Associate Professor of Government and Political Science at University College, Dublin. He is the author of *The Founding of Dáil Éireann* (1971), *Chairman or Chief?: the Role of Taoiseach in Irish Government* (1971) and *Seán Lemass* (1983), and contributing editor to two earlier Thomas Davis series, *The Parliamentary Tradition* (1973) and *Communications and Community* (1984). He is also senior presenter on RTE television current affairs programmes.

IN 1938 Ireland was still getting used to its brand-new constitution. De Valera's Bunreacht was not the first effort to provide a fundamental law for the Irish state. It replaced the Constitution of the Irish Free State, and that, in turn, replaced the often-forgotten Constitution of Dáil Éireann drafted in 1919. It is difficult to understand the present Constitution, and impossible to assess the balance of continuity and innovation in its provisions, without some examination of these earlier constitutions. On the one hand, they illustrate the strength of an enduring constitutional tradition within which de Valera framed his Bunreacht; on the other, they provide a comparison against which to measure his contribution to Irish constitution-making.

Ireland in the early twentieth century was already well set along the road of constitutional development.[1] Within the United Kingdom, of which it was still part, a recognisable—if uniquely traditionalist—modern democratic state was emerging; the old claims of divine right of kings and the pretensions of the Lords were well and truly becoming subordinated to the will of elected representatives of the people. Elections and parties were elbowing aside older sources of parliamentary sovereignty.[2] Ireland, through its representatives at Westminster, played an important part in that process; it also benefited from a democratisation that gave the vote to a wider public and that pointed up the anomaly of an Irish population subject to an alien and imposed administration.

Home Rule, vigorously championed by the Irish Parliamentary Party at Westminster, represented one solution to that dilemma. It also, of course, provoked a militant reaction, especially among Northern Unionists, which was an augury of troubles ahead for Irish constitutional development.[3] But the Irish Parliamentary Party was not alone in planning a new constitutional future for Ireland.

Arthur Griffith's original Sinn Féin proposed, as a variant, the restoration of the 'constitution of 1782', the re-creation of Irish legislative independence historically enshrined in Grattan's Parliament.[4] In brief, his proposal was to apply the Hungarian solution, which had been used to resolve a similar tension between Austria and Hungary: a dual monarchy symbolically representing the common interests of the people of these two islands, but an independent Irish parliament in which popularly elected representatives would control the government. Many saw Griffith's ground-plan as an illusion, set against the promise of immediate Home Rule.

The militant minority involved in Irish-Ireland were impatient with any solution short of complete independence; symbolically their case was asserted in the Easter Rising of 1916, which instituted a Provisional Government to 'administer the civil and military affairs of the Republic in trust for the people,' pending 'the establishment of a permanent National Government, representative of the whole people of Ireland, and elected by the suffrages of all her men and women.'[5] It may be objected that this language of the Proclamation is the rhetoric of military coups the world over: a direct intervention claiming to create or restore a proper order, reform existing maladministration, and the promise to restore 'normal democracy', including elections. But the 1916 leaders were not the military élite of a professional, established army: they proposed a specifically advanced franchise, embracing women as well as men; their attempt to destroy one administration and simultaneously substitute a new one became a model for what followed after. In reality their political ideas reflected as much the socialisation effects of Sinn Féin as the inherited militant tradition of Fenianism.

The important point to register is that all strands of Irish nationalist opinion, from the most radical militants of 1916, through the ranks of Griffith's Sinn Féin to the widely diffused supporters of the Irish Parliamentary Party and Home Rule, were inherently constitutionalists.

That was scarcely surprising. Constitution-making was in the air in the turbulent world of early twentieth-century Europe. Great empires crumbled and cracked apart during the First World War, and everywhere the ideology of popular democracy created experiments in writing new rule-books for government. What was surprising was that the Irish constitution-makers—then and later—remained remarkably conservative in their choice of models. When it came to the issue of framing institutional arrangements for government and providing safeguards for citizens, the rhetoric of political platforms and ritual denunciation of centuries of British persecution was quickly dropped. They were not adventurous in setting up new structures nor in defining new rights. They adopted the model they knew best: a model that was familiar, which they had helped to shape. They built on existing foundations a replica of the British parliamentary-based cabinet system of government.

In the troubled months that followed the failure of the 1916 Rising, the major preoccupation of those thrust into leadership was with political organisation. They were determined to challenge the claim of the Irish Parliamentary Party to speak for the Irish people. To do so, they formed a new party, the Second Sinn Féin.[6] It embraced a wide range of opinion, interest and ideology into a single umbrella organisation that could claim widespread popular support and become the majority party. The general election of 1918 provided the opportunity to achieve its objectives.

This was an election to the United Kingdom parliament. Because of the war, there had not been a general election since

1910. In the meantime a new Representation of the People Act created, for practical purposes, a new electorate: property qualifications were removed, all adult males and some females over thirty became eligible to vote, and the size of the register was trebled. In Ireland, Sinn Féin offered itself on a policy of withdrawal from Westminster and promised to establish an independent Irish parliament. The result was decisive; the *Freeman's Journal* editorialised: 'The meaning of the Irish vote is clear as it is emphatic. More than two-thirds of the electors throughout nationalist Ireland have endorsed the Sinn Fein programme.'[7]

Swept to power, with many of its prominent leaders (including de Valera and Griffith) in jail, it was left to the twenty-nine newly elected members still at liberty to organise matters.

A secret session of these representatives met on 7 January 1919 and appointed a group (described, in parliamentary parlance, as a 'Select Committee') to draw up standing orders and a constitution.[8] The members were: George Gavan Duffy, J. O'Mara, Seán T. Ó Ceallaigh, E. J. Duggan, Piaras Béaslaoi, and Eoin MacNeill. They were a heavyweight team of experienced and qualified men, and obviously set to work immediately. Among documents seized in a raid on Sinn Féin headquarters four days later was a document described in an *Irish Times* report as 'Draft of the Constitution of the Dail Eriann [*sic*] (Irish Constituent Assembly)'. Despite such interruptions, preparations went ahead, and when the First Dáil met for the first time in the Mansion House, Dublin, on 21 January 1919 it was presented with a quartet of documents: a Declaration of Independence, a Message to the Free Nations of the World, the Constitution, and the Democratic Programme.

They were all documents of a constitutional character. Most attention has been paid to the Democratic Programme, a statement of advanced social and economic policy often quoted as evidence of the revolutionary intentions of the First Dáil. It was, in fact, a Labour Party manifesto, which did not represent Sinn Féin ideology, had been accepted for essentially propagandist reasons, and was never implemented.

The Constitution itself is of more enduring significance. In five short, simple articles it sketched the provisional scheme of government for the embryonic Irish state. It was to remain the basic law of that emerging state until the adoption of the Irish Free State Constitution. It was, to adapt Bagehot's famous phrase, a buckle which fastened, a hyphen that joined, the institutions of the new Irish state to the structures, processes and values of the British system. In particular it enshrined the British cabinet model in the central, strategic location it has continued to hold in the Irish political system down to our own day.

Briefly, the Constitution declared that 'all legislative powers shall be vested in Dáil Éireann'; that all executive powers were vested in a Ministry composed of Dáil Deputies approved of, and dismissible by, the Dáil; that the Ministry was financially responsible to the Dáil; and that this provisional Constitution could be altered by vote of the Dáil. Fundamentally, then, it was—in the words of Hugh Kennedy, the first Free State Attorney General and Chief Justice—founded on the great principle 'that all legislative, executive, administrative and judicial power had its source in and was derived from the sovereign people.'[9]

Kennedy suggested that this emphasis on the sovereign people was 'a return, in a sense, to the idea behind the old Irish state.' But this is to ignore the representative emphasis in article 1; the new Ireland was not committing itself to some restored system of primitive direct democracy. On the contrary, it was copying and codifying (admittedly in a simplified way) the three fundamental principles of British constitutional convention: parliamentary sovereignty, untrammelled by any reference to any higher law; a cabinet sustained by its parliamentary support; and a constitution as flexible as ordinary statute law.

The Dáil Constitution, the first Irish twentieth-century constitution, the seed-bed in which de Valera was to root Bunreacht na hÉireann, is a significant document in Irish political development. It reflects the timidity of the 'Irish revolution', confirms the innate conservatism of its leaders, is an enduring monument to the anglicisation of Irish political institutions. There is here none of the crusading fervour, radical optimism, creative experimentation of the American founding fathers. Efforts to moderate the entrenched cabinet model and provide for greater legislative involvement by ordinary deputies through a committee system similar to the US Congress were twice raised. The Acting President, Arthur Griffith, described the scheme as 'a complete revolution of the Constitution of Dáil Éireann. It meant taking away the responsibility of the Ministers and placing it in the hands of Committees.'[10] The same sentiments were echoed by Eoin MacNeill: it was 'a very revolutionary proposal' and he 'did not believe that the country would approve of it.'

The Dáil took the hint. Similarly the actual legislation proclaimed in the decrees of the First and Second Dálaí, between 1919 and 1922, was modest and moderate.[11] The emphasis throughout was on continuity and, at most, incremental change.

A similar caution and restraint is evident in the next Irish exercise in constitution-making. This arose in January 1922, after the Dáil—by a narrow vote—accepted the Treaty. De Valera resigned; Griffith was elected head of the Dáil Government, and Collins head of the Provisional Government established under the terms of the Treaty. In fact, although the formal existence of two governments was contentious and confusing, their personnel was virtually identical and they met as a single body. One of their very first decisions was to establish a committee to draft a constitution for the new Irish state.[12] A distinguished, experienced, professional group was chosen. It included three future Supreme Court judges: Hugh Kennedy, James Murnaghan, and John O'Byrne; James McNeill, a future representative in London and future Governor-General, and the Cork-based academic polymath, Alfred O'Rahilly, as well as the Dublin Quaker businessman James Douglas and an American lawyer, C. J. France. Officially Michael Collins was chairman of the committee but in reality that task was left to Darrell Figgis, a well-known literary figure, protégé of Griffith, and a troublesome colleague.

Collins gave the group, which met in the Shelbourne Hotel in Dublin, its terms of reference: 'They were not to be bound up by legal formalities, but were to put up a constitution of a Free State . . . they wanted definitely to produce and define a free democratic constitution. They were to bear in mind, not the legalities of the past, but the practicabilities of the future.'

The committee was told to ignore articles 3, 4 and 6 of the Treaty (dealing with the Governor-General, the Oath, and coastal defences). They were also apparently advised to 'leave out all points in the Treaty concerning the relations between the two countries.' It was an omission that would cause problems in a matter of months.

The committee met for the first time on 24 January 1922. They were asked to complete drafting in one month. In fact, the final drafts were completed by 7 March, after twenty-seven meetings had considered over fifty documents and consulted a number of experts called to give evidence. The range of topics considered was comprehensive, and some of the topics discussed were noticeably modern. The committee clearly shared the optimistic enthusiasm about constitutional engineering that was such a marked feature of post-First World War thinking. But it was tempered with a considerable degree of political realism, hard-headed practicality, and legal experience. Some members were undoubtedly critical of the British system with its maintenance of archaic forms and titles, its highly disciplined (but almost indistinguishable) parliamentary parties, and its marked concentration of power in the hands of prime minister and cabinet.

They tried to devise some constraints and provide for institutional amendments. Proportional representation, the referendum and the initiative were designed to weaken the stranglehold of mass parties and encourage popular participation. The idea of a second chamber—required by undertakings already given to Southern Unionist leaders—was accepted reluctantly but some serious effort was made to give the Senate real functions. The committee also discussed some method of reducing the cabinet's control of parliament; it was a debate that became acrimonious, revealing some of the inherent personality tensions and suspicions in the group. In the end the committee split between two distinct, but not radically different, drafts. Alfred O'Rahilly, summoned from

Cork, proclaimed his dissatisfaction with both versions and produced a totally new draft with articles on marriage, the family and education that foreshadow, in a remarkable way, some of the new provisions of Bunreacht na hÉireann fifteen years later.[13]

Faced now with three drafts in early March 1922, and under pressure to complete the work, the Provisional Government sought further advice. Tim Healy, veteran Westminster parliamentarian and future Governor-General, regarded all three versions 'as pure Fudge, which must make us a laughing stock... what is wanted is dry, unassailable frigid technique... which by its generality imports and attracts the utmost sovereignty without saying so'; his advice was not regarded as helpful. More usefully George O'Brien, a young lawyer who was subsequently the distinguished and influential Professor of Economics at UCD, offered a detailed critique of specific articles. The Provisional Government also consulted some Roman Catholic bishops. Between April and the end of May it scrutinised and amended the draft Constitution at twelve cabinet meetings, and on 26 May Collins brought their new, agreed version to London.

This provoked an immediate crisis in Anglo-Irish relations. The assertions in the opening articles that 'Ireland is a free and sovereign nation' and 'all powers of Government in Ireland are derived from the people,' the omission of the Oath and the downgrading of the British representative to a titular diplomatic post as 'Commissioner of the British Commonwealth', were seen by the British government as a repudiation of the Treaty.[14] Already concerned with growing unrest in Ireland and suspicious of Irish intentions, London was in no mood to make concessions. Besides, political leaders and officials were conscious that there were other nations in the British Commonwealth that would seek a precedent in any special arrangements between London and Dublin.[15]

There were hurried consultations. The British Law Officers subjected the draft constitution to hostile scrutiny and demonstrated the inconsistencies between it and the Treaty. The British government demanded that it be amended, and insisted on a catalogue of specific questions to be answered by the

Provisional Government. After further discussion, Griffith and his colleagues conceded. In mid-June a revised draft, incorporating the Oath, the Governor-General and the right of appeal to the Privy Council, and symbolically vesting executive authority in the King, was agreed. It was published on the morning of 18 June, polling-day in the Irish general election. The draft constitution was another wedge hammered into the split that was already tearing pro and anti-Treaty politicians and their supporters further and further apart.

Anathema to the Republicans, who had already refused to take their seats in the new Dáil, the draft was debated in September-October 1922. At the outset it was made clear that articles regarded as vital to the Treaty (in effect, those already negotiated with London) could not be changed. However, there were some minor amendments.

These were not always fully explained. The treatment of article 8, dealing with religious freedom, takes up a single column of the *Dáil Debates* for 25 September 1922.[16] Kevin O'Higgins quite correctly told the Dáil that this was 'practically a repetition of a Clause of the Treaty'. He did not say that the British negotiators had insisted on incorporating the whole of article 16 of the Treaty. Nor did he reveal that, at the request of the Provost of Trinity College, a phrase spelling out the specific works of public utility that might justify interference with church or educational property was incorporated from the Home Rule Act, 1914. O'Higgins did announce that Éamon Duggan (a signatory to the Treaty serving as parliamentary secretary) would propose a 'slight change in the wording to meet a particular point of view which we did not expect'. This was to change the declaration of religious freedom and practice as 'inviolable rights' to a formula 'that guaranteed to every citizen subject to public order and morality' the same rights. Duggan explained that this was to meet criticisms that the original version enunciated moral rather than constitutional principles, and to withhold protection from 'certain illegal practices, such, for instance, as Mormonism and things of that sort.' This was, at least, disingenuous. The amendment was in deference to the objection of Roman Catholic bishops to the 'inviolable rights' claim, and was drafted by Archbishop O'Donnell.

The Dáil accepted this and other Government-sponsored amendments. It completed the Constitutional Bill on 25 October. There was a formal, brief debate in the British parliament, and on 6 December, just within the time-scale laid down in the Treaty, the Irish Free State and its Constitution came officially into existence.

There were some changes from the Dáil Constitution. Notably, the acknowledgment of Treaty obligations built symbolically important Dominion elements into the Irish Free State Constitution. While article 2 proclaimed that 'all powers of government and all authority legislative, executive and judicial in Ireland, are derived from the people of Ireland,' the assertion was contradicted by the existence of the Oath, the vesting of executive authority in the King, the creation of a Governor-General, and the right of appeal to the Privy Council. This was a fundamental flaw in the Constitution that made it a target for Republican attacks on the institutions, operations and leaders of the Irish Free State. It was not genuinely the fundamental law desired by the Irish nationalist people, and not expressed in a language or set of institutions that they would have freely chosen. That ambiguity in the Constitution lies behind the often-quoted (and frequently misinterpreted) later remark of Seán Lemass that Fianna Fáil was 'a slightly constitutional party'.[17]

Nevertheless the pro-Treaty upholders of the Constitution had a strong point when they argued that the Irish Free State was, for practical purposes, an independent, democratic, sovereign state. It had achieved the same status as Canada, which nullified any question of a royal veto. The imposition of archaic, monarchic forms was an irritant. Lloyd George had recognised that it would be: he told his English cabinet colleagues that 'the Irish were fed up with the Crown this, and the Crown that, and no wonder,' since it was a potent symbol of alien oppression.[18] But this unwanted and obtrusive political liturgy made little difference to the reality of national sovereignty.

The basic provisions of the Constitution created some deviations from traditional British constitutional practice. There were to be two tiers of Government ministers: cabinet ministers, who would be party men chosen by the head of Government, and 'extern ministers', to be selected by the Dáil itself and not subject to automatic resignation if the Government fell. There were important rights—freedom from arbitrary arrest, habeas corpus, freedom of assembly, and freedom to form unions—which codified traditional common-law practice; also the right to free elementary education and the elaborated guarantee of religious freedom and property. There were articles to encourage the use of the popular referendum and to permit electors, on petition, to initiate legislation. An independent, professional judiciary was established, with the right to determine 'the validity of any law having regard to the provisions of the Constitution.' The Irish Free State Constitution, as adopted, was a model, modern fundamental law very much to the fore in British Commonwealth development. It attracted high praise.

The Irish Free State Constitution was, in the words of Dr Leo Kohn, a German legal scholar,

> a most comprehensive and, in spirit, essentially republican constitution on continental lines... it postulated fundamental rights. It defined in detail the scope and the functions of the several constitutional powers. It reduced to precise terms the conventional rules of the British constitution. Its archaic symbols had to be introduced, but their meaninglessness for Ireland was writ large on every page. The monarchical forms paled into insignificance in the light of the formal enunciation of the principle of the people as the fundamental and the exclusive source of all political authority.[19]

This is, perhaps, an unduly positive interpretation, which underemphasises the resentment created by the inclusion of an enforced Oath and the rigmarole of royalty. It also understates the extent to which, in operation, the Irish Free State Constitution practice (and indeed, for long enough, Bunreacht na hÉireann) continued to cleave to what Dr Kohn termed the 'time-honoured empiricism of the British Constitution' and avoided any rigid application of immutable principles. Certainly the innovations developed during the detailed and exhaustive drafting period were soon dissipated when the Constitution came into operation. This was made possible by the terms of article 50 of the Irish Free State Constitution.

This article provided that the Constitution could be amended by simple act of the Oireachtas. Initially it had been intended that all amendments would require a referendum. During the Dáil debate this was changed to allow for parliamentary amendment of defects that might become obvious during its first eight years. Subsequently this period of flexible amendment was extended to sixteen years. So, during the whole of its life, the Irish Free State Constitution could be changed as easily as any other law, without any direct reference to the people. Both the Cosgrave and de Valera governments took full advantage of the latitude, and between 1923 and 1936 twenty-five Acts were passed amending many provisions of the original text.[20] The record of these changes documents some important markers in Irish constitutional development.

Some amendments were purely technical, for instance the Third Amendment removed the requirement that election day be proclaimed a public holiday. Changes in the electoral procedures, composition, powers and duration of the Irish Free State Senate were incorporated in eleven amendments. But two sets of amendments are of particular importance.

The first were a group passed during the period of the Cumann na nGaedheal government. They had the cumulative effect of strengthening the powers of the executive and effectively removing the various innovations that marked the Irish Free State Constitution as different from the basic British model. So, in 1927, an amendment made the appointment of extern ministers optional; no more were appointed. In 1928, after Fianna Fáil organised a popular petition to abolish the Oath, the referendum and the initiative were abolished. In 1929 the process of flexible amendment in article 50 was extended for a further eight years. In 1931 the Constitution (Amendment No. 17) Act incorporated a Public Safety Act, which, like subsequent Emergency Powers Acts, could effectively set aside all the guarantees of the Constitution.

When Fianna Fáil came to power in 1932 they continued this tradition of wholesale amendment. The cumulative effect of

Fianna Fáil amendments was to reduce, and eventually eliminate, the archaic Crown symbolism incorporated at British insistence in 1922. So, in 1933 the Oath was removed; in 1933 the limited right of appeal to the Privy Council was abolished; in 1936, taking advantage of the abdication crisis, the remaining references to the Crown in terms of domestic arrangements, and the office of Governor-General, disappeared.

By this time the original Irish Free State Constitution was a thing of shreds and tatters. Virtually every page was cluttered with deletions, additions, and amendments: forty-one of its eighty-three articles had been altered. The promise of a codified, modern fundamental law with explicitly defined relationships between its various institutions had given way to a traditional British-type cabinet system. Entrenched rights upheld by a Supreme Court reviewing legislation had not developed. The panoply of measures designed to encourage popular participation had been abandoned.

In the wrong hands Ireland could have gone the way of other European states in the dangerous Europe of the mid-thirties. De Valera by now had abolished the Senate, had an overall majority in the Dáil and a totally flexible Constitution with neither effective judicial review nor the requirements of a popular referendum to restrain his will. He could, by simple act of the single parliamentary chamber dominated by his party, make whatever constitutional changes he wished. It was a classic opportunity to establish a dictatorship. Instead his mind had already turned to writing a new constitution for modern Ireland.

NOTES

1. For a comprehensive development of this view see Brian Farrell (ed.), *The Irish Parliamentary Tradition*, Dublin: Gill and Macmillan 1973.
2. A recent general account of British constitutional development, with further references noted, is R. M. Punnett, *British Government and Politics*, 5th ed., London: Gower 1987, chap. 6.
3. A thorough account, distinguishing the responses of Southern and Northern Unionists, is contained in Patrick Buckland, *Irish Unionism*, I: *The Anglo-Irish and the New Ireland, 1885-1922*, Dublin: Gill and Macmillan 1972, and *Irish Unionism*, II: *Ulster Unionism and the Origins of Northern Ireland, 1886-1922*, Dublin: Gill and Macmillan

1973. See also D. W. Miller, *Queen's Rebels: Ulster Loyalism in Historical Perspective*, Dublin: Gill and Macmillan 1978.
4. Griffith's ideas are discussed in R. M. Henry, *The Evolution of Sinn Féin*, Dublin: Talbot Press 1920.
5. The quotations are from the Proclamation of 1916.
6. On the second Sinn Féin see Michael Laffan, 'The Unification of Sinn Féin in 1917' in *Irish Historical Studies*, XVII/67 (March 1971) and Brian Farrell, *The Founding of Dáil Éireann: Parliament and Nation-Building*, Dublin: Gill and Macmillan 1971.
7. *Freeman's Journal*, 30 December 1918, quoted in G. M. Golding, *George Gavan Duffy, 1882-1951*, Dublin: Irish Academic Press 1982, 19.
8. For a fuller account of the drafting and content of the Dáil Constitution and Democratic Programme see Brian Farrell, 'A Note on the Dáil Constitution, 1919' in *Irish Jurist*, IV (1969), 1.
9. Hugh Kennedy, memorandum to the Acting Chairman, 'Re: the Creation, Source of Authority and Powers of the Three Dails [*sic*], and certain other matters bearing thereon', 5 August 1922, in UCD Archives.
10. The full debate is reported in Dáil Éireann, *Miontuairisc an Chéad Dála*, 17 September 1920, 213-4.
11. These Dáil decrees are listed and discussed in Brian Farrell, 'The Legislation of a "Revolutionary" Assembly: Dáil Decrees, 1919-1922' in *Irish Jurist*, X (1975), 1.
12. For a fuller account of the early phases of the drafting, with references, see four articles by Brian Farrell, 'The Drafting of the Irish Free State Constitution' in *Irish Jurist*, V, VI, 1-2 (summer-winter 1970-71); also D. H. Akenson and J. F. Fallin, 'The Irish Civil War and the Drafting of the Irish Free State Constitution' in *Éire-Ireland*, V, 2 (summer 1970).
13. These are quoted and discussed in the Farrell articles referred to above, which also quote a note from de Valera to O'Rahilly returning 'the drafts for the constitution which you were so kind enough to lend me some time ago,' 27 March 1934.
14. The extensive documentation on official British reactions is collated in a narrative account, 'The Draft Irish Constitution: History of Negotiations between the Signatories of the Articles of Agreement for a Treaty between Great Britain and Ireland. May-June 1922,' Public Record Office, London (CAB 43/7).
15. On imperial implications see D. W. Harkness, *The Restless Dominion*, London: Macmillan 1969.
16. This account is based on a set of notes for the committee stage of the Constitution Bill prepared by Hugh Kennedy and preserved in his papers in the UCD Archives, and on *Dáil Debates*.
17. See Brian Farrell, *Seán Lemass*, Dublin: Gill and Macmillan 1983, 21 ff.
18. The remark is quoted in K. Middlemas (ed.), *Thomas Jones: Whitehall Diary, III: Ireland 1918-1925*, London: Oxford University Press 1971, 208.
19. Leo Kohn, *The Constitution of the Irish Free State*, London: George

Allen and Unwin 1932, 80. Kohn's interpretation is clearly influenced by Hugh Kennedy, who contributed a foreword.

20. The complete list is given in Saorstát Éireann, *Constitution of the Irish Free State (Saorstát Éireann) Act, 1922, Embodying the Constitution as Amended by Subsequent Enactments Presented to Dáil Éireann by the Ceann Comhairle*, Dublin: Stationery Office 1936 (P No. 2538), 4. See also P. Fay, 'The Amendments to the Constitution Committee, 1926' in *Administration*, 26 (1978), 5.

PROFESSOR RONAN FANNING

3. *Mr de Valera Drafts a Constitution*

Ronan Fanning is Professor of Modern History at University College, Dublin. His major publications are *The Irish Department of Finance, 1922-58* (1978) and *Independent Ireland* (1983).

THE historian addressing this topic must first face a problem peculiar to the historical profession.

That problem is neatly summarised in the title of this volume: *De Valera's Constitution and Ours*. For while *our* Constitution, the Constitution of 1937, is a concern of the present, if we would properly understand Éamon de Valera's Constitution it is imperative that we ignore the present and look to the past.

Many of the other contributors to this volume—political scientists, lawyers and judges, politicians—are not subject to the same imperative. This is because the perspectives of political science, of law, of politics, are essentially perspectives of the present. The historian's, however, is the perspective of the past. And for the historian the present is essentially an enemy obstructing a proper perspective on the past. The point was best made, perhaps, by an eminent German historian who insisted that the first duty of all historians is to give to each past the open future it once had.[1]

That is why it is the historian's task to explore the world in which, and for which, Éamon de Valera drafted the Constitution *of* 1937, without regard to what has happened *since* 1937.

Our point of departure for that exploration is the paradox that de Valera saw the 1937 Constitution more as an end than as a beginning. The dynamic that impelled him in his constitutional designs had less to do with inaugurating a brave new world than with bringing an old and—from de Valera's perspective—desperately unhappy world to a close. His impulse, in short, was as much negative as positive.

What de Valera wanted to bring to an end, of course, was the Constitution of 1922. What he wanted to rewrite, as he thought it should have been written in the first place, was the Anglo-Irish Treaty of 1921. What he wanted to destroy was the Irish Free State.

One of de Valera's senior cabinet colleagues, Seán MacEntee, summed it up well in an interview forty years later: 'Now, look, here is what has to be remembered in relation to the Constitution. The purpose of the Constitution was to get rid of the Oath, and the Irish Free State constitution.'[2] Everything that de Valera did after 1922 was directed towards these objectives. His regathering of the reins of political leadership after the Republicans had suffered a crushing defeat in the Civil War; his establishment of Fianna Fáil in 1926; Fianna Fáil's entry into the Dáil in 1927; their victory in the 1932 election—all alike were motivated by a single-minded determination to undo what had been done in 1921-2.

Hence the primary historical significance of the 1937 Constitution is that it represents the apotheosis of all those efforts, the ultimate vindication of de Valera's brand of Irish republicanism. That is why, in the eyes of its principal architect at least, what is omitted from the 1937 Constitution is as important as what is included.

The steps by which de Valera proceeded on his self-appointed task of destruction by omission were slow and cautious, and were well in train before 1937. The hated Oath of Allegiance to the British Crown incorporated in article 17 of the 1922 Constitution had been deleted by 1933. And it was at a commemoration of the Easter Rising in April 1933 that de Valera publicly outlined his strategy:

> Let it be made clear that we yield no willing assent to any form or symbol that is out of keeping with Ireland's right as a sovereign nation. Let us remove these forms one by

> one, so that this state we control may become a Republic in fact; and that, when the time comes, the proclaiming of the Republic may involve no more than a ceremony, the formal confirmation of a status already attained.[3]

De Valera's strategy was one of piecemeal destruction, and 1933 witnessed three more constitutional amendments: one abolished the right of appeal to the King's Privy Council; the other two reduced the powers of the Governor-General, the King's representative in Ireland.

De Valera's objection to the 1922 Constitution, he reminded the Dáil in May 1935, was that it did not represent the free expression of Irish opinions, but that it had been 'imposed from without' by the British. He took his stand on the fact that

> we have undoubtedly been elected by the majority of the Irish people. We do not recognise any authority coming from any other source except, under God, through the Irish people to us.... At the moment, we are operating a constitution which has not been wholly ours. I hope, before our term expires, that we will be able to bring in a Constitution which, so far as internal affairs at any rate are concerned, will be absolutely ours.[4]

By then, John Hearne, the legal adviser in the Department of External Affairs, acting on de Valera's instructions, had already prepared the draft heads of a constitution. These draft heads were an endeavour to insert de Valera's instructions 'into the text of the existing Constitution rather than an effort to construct—at this stage—a completely new Constitution.'[5]

But by August 1936 de Valera's mind had hardened against further tinkering with the 1922 Constitution. He now favoured a new constitution, and the cabinet minutes reveal that de Valera 'mentioned' his intention of writing to the new king, Edward VIII, informing him (*a*) that the constitution would deal with the internal affairs of Saorstát Éireann, and (*b*) that amongst the provisions of the new constitution would be the creation of the office of President, elected by the people, and the abolition of the office of Governor-General.[6]

The wording of that entry in the cabinet minutes—that de

Valera, in his capacity as President of the Executive Council and Minister for External Affairs, should merely *mention* so significant a step to his cabinet colleagues, and that he rightly assumed their acquiescence in his wishes—well illustrates his predominance over his ministers.

It is historically accurate to speak of the 1937 Constitution as de Valera's constitution, not merely because he was the head of the government that enacted it but because the records recently released by the Department of the Taoiseach and by the Franciscan Institute in Killiney, where de Valera's own papers are housed, put his personal predominance beyond any shadow of doubt.

Acting on his own initiative, often in advance of informing or consulting cabinet colleagues in respect of matters he adjudged especially sensitive, Éamon de Valera personally controlled every detail of the process of drafting a new constitution. His two most important assistants in that process were civil servants: the first, John Hearne, has already been mentioned; the second was Maurice Moynihan, the secretary to the Executive Council, who ran the committee responsible for drafting the constitution.

The dimensions of the process of constitutional change were significantly widened as a result of the abdication crisis of November 1936 that engulfed Edward VIII. Although John Hearne's draft heads of May 1935 show that de Valera then intended that the constitution 'contain provision for the retention of the King as a constitutional officer of Saorstát Éireann in the domain of international relations,'[7] he now seized the opportunity to complete one of the most delicate manoeuvres in his restructuring of Anglo-Irish constitutional relations: taking the King out of the constitution.

De Valera did this by two acts rushed through the cabinet and the Dáil between 9 and 12 December 1936. The first, the Constitution (Amendment No. 27) Act, struck out of the constitution all mention of the King and of the Governor-General. The second, the External Relations Act, provided by ordinary law for the continued exercise by the King of certain functions in external matters as and when advised by the Irish government—in practice this meant that all foreign diplomats in

Dublin continued to be accredited to the King until the External Relations Act was repealed in 1948. But the External Relations Act, as de Valera frequently insisted, was 'a simple statute repealable by the legislature and not a fundamental law,'[8] and the way was now clear for the introduction of a new constitution.

Again, de Valera moved swiftly. He circulated the draft constitution to his cabinet colleagues and to certain of the more sympathetic members of the judiciary on 16 March 1937. He also established a small, four-member committee to examine and revise the draft in the light of observations that might be received from ministers or from their departments. Few ministers bothered. Even so energetic and independent-minded a cabinet colleague as Seán Lemass contented himself with some minor and anodyne comments relating to social policy.[9]

Indeed, it well illustrated the extraordinary reluctance of Fianna Fáil ministers to question de Valera's authority that the only trenchant criticism of his draft constitution came, not from a cabinet colleague but from a civil servant: J. J. McElligott, the Secretary of the Department of Finance.

Although McElligott had been appointed to Finance by the Cosgrave government, first as Assistant Secretary in 1923 and then as Secretary in 1927, his republican credentials were impeccable. He had joined the rebels in the GPO on his return to Dublin from Fairyhouse races on Easter Monday 1916, and was jailed and dismissed from the civil service in consequence. He then worked in London as a financial journalist until his reinstatement in 1923.

McElligott's response to the request for departmental observations on the draft constitution began by taking the line that his department 'was not called upon to praise but rather to point out possible defects and difficulties.' He then launched a savage attack on the political core of the constitution, articles 1-4.

> These Articles, dealing with the Nation as distinct from the State, (a distinction which many political scientists would not admit), seem rather to vitiate the Constitution, by stating at the outset what will be described, and with

> some justice, as a fiction, and one which will give offence to neighbouring countries with whom we are constantly protesting our desire to live on terms of friendship.
>
> Having been at such pains to expel fictions from the existing Constitution and to bring theory into line with practice, it seems inconsistent now to import an even greater fiction.
>
> Further, from the point of view of international law, it is not clear whether we are on safe grounds in claiming sovereignty and jurisdiction over land recognised internationally, de jure and de facto, as belonging to another country . . .
>
> From the practical point of view, apart from the fear of consequences, these Articles will not contribute anything to effecting the unity of Ireland, but rather the reverse. Besides they will impose an additional and more severe strain on our relations with the members of the British Commonwealth of Nations, relations which are already difficult enough, and which coming events, apart from the Constitution, will make even more difficult.

McElligott displayed a similar pragmatic distaste for the 'adoption of the name of Éire' and the consequent expense of the 'alteration of currency and bank notes, coinage, seals of state and of government departments, and of all kinds of government stationery.'

He also objected to the articles on private property and social policy, on the grounds that they were

> not of a kind usually enshrined in a Constitution. They will not be helpful to Ministers in the future but will provide a breeding ground for discontent, and so create instability and insecurity. They are consequently objectionable and even dangerous. Their provisions are too vague to be of positive assistance to any Government and are yet sufficiently definite to afford grounds for disaffection to sections of the community, who might claim that the Government were not living up to the Constitution.

He argued that 'various declaratory phrases' were objectionable because of their 'idealistic tendency which, individually unobjectionable as a statement of social policy, may, if launched out into the void in the draft constitution, recoil like a boomerang on the Government of some future day in circumstances not anticipated by the originators.'[10]

But McElligott's was a voice crying in the wilderness, the exception to the rule of deference that generally characterised the response of ministers and civil servants to de Valera's constitution. The draft articles he found repugnant remained essentially unchanged for, as another official, Michael McDunphy, minuted in response to McElligott's memorandum: 'This is a matter of policy.'[11] It was more than that. It was the essence of de Valera's constitution.

The very composition of the drafting committee again demonstrates de Valera's determination to retain the process in his own hands. It included no ministers but consisted exclusively of civil servants: Maurice Moynihan, John Hearne, Philip O'Donoghue (the legal adviser in the Attorney General's department) and Michael McDunphy (Assistant Secretary under Maurice Moynihan). None of the four worked in an outside department under the direction of any other minister, and all but O'Donoghue worked directly to de Valera. They were in constant touch with de Valera throughout the drafting process, which was completed by the end of April.

The papers recently released from the de Valera archives reveal the extent to which he personally controlled the drafting process. The procedure followed in regard to the religious provisions of the constitution (article 44) offers a particularly dramatic illustration of this point.[12]

The religious article was omitted from the first draft of the constitution as circulated on 16 March. It was likewise omitted from the revised draft circulated on 1 April and from the second revised draft, circulated on 10 April. Nor were the members of de Valera's small and select constitutional committee charged with responsibility for the draft religious article, which de Valera retained in his own possession. Again, McElligott alone saw fit to complain about the lack of time for departments to offer a mature, reflective response.

The wording of the article was only revealed when it was

included in the final text printed on 26 April. There is no evidence whatever that any of de Valera's cabinet colleagues offered, or were invited to offer, any observations on the religious article before that point. They considered its text once—on 27 April—and it went unchanged for final printing on the very next day.

The absolutism of de Valera's control was likewise demonstrated by his rejection of representations made by many of the leading Catholic churchmen whom he did consult. Among those who pressed de Valera to adopt a wording more fully consonant with the teaching of the Catholic Church were Cardinal Joseph MacRory, the Archbishop of Armagh, and Dr John Charles McQuaid, the President of Blackrock College and later—from 1940 until 1972—Archbishop of Dublin.

So determined was de Valera to resist a wording that would exclude all references to other churches or religions that he sent the Secretary of his Department of External Affairs, Joe Walshe, on a special mission to the Vatican to argue his case. Both the Pope, Pius XI, and the Secretary of State, Cardinal Pacelli (who was elevated to the Papacy as Pius XII in 1939), took the view 'that the "special position" given to the Catholic church had no real value so long as there was not a formal acknowledgement of the Roman Catholic Church as the church founded by Christ.' Indeed at one point Cardinal Pacelli smilingly told Walshe, who was a former Jesuit seminarian, 'that according to the strict teaching of the Church we were heretics to recognise any Church but the one true Church of Christ,' although he assured him 'at once that the Church would not take our heresy too seriously'![13]

The story behind the drafting of the religious article is also of interest because of what is said at the beginning of this essay about contrasting perspectives.

From the more liberal, secularist perspective of the 1980s, what strikes most observers about article 44 is the 'special position' it conferred upon the Catholic Church: a position that obtained until December 1972, when the clauses in question were deleted by referendum as a gesture towards Protestant susceptibilities under the impact of the Northern Ireland crisis. From de Valera's perspective in 1937, however, article 44 was a compromise that denied the Catholic Church the kind of exclusive recognition it would have preferred.

Nor was this the only respect in which de Valera saw his new constitution as a compromise. This was also why article 4 declared that 'the name of the State is Éire, or in the English language, Ireland'—*not* Poblacht na hÉireann or the Republic of Ireland.

De Valera's reasoning was based on that aspect of Anglo-Irish relations that he was unable to influence: the continuance of partition. 'When the name of the State is changed from "Éire" to "Poblacht na hÉireann",' he told the Fianna Fáil ard-fheis in October 1937, 'we want to see it in operation, not for the twenty-six counties alone, but for the whole thirty-two counties.'[14] Similar reasoning lay behind the retention of the vestigial link with the Commonwealth for diplomatic purposes embodied in the External Relations Act of 1936: 'in order that, when Northern Ireland came in,' as de Valera over-optimistically explained, 'the contact with the Crown which they valued so highly should not be entirely severed.'[15]

How, then, did de Valera reconcile this quest for compromise, this anxiety to assuage the Ulster Unionists, with other apparently uncompromising constitutional assertions: the assertion of article 2, for example, that 'the national territory consists of the whole island of Ireland,' and the declaration in article 8 that 'the Irish language as the national language is the first official language'?

The explanation lies in the fact that there was a point beyond which de Valera was not prepared to compromise the beliefs of the majority in the interests of conciliating the minority. He distinguished, too, between the nation and the state. Although he saw the first section of the Constitution—on the nation—as the appropriate place in which to lay claim, on behalf of the nation, to 'the whole of the national territory', it was also 'clearly laid down' in article 3 'that the area of jurisdiction of the government which is provided by this constitution shall be of the same extent as that of the State.'

Contemporary critics of the state's identification with the Catholic religion and with the Irish language as embodied in the 1937 Constitution too readily lose sight of their function as devices for bonding together a deeply divided people.

Here again we must resist the temptation to look forward to our own time and our present discontents, and instead look backwards to the traumas of 1921-2. The amputation of partition compounded the savage and bloody injuries inflicted on the body politic by the Civil War. Together they created not merely a divided nation but a state so bitterly split that a large proportion of its citizens paid it no more than a grudging allegiance, while a smaller number continued to claim the right to bear arms against it.

In so deeply riven a state there was a pressing need for common ground where citizens could gather irrespective of political affiliation, which found expression in a search for marks of national identity. Religion and language—identifiably different from those that have long characterised the British national ethos—were but the two most obvious hallmarks of independent Ireland. And it was as such that they were embodied in de Valera's constitution. Catholic triumphalism and language revivalism alike were rooted in the necessity to find something to celebrate in an infant state scarred by political disappointments and economic austerities and by the general disenchantment typical of a neo-revolutionary age.

Neither should those who damn the Catholic triumphalism they so readily identify in the 1937 Constitution ignore the residual impact of that ingrained anti-Catholicism that had so characterised British dealings with Ireland since the sixteenth century. Nor should they forget that an especially vicious form of anti-Catholic prejudice and discrimination was an outstanding feature of that part of Ireland still within the United Kingdom.

These considerations of alienation and allegiance bring us directly to the rationale that underpinned de Valera's constitution.

The matter may be simply put. De Valera accepted that his fellow-citizens had a right to dispute the legitimacy of the 1922 Constitution and, consequently, to withhold their allegiance from the institutions of the state. That, indeed, had been his own position—certainly from 1922 until 1926, arguably between 1927 and 1932. His aim was to enact a constitution that would satisfy what he regarded as justifiable republican aspirations and thereby secure the legitimacy of the state.

Once the Irish people 'had established a state in accordance with their wishes, those who tried by violent means, to overthrow that state should be held here, as in other countries, to be guilty of the most terrible crime of a public character which is known in civilised society.'[16]

This, then, was the stark, unambiguous language in which members of the IRA who took up arms against de Valera's state could expect to be unequivocally condemned: language very different from that with which de Valera responded to their campaign against the Irish Free State, detested by all republicans. The upshot was the Offences Against the State Acts of 1939 and of 1940, and the execution of convicted IRA men during the Second World War.

What is perhaps most striking about this exploration of de Valera's priorities is how very different they are from most—although not all—of our contemporary concerns.

To de Valera, the recent constitutional referenda on divorce and abortion would have seemed profoundly distasteful and, probably, irrelevant. Nor would he have been able to understand, let alone sympathise with, the aspiration of today's left-wing parties to enshrine neutrality in the Constitution. The idea of his Constitution, he informed the Dáil, was

> to put the matter of our external relations in its proper position relatively to the Constitution, and that is outside it, as a matter of foreign policy, to be determined from time to time according as the people's interests suggest to them that they should put this government or that government into office with powers to implement their will.[17]

To point out our current obsession with such issues as the constitutional regulation of sexual morality, with the role of women, with property rights, with judicial review—even, perhaps, with the role of the North—is not to suggest that these are not appropriate concerns in the present. It is rather to remind ourselves, if I might end as I began, that de Valera's perspective must be distinguished from our own.

De Valera's perspective was framed by the twin pillars of

independence and legitimacy. He drafted a constitution for a sovereign state that had cast off the last constitutional shackles binding Ireland to England—or, in his own words, 'an independent republic, associated as a matter of our external policy with the States of the British Commonwealth.'[18] And that constitution finally legitimised the independent Irish state in as much as it commanded the allegiance of all but a statistically insignificant minority of its citizens.

That few are today disposed to celebrate what is in a very real sense the fiftieth anniversary of Irish independence is, perhaps, a measure of how much we have matured as a people during the last fifty years: a measure of how we have gradually rid ourselves of our more fevered Anglophobic insecurities and of our compulsion unrelentingly to beat the national drum. It is a measure, too, of how much we have come to take the sovereignty and legitimacy of our state for granted.

And that, perhaps, is the largest tribute that we owe to the constitution Éamon de Valera drafted in 1937.

NOTES

1. Professor Thomas Nipperdey, speaking at the Fourteenth International Congress of the Historical Sciences, San Francisco, 1975.
2. Quoted in Dermot Keogh, 'The Constitutional Revolution: an Analysis of the Making of the Constitution,' in *Administration*, vol. 35 (1987), 58.
3. Maurice Moynihan (ed.), *Speeches and Statements by Éamon de Valera 1917-73*, Dublin 1980, 237. What follows is based on Ronan Fanning, *Independent Ireland*, Dublin 1983, 116-9.
4. Moynihan, *Speeches and Statements*, 264.
5. Keogh, 'The Constitutional Revolution', 9.
6. State Paper Office (SPO), Cabinet Papers (CAB 1/6/315).
7. Keogh, 'The Constitutional Revolution', 9.
8. Moynihan, *Speeches and Statements*, 479.
9. SPO file S10160. I owe this reference to Professor Brian Farrell. See also Keogh, 'The Constitutional Revolution', 83, n. 105: 'The Department of Industry and Commerce did not make any comments on the Constitution. Lemass made one personal intervention at the last minute.'
10. See Ronan Fanning, *The Irish Department of Finance 1922-58*, Dublin 1978, 266-9, for a fuller account.
11. Keogh, 'The Constitutional Revolution', 27.
12. What follows is based on Ronan Fanning, 'The Politics of Appeasement and Éamon de Valera's Constitution', two articles published in the *Irish*

Times on 30-31 July 1987. The theme of church and state is more extensively treated in Dr Keogh's contribution to this volume. My concern is not with that theme *per se* but with what it shows of de Valera's determination to retain control of the drafting process in his own hands.

13. De Valera Papers (1995/1D).
14. Moynihan, *Speeches and Statements*, 331.
15. Robert Fisk, *In Time of War: Ireland, Ulster and the Price of Neutrality*, London 1983, 63.
16. *Dáil Debates*, vol. 74, col. 967, 23 February 1939.
17. Moynihan, *Speeches and Statements*, 319.
18. ibid., 480.

GEARÓID Ó TUATHAIGH

4. *The Irish Nation-State in the Constitution*

Gearóid Ó Tuathaigh lectures in modern history at University College, Galway. He is the author of *Ireland Before the Famine, 1798-1848* (1972) and (with Joseph Lee) *The Age of de Valera* (1982).

IN the dying days of 1987, in a special issue commemorating the fiftieth anniversary of de Valera's Constitution, an editorial in the *Irish Times* called for a major constitutional review, a task the editorial described as one of 'bringing the state out of de Valera's idealised, pastoral political culture, of freeing it from a great deal of the now empty rhetoric of the 1930s and of taking it into the world of the 1990s and of the third millennium.' The editorial concluded with a commentary on two articles in particular:

> The most difficult and the most urgent aspect of that project, in so far as it will depend on constitutional reform, concerns Articles 2 and 3, which purport to claim jurisdiction over the North. It is a claim which is expressed in a dangerously simplistic idiom, in terms which are suggestive of a desire for conquest, subjugation indeed, and which can have no place in the dialogue which must come about with the Unionist majority in the North. The concept of territorial occupation, of the Gall flying to the sea before the conquering might—military, social or cultural—of the Gael, may well have had its place as part of a necessary political or cultural mythology in 1937. It has none to-day. And it contradicts the declared desire of the great majority of people on this island for the achievement of unity by peaceful means alone.[1]

Leaving aside the rather colourful and questionable interpretation of this editorial, it is certainly the case that most commentators on the Constitution in recent years—in fact for twenty years now—whether favouring partial amendment or replacement, have identified articles 2 and 3 as being especially problematic, particularly in the context of the conflict in Northern Ireland and the various political initiatives—within Ireland and in Anglo-Irish relations—that that conflict has prompted. The articles are variously described as a provocation to Unionists; incompatible with peace and reconciliation between Irishmen; an impediment to good relations between the communities within Northern Ireland and in the island as a whole; an unenforceable territorial claim; a dangerous indulgence in the obsolete rhetoric of nationalist irredentism. It is suggested that the articles be amended, replaced, simply removed, or, in the event of a new constitution, simply omitted.

In this short essay I should like to look at articles 2 and 3, not in isolation but as part of the general attempt—in the Preamble and in articles 1 to 8—to incorporate the concept of an Irish nation into constitutional form in de Valera's document. The articles on the nation and the state, then, are the articles that concern me in this essay.

These articles are concerned with the sources of all political authority in Ireland (article 1 affirms the inalienable and indefeasible right of 'the Irish nation' to political sovereignty); the national territory and the jurisdiction of the institutions of the state; the name of the state (Éire or, in the English language, Ireland); the form of state being established (a 'sovereign, independent, democratic state'); the people as the source of authority for the exercise of power by all the organs of the state; the national flag (the Tricolour); and the national and official languages (Irish and English).

On the matter of the form and designation of the state, it is interesting that de Valera refrained from calling the state explicitly a republic. His reasons for this were complex, but included a desire to hold the title 'republic' for a 32-county state rather than confer it on anything less; and also, perhaps, to allow some scope for an initiative and dialogue on the partition question within a British Commonwealth context. In 1948, of course, a later government did indeed declare the state a republic—but the title, 'the Republic of Ireland', was provided for in statute law rather than through constitutional amendment. The Tricolour (article 7) was meant to symbolise peace and harmony in the bonding of the Orange and Green traditions in Ireland—even though the Ulster Unionists refused to accept its validity as an appropriate symbol for all the people of Ireland.

In affirming the democratic nature of the state and its sovereignty, what was being asserted was the sovereignty of the Irish state in respect of other states, not that the state was above the law in respect of its transactions with its own citizens.[2] When we turn to examine the effects—the real, practical significance—of article 8, the article that declares that 'the Irish language as the national language is the first official language,' we encounter a surprising lack of clarity, and a large number of paradoxes and contradictions. Article 8 goes on to state that 'the English language is recognised as a second official language,' and further states that 'provision may, however, be made by law for the exclusive use of either of the said languages for any one or more official purposes, either throughout the State or in any part thereof.'

This article in de Valera's Constitution replaced article 4 of the old Free State Constitution of 1922, which had read: 'The National language of the Irish Free State . . . is the Irish language, but the English language shall be equally recognised as an official language. Nothing in this Article shall prevent special provisions being made by the [Oireachtas] for districts or areas in which only one language is in general use.'

It should not surprise us that both the 1922 and 1937 constitutions acknowledged Irish as the national language of the new Irish state. The post-1916 Sinn Féin political élite, from which many of the leading figures in both Cumann na nGaedheal and Fianna Fáil emerged, was deeply and widely influenced by the Gaelic League ideal, and shared a belief that the Irish language was the most irrefutable authenticating mark of the Irish nation, on whose behalf a national state had been demanded; that the loss of the language had been one of the most grievous aspects of the conquest; and that the restoration of Irish as the main vernacular of the people ought to be the objective, not to say obligation, of an independent Irish national state. This view—this philosophy, if you like—informed state language policy in education and in recruitment to various branches of the civil service under successive governments of the Free State. Fianna Fáil policy in these areas in the 1930s was largely a matter of reinforcing the language policy laid down during the 1920s. So also in the matter of the constitutional status of the language; the 1937 Constitution reinforced and enhanced the formal status accorded to Irish.

But what have been, indeed what are, the practical effects of this constitutional status enjoyed by the Irish language? It might reasonably be supposed that it would mean that the Irish-speaker would enjoy equal rights with the speaker of English in the conduct of his or her business, legal and administrative, with the state. That this is far from being the case is revealed in an important report on *Irish and the Law* published by the distinguished legal group Fásach in June 1986. This report made the following observations:

> Very little if any consideration would appear to have been given to the whole area of the legal and administrative systems and the use of the Irish language . . . Successive governments have to a greater or lesser extent ignored the existence of the Irish language (prescinding from any reference to its pre-eminent status), in the official and daily use of the legal and associated administrative systems. This is evidenced by the almost exclusive use of the English language by the State in all matters relating to Court procedures, land and property transactions and the functioning of state Departments and Agencies . . . The Irish language is a recognised procedural language of the European Court of Justice. The language of the proceedings before the Court will as a rule be selected by the Plaintiff. To date, however, the Irish government have adopted the English language when faced with choice of language in any case in which they were involved.[3]

The Fásach report found that over a wide range of state services, in law and administration, from the practice of the courts of law to the supply of various kinds of documentation, the Irish-speaker was effectively precluded from choosing the language through which he or she wished to conduct business. It documented the state's delinquency in this matter in some detail, and concluded:

> Generally speaking, until such time as the Irish-speaker feels with confidence that socially and economically he will not suffer, and that he has equal opportunity to process his affairs without difficulty or delay, in a similar manner to the English-speaking citizen of the State, that Irish-speaking citizen is labouring under a disadvantage and is not equal before the law . . . In a bilingual society the free availability of the Legal and Administrative systems in both languages is an essential prerequisite to the continued survival of the lesser-used language.[4]

In view of the findings of this report, and in the light of the somewhat limited elaboration of language rights under the Constitution that has emerged from the handful of test cases taken to the superior courts, it is not surprising that the Fásach report recommended major reforms, including the proposal that 'in similar manner to Canada an appointment be made to the position of Commissioner for Languages with supporting legislation to enable the concept of equality before the law to be implemented clearly and fully for the citizen equally in both languages.' Nor, indeed, in the light of these findings, is it surprising that many Irish-language groups (including Conradh na Gaeilge) have called for a full Bill of Language Rights to give practical effect to the constitutional statement on language contained in article 8.

Whatever one may think of the particular remedies being proposed, it seems clear that, fifty years after the enactment of de Valera's Constitution, the position of comprehensive disadvantage under which Irish-speakers currently operate in this state ought to be a source of grave concern to all those seriously concerned with the protection of minority rights or with any real commitment to the concept of cultural pluralism in Ireland.

This concept of cultural pluralism has, in fact, emerged very strongly in discussions of nationality and national identity in Ireland during the past twenty-five years; and this has inevitably affected thinking on and public discussion of those articles in de Valera's Constitution that incorporate the concept of 'the Irish nation'. In particular, articles 2 and 3 have come in for considerable attention and comment. Article 2 declares that 'the national territory consists of the whole island of Ireland, its islands and the territorial seas,' while article 3 states that 'pending the re-integration of the national territory, and without prejudice to the right of the Parliament and Government established by this Constitution to exercise jurisdiction over the whole of that territory, the laws enacted by that Parliament shall have the like area and extent of application as the laws of Saorstát Éireann and the like extra-territorial effect.'

In seeking to understand both the substance and the tone of articles 2 and 3, we need to remind ourselves of at least a few of the main features of the historical context in which these articles were framed. Firstly, in declaring the national territory to be the whole island, de Valera was expressing the consensus view of Irish nationalists, not only in his own time but for at least fifty years before, when the 'Ulster problem' (i.e. the problem of a politically divided community in Ulster) first emerged clearly during the Home Rule crisis of 1885-6. John Redmond in his day was as outraged at the prospect of a permanent division or partition of Ireland as de Valera was in his. Nationalists of all shades of green shared the view that partition was wrong, morally and historically, and that the passage of time would not make it acceptable. The Preamble to the 1922 Constitution had expressed confidence 'that the National life and unity of Ireland shall . . . be restored.' In his article 2, therefore, de Valera was saying nothing that was new or controversial in Irish nationalist thinking; and it is significant that this article caused little or no comment, in the Dáil or in public debate, in the Free State at the time.

Article 3, on the other hand, does need closer scrutiny. De Valera was aware of the criticisms that could be made of a constitution claiming jurisdiction as of right over territory in which the people were not being afforded the opportunity of voting on the constitution, or who would not be sending representatives to the parliament that article 3 claimed as having the right to legislate for the whole island. But, as John Bowman has demonstrated, de Valera's attitudes and strategies on partition during the 1930s—indeed throughout his life—were full of complexity.[5] While accepting that little practical could be done in the short term to end partition, and while ruling out any suggestion of the use of force, de Valera was utterly convinced that the *right* of the Irish people to exercise full sovereignty over all of the 'national territory' had to be solemnly declared in the Constitution to be enacted by the people of 'free Ireland', that is, of that part of Ireland that was not 'occupied'. This assertion or claim would be a vital card in any future negotiations with the British, the *de facto* sovereign power, on partition, and de Valera remained convinced that such direct dealings with the British would be the vital arena if and when any real movement would take place towards ending partition.

In addition to his own deep feelings on the matter of partition, it is possible that the extraordinary speed and ease with which de Valera had succeeded during 1932-7 in dismantling so much of the Treaty of 1921 encouraged him to feel that in working through the agenda of outstanding political problems in Anglo-Irish relations it would be important for the Irish to take the high moral (and historical) ground. Whenever an Irish government might get round to serious negotiations with the British, then article 2 would be a great support to the Irish nationalist negotiators of that day.

So far as Unionist fears and demands were concerned, de Valera, in common with many nationalist leaders, insisted that there was considerable scope for flexibility in devising special structures, of government and administration, that would accommodate the Ulster Unionists within an all-Ireland framework. Moreover, the fact that article 3 explicitly limited the jurisdiction of legislation passed by the Oireachtas to the 26 Counties, 'pending the re-integration of the national territory'; that the use of force in ending partition was regularly and forcefully rejected by de Valera; that the decision not to describe the state as a republic, theoretically at least, seemed to leave the door slightly open to some initiative on the resolution of the partition question within a British Commonwealth setting; the fact that article 29 affirmed Ireland's 'adherence to the principle of the pacific settlement of international disputes by international arbitration or judicial determination'—all of these could be cited, and from time to time were cited by de Valera's supporters, as evidence that the controversial claims of articles 2 and 3 in no way indicated or justified an aggressive posture towards the Ulster Unionists in the resolution of the partition problem. Indeed, the real meaning of the claims of articles 2 and 3, according to some admirers of the Constitution, was not a claim for the right of the people of the 26 Counties to take over the Six Counties, but the claim on behalf of the Irish nation, the Irish people, to unfettered sovereignty over the entire national territory of Ireland.

The problem with this line of argument was the way in which 'the Irish nation' or 'the Irish people' were defined and identified elsewhere in the Constitution. In the reference in the Preamble to 'the people of Éire, humbly acknowledging all our obligations to our Divine Lord, Jesus Christ, who sustained our fathers through centuries of trial, gratefully remembering their heroic and unremitting struggle to regain the rightful independence of our Nation'; in the symbols of nationhood acknowledged in the Constitution (including the flag and the national language, and excluding all monarchical symbols), to say nothing of the confessional colouring of some of the articles on social policy—in these and other references to 'the sovereign Irish nation' of de Valera's Constitution, most Ulster Unionists did not recognise themselves easily, or fully, or, in most cases, at all.

It was to be expected that Unionists would point out these contradictions: and this they did, regularly and trenchantly (with a mixture of outrage and satisfaction), in the half-century after 1937. But at the time of its enactment these contradictions were pointed out by the most cogent critic who took part in the Dáil debate on the draft constitution, Deputy Frank McDermott. However, the protracted, and at times heated, debate in the Dáil and in public on the 1937 Constitution was chiefly centred on the proposed powers of the President (would de Valera become a dictator?), the status, role and rights of women under the Constitution, and church-state relations. The incorporation of 'the nation' into the Constitution was not a significantly divisive or, as it seems, a significantly controversial issue in the debate, which concluded with the adoption of the Constitution in a plebiscite among the voters of the 26-county Saorstát Éireann.[6] The turnout was 76 per cent of those entitled to vote; of the 1.2 million who voted, 685,105 were in favour of the Constitution, while 526,945 voted against.

The first major review of de Valera's Constitution took place under the promptings of Seán Lemass in the confident mid-sixties. An all-party Oireachtas committee, chaired by George Colley, reviewed the Constitution. Its report, published in December 1967, recommended (among other changes) the replacement of the by now controversial articles 2 and 3 with the following statement:

> The Irish nation hereby proclaims its firm will that its territory be re-united in brotherly affection between all Irishmen. The laws enacted by the Parliament established by this Constitution shall, until the achievement of the nation's unity shall otherwise require, have the like area and extent of application as the laws of the Parliament which existed prior to the adoption of this Constitution.[7]

The mood of the mid-1960s in the Republic is nowadays generally described in terms of its note of optimism, openness, cultural and intellectual curiosity, and a general questioning of the conventional wisdom of the older generation on all important questions: church-state relations, the conditions for economic growth, the relationship between economic growth and social and cultural change. Many developments affected values and attitudes in Ireland in the 1960s: the impact of economic (and demographic) growth, of television and the communications revolution, of Vatican II; the debate on the manifold implications of our impending entry to the EEC; the fact that the historic Lemass-O'Neill meetings had begun to thaw the long-frozen relationship between the political élites in Dublin and Belfast.

So far as national identity was concerned, it is probably fair to say that by the late 1960s most citizens of the Republic took their Irish nationality for granted; their Irishness was a 'given', uncomplicated and inseparable aspect of their citizenship of the independent Irish republic. It is true, of course, that the 'essence' of Irish nationality—its authenticating marks, the particularity of the Irish witness in literature and the arts, for example—continued to exercise the minds of intellectuals and cultural groups concerned with the preservation and cultivation of a distinctive Irish cultural and political identity. Indeed, the greater openness of society to external cultural influences, notably through television and the communications revolution in general, probably gave an extra stimulus to the discussion of what was distinctive in Irish national culture and identity, and how much of this distinctiveness could or should be preserved in a changing society, and by what means. But whatever the intellectuals may have been thinking and writing, the majority of the citizens in the Republic, particularly the younger generation, probably took their Irishness for granted by the late 1960s, when the all-party Oireachtas committee published its review of the Constitution.

The recommendations of the 1967 report, whatever their merits, were quickly overtaken by the outbreak of the conflict in Northern Ireland in the later 1960s.[8] As the conflict in Northern Ireland began to affect every aspect of life throughout Ireland, the question of national identity returned to centre-stage in the debate among politicians, churchmen and intellectuals about the current predicament and future prospects of the people of Ireland, the people of Northern Ireland in particular. This conflict and this debate have had consequences for every aspect of our public affairs. Three in particular seem to me to have a particular bearing on our consideration of articles 1 to 8 of the Constitution.

Firstly, nationalists, especially in the Republic, are now much more aware of and concerned with the complex identity, attitudes and predicament of the Ulster Unionists than was the case twenty years ago. (Indeed, it has sometimes seemed that this concern with and for the Unionists has eclipsed entirely concern with other vital aspects of the partition problem.)

Secondly, up to the present time articles 2 and 3 have not

proved an impediment to important initiatives being taken by the Dublin government to find a formula for reconciling nationalist and Unionist demands. The Sunningdale agreement of 1973 was challenged in the courts, in particular the clause that declared that 'the Irish Government fully accepted and solemnly declared that there could be no change in the status of Northern Ireland, until a majority of the people of Northern Ireland desired a change in that status.' When Kevin Boland claimed that this would have the effect of limiting the sovereignty and prejudicing the rights to jurisdiction claimed in articles 2 and 3, the case was rejected, essentially on the grounds that the statement of a government's policy on a *de facto* situation was not a denial or a repudiation of the *rights* claimed in the relevant articles.[9]

More recently, opinion has divided on whether or not article 1 of the Anglo-Irish Agreement of 1985 is repugnant to articles 2 and 3 of our present Constitution. Article 1 of the 1985 Anglo-Irish Agreement states that the two governments

(*a*) affirm that any change in the status of Northern Ireland would only come about with the consent of a majority of the people of Northern Ireland;

(*b*) recognise that the present wish of a majority of the people of Northern Ireland is for no change in the status of Northern Ireland;

(*c*) declare that, if in the future a majority of the people of Northern Ireland clearly wish for and formally consent to the establishment of a united Ireland, they will introduce and support in the respective Parliaments legislation to give effect to that wish.

The courts have yet to pronounce on this issue; but whatever the outcome, articles 2 and 3 in the Constitution cannot be altered by the courts or by the Oireachtas; they can only be altered by the voters of the state in a referendum.[10]

This brings me to the third aspect of the recent debate on nationality that seems to call for comment. This is the fact that, even as the notion of cultural pluralism took firm root among key sections of the population, and as the commitment to peaceful unification by consent came to be the declared policy of most of the nationalist parties and groups on the island, at the same time there is clear evidence that mainstream nationalist thinking and policy continues to see the national territory as the whole island of Ireland.

This emerged clearly in the report of the New Ireland Forum. Acknowledging that 'a new Ireland will require a new constitution which will ensure that the needs of all traditions are fully met,' the Forum report went on to claim that 'a united Ireland in the form of a sovereign, independent Irish state to be achieved peacefully and by consent . . . would offer the best and most durable basis for peace and stability.' And while the report recognised that 'such a form of unity would require a general and explicit acknowledgement of a broader and more comprehensive Irish identity,' and that 'such unity would . . . be different from both the existing Irish state and the existing arrangements in Northern Ireland because it would necessarily accommodate all the fundamental elements in both traditions,' in the final analysis 'the particular structure of political unity which the Forum would wish to see established is a unitary state, achieved by agreement and consent, embracing the whole island of Ireland and providing irrevocable guarantees for the protection and preservation of both the unionist and nationalist identities. A unitary state on which agreement had been reached would also provide the ideal framework for the constructive interaction of the diverse cultures and values of the people of Ireland.'[11]

In more recent days, the Progressive Democrats have published a draft constitution, which will, no doubt, generate further debate in the months ahead. It suggests several important changes in the articles and clauses that describe or invoke 'the nation'; but its suggested alternative to the existing articles 2 and 3 is worth quoting in full:

> The people of Ireland hereby proclaim their firm will that the national territory, which consists of the whole island of Ireland, its islands and territorial seas, be reunited in harmony and by consent. The laws enacted by the Parliament established by this Constitution, until the achievement of the Nation's unity may otherwise require, shall have the like area and extent of application as the

> laws of the Parliament which existed prior to the adoption of this Constitution. Provision may be made by law to give extra-territorial effect to such laws.

Whatever the flexibility on political structures, or however 'open' the version of cultural pluralism or diversity, it seems that the desire for territorial integrity is still close to the core of mainstream nationalist thinking.

Whether the public at large share this conviction is a question that only a referendum on articles 2 and 3 could answer definitively. But recent public opinion polls, most notably the MRBI surveys of 1983 and 1987, give us some intriguing clues. The 1987 survey found in its sample that only 56 per cent of the people in the Republic considered the Irish nation to consist of thirty-two counties (down from 63 per cent in 1983), with 38 per cent opting for the twenty-six counties as the extent of the Irish nation (up from 34 per cent in 1983); only 33 per cent of those questioned considered the people of Northern Ireland unambiguously Irish (down from 41 per cent in 1983), with 42 per cent of the sample considering the people of Northern Ireland both Irish *and* British (up from 39 per cent in 1983); a 15 per cent minority considered the Northern people to be unambiguously British. So far as reunification is concerned, 67 per cent of the 1987 sample hoped for reunification (down from 76 per cent in 1983), with 19 per cent not wanting unification; but about half of those questioned believed that the North would never be united with the rest of the country.[12]

Those who might be prompted by these figures to talk of constitutional change or amendment would do well to remember that a constitutional referendum (or an election) is a different matter from an opinion or attitude survey taken at a given point in time. As recent experience of referenda has shown, the precise wording of a constitutional amendment, the particular configuration of political parties and interests on the issue in question, and the general political management of a constitutional amendment, are all vital to the outcome.[13]

In present circumstances it seems to me to be most unlikely that articles 1 to 8 will be removed or amended as a result of piecemeal constitutional amendment of the existing document. The drafting of a new constitution would, of course, afford an opportunity for a reconsideration of the manner, and the wording, that might best describe the relationship between state and nation in late-twentieth-century Ireland; and here the experience of other peoples with broadly similar problems would merit careful attention (one thinks immediately of Germany). However, all commentators agree that every constitutional document, however timeless some of its fundamental truths and tenets may be, reflects in some way the times in which it is written. De Valera's Constitution, by and large, reflected the Irish nationalist consensus view of what constituted 'the Irish nation', and how it should be incorporated into the Constitution. We would do well to ask ourselves the question what, if any, would be a consensus view on this complex matter of the Irish nation and the state that might be incorporated into a new constitution drafted in the somewhat unsettled ideological climate of Ireland in the late 1980s.

NOTES

1. *Irish Times*, 29 December 1987.
2. A point made in the standard commentary on the Constitution: John Kelly, *The Irish Constitution*, Dublin: Jurist Publishing Company 1980, 22-3.
3. *An Ghaeilge agus an Dlí: Tuarascáil*, Dublin: Fásach 1986.
4. ibid.
5. John Bowman, *De Valera and the Ulster Question, 1917-1973*, Oxford: Clarendon Press 1982.
6. An analysis of aspects of the public debate on the 1937 Constitution is Mary McGinty, 'A Study of the Campaign For and Against the Constitution', unpublished MA dissertation, UCG, 1987.
7. For a full report on the review, see the *Irish Times*, 23 December 1967.
8. Two recent works that cover developments since 1960 are Frank Litton (ed.), *Unequal Achievement*, Dublin: Institute of Public Administration 1982, and Kieran Kennedy (ed.), *Ireland in Transition: Economic and Social Change in Ireland Since 1960*, Cork and Dublin: Mercier Press 1986.
9. See Kelly, *The Irish Constitution*, 13-17.
10. A critical view of the agreement (which includes the full text of the agreement as an appendix) is Anthony Coughlan, *Fooled Again?: the Anglo-Irish Agreement and After*, Cork and Dublin: Mercier Press 1986.

11. *New Ireland Forum: Report*, Dublin: Stationery Office 1984.
12. *MRBI Twenty-First Anniversary Poll*, Dublin: Market Research Bureau of Ireland 1983, and *Éire Nua: an MRBI Perspective on Irish Society Today*, Dublin: Market Research Bureau of Ireland 1987.
13. This is especially true of the referendum on the divorce issue in 1985.

MR JUSTICE DÓNAL BARRINGTON

5. *The North and the Constitution*

Dónal Barrington was called to the Bar in 1951, to the Inner Bar in 1968 and to the Northern Ireland Bar in 1971. He was appointed a judge of the High Court in 1979.

WALTER BAGEHOT divided the British constitution into the 'efficient' parts and the 'dignified' parts. One might divide the Irish Constitution into the 'efficient' parts and the 'confessional' parts. The 'efficient' parts are concerned with the workings of government and with the protection of citizens' rights, and, by and large, are working reasonably well. Most public controversy has centred on the 'confessional' parts.

One cannot deal with the subject of the North and the Constitution without getting involved in the confessional parts of the Constitution. Articles 2 and 3 of the Constitution certainly raise matters of political controversy in which I do not wish to get involved. It may, however, be helpful to offer a personal opinion on what the articles mean. In many ways Gearóid Ó Tuathaigh's paper has set the historical and political background to what I have to say. I wish to attempt a legal analysis. It is not an easy matter, and I am conscious that what I have to say may be too simple for the lawyer and too complex for the layman. With these few words of warning I shall begin.

The first reference to the North appears in the Preamble to the Constitution, which says that the people adopted the Constitution so that the dignity and freedom of the individual may be assured, true social order attained, and the unity of our country restored. So it is clear, even from the Preamble, that the Constitution accepts that the country is divided and sets reunification as a national objective.

The next reference to the North comes in articles 2 and 3. It is important to remember that articles 2 and 3 appear in a section of the Constitution headed 'The Nation'. The next section of the Constitution (beginning with article 4) is headed 'The State'. There can be no doubt that this distinction was deliberately drawn by the drafters of the Constitution. It is clear from the layout of the Constitution itself. It is also clear from a trenchant memorandum to Mr de Valera, at the time the Constitution was being drafted, from J. J. McElligott, the Secretary of the Department of Finance, who doubted if it was wise to distinguish between the nation and the state in this way.[1]

Articles 2 and 3 read as follows:

> [2] The national territory consists of the whole island of Ireland, its islands and the territorial seas.
> [3] Pending the re-integration of the national territory, and without prejudice to the right of the Parliament and Government established by this Constitution to exercise jurisdiction over the whole of that territory, the laws enacted by that Parliament shall have the like area and extent of application as the laws of Saorstát Éireann and the like extra-territorial effect.

Very few people have attempted to analyse these articles or to relate them to other articles in the Constitution before either praising or condemning them. It is probably true to say that nationalists draw some consolation from the articles while unionists see in them a threat by the South to take over the North.

If article 2 stood alone, its meaning would be clear: the national territory consists of the whole island of Ireland. But it does not stand alone. Article 3 provides that, 'pending the re-integration of the national territory,' laws passed by the Oireachtas are to have the same area and extent of application as the laws passed by the parliament of the Free State. In other words, until such time as Ireland is reunited, laws passed by the Oireachtas are to apply in the 26-county area only. But this is declared to be 'without prejudice to the right of the Parliament and Government . . . to exercise jurisdiction over the whole of that territory'. But, it could be asked, what value is a right to legislate for the whole of Ireland if laws passed by the Oireachtas are to apply only to the 26-county area until such time as Ireland is united? What kind of right is the Constitution referring to, and what kind of threat to the North is contained in a provision of our Constitution that provides that laws enacted by the Oireachtas are to apply only to the 26-county area?

It used at one time be said that these articles amounted to a *de facto* but not *de jure* recognition of the Northern regime. Both interpretations are, I suggest, incorrect. The terms '*de facto* recognition' and '*de jure* recognition' are terms of international law, and have no relevance in a discussion of relationships between the Republic of Ireland, which is a sovereign state, and the local administration in Northern Ireland, exercising limited powers devolved from the British Parliament in Westminster. Moreover, it should be recalled that the Constitution is a domestic document, not an instrument of international law.

Our Supreme Court, in 1976, had some important things to say about articles 2 and 3. These articles, it said,

> can be understood only if their background of law and political theory is appreciated.... One of the theories held in 1937 by a substantial number of citizens was that a nation, as distinct from a State, had rights; that the Irish people living in what is now called the Republic of Ireland and in Northern Ireland together formed the Irish Nation; that a Nation has a right to unity of territory in some form, be it as a unitary or federal State; that the Government of Ireland Act, 1920, though legally binding, was a violation of that national right to unity which was superior to positive law. The national claim to unity exists not in the legal but in the political order and is one of the rights which are envisaged in Article 2; it is expressly saved by Article 3 which states the area to which the laws enacted by the Parliament established by the Constitution apply. The effect of Article 3 is that, until the division of the island of Ireland is ended, the laws enacted by the Parliament established by the Constitution are to apply to

> the same area and have the same extent of application as the laws of Saorstát Éireann had. The area to which the laws of Saorstát Éireann applied was, having regard to the Articles of Agreement of 1921 and the Act of 1925, unquestionably the area known as the Republic of Ireland.[2]

The late Mr Justice Kenny, who was a member of the court that handed down this judgment, later referred to this passage in the course of an address he delivered in Belfast, which was subsequently published in the *Northern Ireland Law Quarterly*.[3] He drew attention to this passage, and lamented the fact that it had received so little attention in public.

In the same address, Mr Justice Kenny discussed some of what he referred to as the 'fundamental doctrines' of Irish nationalism as a political creed, and summarised four of them as follows:

1. That the Irish nation comprehends all those living in the island of Ireland, except aliens.
2. That a nation, as distinct from the legal entity called the state, has rights, even though these are not recognised by law.
3. That a nation has a right to territorial unity in some form. This may take the form of a confederation in which the central government has little power, or it may be a federal state in which the central government has considerable jurisdiction.
4. That the division of the island of Ireland into two entirely separate states was a wrong against the Irish nation and had no justification in political theory, despite anything the treaties or the law provided.

The point is that while these doctrines of political nationalism are reflected in article 2 of the Constitution, the Constitution is primarily concerned with the establishment of a parliament and system of government, and that that parliament, whatever the creeds of Irish nationalism, is expressly prohibited from attempting to legislate for Northern Ireland until such time as the partition problem has been resolved.

It appears to me that this matter becomes clearer if viewed, as it should be, from the perspective of international law rather than that of national law. The term 'international law' unfortunately raises a further difficulty, because international law governs, not the relations between nations but the relations between states.

It is also important to remember that in 1936, when the Constitution was being drafted, Mr de Valera was President of the League of Nations, and that some of the values of the Covenant of the League of Nations are reflected in the Constitution itself and in particular in article 29. It appears to me to be important to relate articles 2 and 3 of the Constitution to article 29, which provides that Ireland accepts the generally recognised principles of international law as its rule of conduct in its relations with other states. Article 29 also provides that Ireland affirms its devotion to the ideal of peace and friendly co-operation amongst nations founded on international justice and morality. It then continues: 'Ireland affirms its adherence to the principle of the pacific settlement of international disputes by international arbitration or judicial determination.'

To fully understand the significance of these statements it is necessary to go to the Covenant of the League of Nations and to the 1925 Boundary Agreement, which, unlike the Constitution, is an international agreement and registered as such under the auspices of the League of Nations.

The Boundary Agreement, having referred to the Articles of Agreement for a Treaty between Great Britain and Ireland, and to the Government of Ireland Act, 1920, goes on to state, at paragraph 1: 'The extent of Northern Ireland for the purposes of the Government of Ireland Act, 1920, and of the said Articles of Agreement shall be such as was fixed by subsection (2) of Section 1 of that Act.' Subsection 2 of section 1 of the Government of Ireland Act provides that 'Northern Ireland shall consist of the parliamentary counties of Antrim, Armagh, Down, Fermanagh, Londonderry and Tyrone and the parliamentary boroughs of Belfast and Londonderry . . . '

Turning now to the Covenant of the League of Nations, one can easily see where the provisions of article 29 of the Constitution came from. Under article 12 of the Covenant, the members of the League agree that if there should arise between them any dispute likely to lead to a rupture, they will submit the matter either to arbitration or to an inquiry by the Council of the League. Under the provisions of article 13, they agree to accept the findings of any such arbitration.

It appears to me that articles 2 and 3 must be read in the light of these facts. Whatever political doctrine is stated in article 2, the state established by the Constitution has pledged to respect its international obligations and the peaceful settlement of international disputes. Article 3 accordingly prohibits it from attempting to legislate for Northern Ireland. Had article 2 stood, without article 3, it might have amounted to a claim by the South to territory that was, in international law, part of the United Kingdom. It would have amounted to an international dispute that Ireland, as a member of the League of Nations, could have been called upon to submit to international arbitration. In view of the fact that the 1925 Boundary Agreement was a treaty registered with the League of Nations, it is not difficult to predict the outcome of such an international arbitration.

It is for these reasons I suggest that the national claim made in article 2 is, for all purposes of domestic and international law, withdrawn in article 3 until such time as the unity of our country is restored. The formula contained in articles 2 and 3 is, I suggest, a subtle one in which Mr de Valera has combined nationalist ideals with common sense and political caution, in a manner not untypical of the man.

But the matter goes much further than this. All Irish governments have appreciated the dangers that beset Ireland as a small, weak country in a violent world. All governments have therefore sought to strengthen international organisations that work for the peaceful resolution of international disputes. I do not know, however, if any other government has actually written into its Constitution the principle of the pacific settlement of international disputes. Our major international dispute is our dispute with Britain about the North, and this must have been present to the minds of the drafters of the Constitution when they wrote the pacific settlement of international disputes as a political principle into our Constitution. It might therefore be said that not only does the Constitution forbid the Oireachtas to attempt to legislate for Northern Ireland until such time as Ireland has been reunited, but that it also commits the state to seek a peaceful method of reunification. There is no mandate in the Constitution for even the Government to attempt to resolve the partition problem by violence. *A fortiori*, there is no mandate for the Provisional IRA or any other organisation to attempt to do so.

The Constitution has not got a particular meaning in article 2 and a different meaning in article 29. It is one document, and has only one meaning. The most remarkable thing about it is its commitment to a peaceful solution to the partition problem. I feel that if this matter were more widely understood it would help to ease the fears and tensions that at present threaten the peace of this island.

As Professor Fanning has said, Mr de Valera, in drafting the Constitution, was hoping to get away from the Treaty of 1921 and the 1922 Constitution. But the legacy of history could not be changed. Nowhere is this more obvious than in the case of the North. The Treaty of 1921 had provided, in article 12, for the setting up of a Boundary Commission in the event of the six counties seceding from the Free State. It was widely assumed by nationalist politicians—and in this they were of course encouraged by Lloyd George—that the Boundary Commission would result in the transfer of substantial territories from North to South. Nationalists hoped for the transfer of Tyrone, Fermanagh, South Down, South Armagh, and Derry city. What remained to the Unionists, they hoped, would not be a workable entity and, sooner or later, the Unionists would have to join the South.

Looking at article 12 now, with the wisdom of hindsight, one cannot but be surprised at how naïve the nationalists were. Nowhere in article 12 is there a reference to the transfer of territories. There is indeed a reference to the wishes of the inhabitants and to economic and geographical conditions. But the task of the commission was not to transfer territories but to determine boundaries. This was capable of the interpretation that the task of the commission was simply to tidy up the existing border between North and South.

It was to be a fatal ambiguity so far as the nationalists were concerned. In 1925 the *Morning Post* claimed to have seen a draft of the commission's report, and claimed that the commission would not only not transfer any substantial portion of the North to the South but would transfer some parts of the South to the North.

The Irish government, in an effort to pre-empt the publication of the commission's report, executed the Boundary Agreement of 1925 and accepted that the border between North and South should remain as set out, in totally different circumstances, in the Government of Ireland Act, 1920. The result has been to leave the North with a significant dissident minority mainly concentrated in the areas adjoining the border and to leave North and South with a frontier that is longer than the Maginot line and traverses much wilder countryside. It bisects farms and houses, and presents opportunities that smugglers and guerrillas have been able to exploit.

I said that the Boundary Agreement of 1925 had accepted that the border should remain as set out, in totally different circumstances, in the Government of Ireland Act, 1920, and I should like to elaborate on this remark. The Government of Ireland Act was rejected by nationalist opinion, and is referred to derisively as the 'Partition Act'. But for that very reason it is worth looking at, because it was the first occasion on which legislators had to worry about how security would be organised in a partitioned Ireland. The Government of Ireland Act was the last of the Home Rule Bills to be enacted into law. Under it, both parts of Ireland would have remained in the United Kingdom. The British army would have moved freely throughout the whole of Ireland so that, from the security point of view, it was not particularly important where the line of the border lay. The Parliament of Northern Ireland and the Parliament of Southern Ireland could each have raised its own police force, but there would have been one Court of Appeal for all Ireland and both police forces would have been subject to this, so that both would have to obey the same standards. By 1925 a totally different situation prevailed. North and South had gone their different ways, with separate armies, separate police forces and separate courts. In these circumstances, whatever one thought of the border from the political point of view, it made no sense from the point of view of security.

One might illustrate the problem by looking, not at the

movements of people but at the movements of livestock on this island. In 1978, because of the malfunctioning of the pricing system in the Common Market, very much higher prices were obtainable for livestock in the Republic than in Northern Ireland. Notionally this should not have had any effect on the movements of livestock, because if the livestock moved through legal channels certain compensatory amounts would be payable by the Northern exporter at the border, which would deprive him of the benefit of the discrepancy between the prices prevailing in the two parts of Ireland. Nevertheless livestock started to move mysteriously from North to South. The Northern meat-processing plants could not obtain a sufficient supply of cattle, and workers in the plants were threatened with unemployment. The British government was advised by an independent firm of consultants that unless they did something, there was a danger that the entire production of fat cattle and pigs in the North of Ireland would disappear over the border into the Republic.

To counteract these movements, the British government introduced a subsidy for the Northern Ireland slaughterhouses. Such a subsidy was, prima facie, a breach of Common Market law. But the European Commission, having studied the matter, decided that the subsidy was, in all the circumstances, justified. The reference in the Commission's report to the border between North and South is revealing:

> This frontier is difficult to patrol and gives scope for clandestine trade. In effect, there is a single market in live cattle in these two regions owing to the structural geographical and political circumstances ... As a result of this situation there has been first of all a marked increase in the 'migration' of live animals from Northern Ireland to Ireland where intervention prices and market prices are higher, to the detriment of slaughterhouses and meat processing industries in the North. Owing to the difficulty of patrolling the common frontier, it has been possible for animals to cross into the South clandestinely in order to avoid paying the monetary compensatory amounts. To remedy these difficulties the Council authorised the

> United Kingdom to grant an employment subsidy to Northern Ireland slaughterhouses ...[4]

The Government of Ireland Act also provided for the setting up of a Council of Ireland, which was to be equally representative of the parliaments of Northern Ireland and Southern Ireland. The two parliaments could agree to confer extra powers upon the Council of Ireland, which might ultimately evolve into a parliament for the whole of Ireland. Initially the Council was to have very little power, being confined to the administration of services throughout the whole of Ireland in connection with railways, fisheries and (significantly enough) the diseases of animals. The Council of Ireland never met, and the Boundary Agreement of 1925 finally provided for its abolition. Yet on both the nationalist and Unionist side there were always people who regretted the abolition of the Council of Ireland. I remember, for instance, Professor Savory, who was a Unionist MP for Queen's University, advocating in the 1950s that the Council of Ireland should be revived.

One possible solution to the partition problem that Mr de Valera appears to have contemplated was for the Stormont parliament to retain the powers it had under the Government of Ireland Act but for the powers retained by London to be transferred to Dublin. This is probably why article 15.2 of the Constitution says that the Oireachtas may make provision by law for the creation or 'recognition' of subordinate legislatures. It was probably to facilitate such a solution that Mr de Valera retained the link with the Commonwealth in the External Relations Act, 1936. This decision, in turn, was probably responsible for article 29.4.2 of the Constitution, which provides that, for the purpose of the exercise of any executive function of the state in or in connection with its external relations, the Government may 'avail of or adopt any organ, instrument, or method of procedure used or adopted for the like purpose by the members of any group or league of nations with which the State is or becomes associated for the purpose of international co-operation in matters of common concern.'

Mr de Valera probably saw the partition problem as a matter

to be resolved, in the first instance at any rate, by the two sovereign powers, in Dublin and London. The fact that the Republic was a sovereign state gave the nationalist community a significant negotiating advantage. The most significant achievement of this approach to the problem is probably contained in the Hillsborough agreement. The trouble is that while, by and large, the nationalist community was prepared to trust the Dublin government to negotiate on its behalf, the Unionist community was not prepared to trust the British government. This is because the primary concern of the Unionist community is with its position in Ireland and not with the wider interests of the United Kingdom. This strange 'Irish dimension' should never be lost sight of.

Seán Lemass was conscious of it at the time of the Lemass-O'Neill meetings in the 1960s. Later, after the fall of O'Neill and the fall of Stormont, an effort was made at a new approach to an interim agreement at Sunningdale. There were three aspects to the Sunningdale agreement. The first was that the two governments should guarantee that there would be no change in the status of Northern Ireland until the majority of the people of Northern Ireland wished it, and that in the meantime the two governments would co-operate to ensure that the Unionist community in Northern Ireland were not forced into a united Ireland against their will. Secondly, the nationalist community, in return for accepting the institutions of Northern Ireland until such a majority evolved, would be allowed to share power in government. In the interval, there should be established an all-Ireland body, known as the Council of Ireland, to give expression to an Irish cultural identity and to attend to matters of common concern to the people of all the island.[5]

It is often said that it was the Council of Ireland that brought down the Sunningdale agreement. Indeed a member of the SDLP, in a foolish speech, said that the Council of Ireland was the wagon that was going to trundle the Unionists into a united Ireland whether they wished it or not. This speech, which was presumably designed to comfort his own supporters, was seized on eagerly by the leaders of the loyalist community.

But in truth the Council of Ireland was a paper tiger. It was different from the Council of Ireland contemplated by the Government of Ireland Act. It would indeed have had equal representation from the Oireachtas and the Northern Ireland Assembly, but it could only act by unanimous agreement, so that if even one Unionist representative objected it could not make a decision. Moreover, an amendment to the Constitution would be necessary before it could exercise any executive power. These matters were well known to the leaders of the loyalist parties, though not perhaps to the leaders of the Ulster Workers' Council strike.

The SDLP had always believed that the real loyalist objection was not to the Council of Ireland but to power-sharing. That was why, after the failure of the Sunningdale experiment, when the British government summoned a constitutional convention to search for an 'internal solution' in Northern Ireland, the SDLP decided to test the loyalists on the question of power-sharing. The SDLP's case for power-sharing was that they represented a community which, for fifty years, had been discriminated against at every level of life in Northern Ireland. If therefore they were to bring the minority community with them in supporting the institutions of Northern Ireland, they had to be able to say that they would be present at every level where important political decisions were made, so that they could assure their followers that there would be no further discrimination. It was not sufficient therefore for them to be on parliamentary committees: they had to be at the inner council of government where the final decision was made. The loyalist position was that any form of institutionalised power-sharing was alien to the British system of cabinet government, and that only a system modelled on the British system would be acceptable for Northern Ireland. The SDLP responded that even the British system contemplated a form of national government to deal with a war or other national crisis. Such a crisis, it was suggested, did in fact exist in Northern Ireland. It was in this way that the idea of the 'voluntary coalition' was born. When the loyalists finally rejected this, it became clear that no progress could be made on an internal settlement, and the convention was dissolved.

It was because no progress could be made on an internal

settlement that the two governments reverted to searching for their own solution to the problem. These matters take somewhat from the Unionists' complaint that they were not consulted about the Hillsborough agreement. At the same time, everyone realises that there can be no effective settlement without their involvement.

The search for such a settlement goes on. In the interval, the two sovereign governments have the task of keeping the peace on this island. In the past, one of the ways both governments used for keeping the peace in troubled times was the introduction of internment. Internment was in fact introduced on both sides of the border in the twenties, the forties, and the fifties. In the seventies the North introduced internment, but the South refused to follow suit. Internment was no longer acceptable to nationalist opinion, North or South. Besides, many people consider that the introduction of internment in the North in the seventies merely made matters worse. Others speculated whether a regime that could only be propped up by such methods was worth preserving.

Since then more imaginative efforts have been made, at Sunningdale and at Hillsborough, to find an acceptable interim solution to the problem. The formulation of policy in relation to such matters is, under our Constitution, a matter for the Government. There is nothing in articles 2 or 3 of the Constitution, I suggest, to inhibit the Government in its quest for an interim solution, provided that the aim of ultimate national unity is preserved. If at any time the question of setting up any form of all-Ireland body exercising executive, legislative or judicial powers should arise, a constitutional referendum would be necessary. But if that were to happen we would be on the road to an ultimate solution.

In the interval, we must all try to keep the peace.

NOTES

1. Ronan Fanning, *The Irish Department of Finance, 1922-58*, Dublin: Institute of Public Administration 1978, 267.
2. *In re Criminal Law (Jurisdiction) Bill, 1975*, [1977] IR 129, 145-8.
3. Mr Justice Kenny, 'Incorporating a Bill of Rights', in *NILQ*, 1979, 189.

4. See *Doyle* v. *An Taoiseach*, [1986] ILRM 693.
5. For the text of the Sunningdale communiqué see *Boland* v. An Taoiseach, [1974] IR 338.

DR MICHAEL GALLAGHER

6. *The President, the People and the Constitution*

Michael Gallagher is a lecturer in the Department of Political Science at Trinity College, Dublin. He is the author of *The Irish Labour Party in Transition* (1982) and *Political Parties in the Republic of Ireland* (1985), and co-editor of *Candidate Selection in Comparative Perspective: the Secret Garden of Politics* (1988).

ALTHOUGH Bunreacht na hÉireann came into operation on 29 December 1937, it was not until 4 May 1938 that the first president, Douglas Hyde, was elected, and not until 25 June of that year that he was inaugurated.

The office, which had no real parallel in the old Irish Free State Constitution, has two aspects. The President is, first and foremost, the head of state (though never explicitly described as such[1]) and as such takes 'precedence over all other persons in the State' (article 12.1). At President Hyde's inauguration ceremony, de Valera described him as 'inheriting the authority and entitled to the respect which the Gaels ever gave to those whom they recognised to be their rightful chiefs . . . In you we greet the successor of our rightful princes, and in your accession to office we hail the closing of the breach that has existed since the undoing of our nation at Kinsale.'[2]

But the President is more than merely a symbol of the nation. He or she is also, as one of the three constituent parts of the Oireachtas (article 15.1.2), a figure with certain potentially important political responsibilities. De Valera's comments on the Presidency when the relevant articles were discussed by the Dáil in 1937 give us an insight into the way—or one of the ways—in which its creator envisaged the President's role. The President, declared de Valera, was there 'to guard the people's rights and mainly to guard the Constitution,' maintaining the 'mastery' of the people and safeguarding their interests between elections.[3] De Valera did not envisage him playing any active part in the day-to-day decision-making process, which was the Government's responsibility; rather, he would fulfil the role of a reserve power, intervening on the people's behalf only if government or parliament appeared to be threatening to violate the letter or the spirit of the Constitution. The President, said Frank Aiken in the same debate, would be 'a person who will guard the rights and liberties of the people against any attempt to set up a dictator by either the Executive Council or the two Houses of the Oireachtas.'[4]

The President's independence from government is guaranteed by the difficulty of removing him from office, which can be achieved in two ways. The first occurs if the Supreme Court declares him 'permanently incapacitated' (article 12.3.1). The second method is impeachment for 'stated misbehaviour', a term not elaborated on and which presumably means only that some specific ground must be cited. A proposal to impeach the President must be supported by two-thirds of the members of one house of the Oireachtas, whereupon the other house investigates the charge; for the President to be removed from office, two-thirds of the members of the investigating house must support a proposal that the charge has been sustained (article 12.10). The impeachment procedure is, then, such that the President can be removed only if there is a broad political consensus to that effect.

To fulfil the role of 'guardian of the Constitution', the President was given six specific discretionary powers, as well as a number of duties that are performed only on the 'advice' (i.e. direction) of the Government (article 13.9). Even collectively, it must be said, they fall far short of what a President would require if his or her role were genuinely to guard the Constitution or to prevent the Government or the Oireachtas attempting to 'set up a dictator'; and in fact Bunreacht na hÉireann clearly assigns these responsibilities to the courts rather than to the President. The contrast between the grandiose phrases in the Dáil debates and the limited powers actually awarded to the office is just one manifestation of de Valera's ambivalence towards it.

In exercising three of the powers, the President is merely one step in a process that could arise in theory but has never done so in practice. First, if the Dáil and the Government wish to restrict the time the Seanad may spend considering a bill, the President's concurrence is needed (article 24.1). Second, if the Seanad wishes to challenge a decision of the Ceann Comhairle that a specific bill is a 'money bill', it needs the agreement of the President before being able to appoint a committee to settle the matter (article 22.2). Third, if the Dáil deems a particular bill to be passed notwithstanding its non-ratification by the Seanad (article 23.1), a majority of senators together with at least a third of all TDs may petition the President to put the bill to a referendum of the people (article 27).

The other three powers are exercisable on the President's initiative. The first is to convene a meeting of either or both houses of the Oireachtas (article 13.2.3). This power is, presumably, intended to cover situations where the Government is unable or unwilling to convene such a meeting; to date, it has not been used in these circumstances. Second, the President has the right, instead of signing a bill into law, to refer it to the Supreme Court for a decision on its constitutionality (article 26). The President can exercise this power, like all the others we have so far mentioned, only after consulting the Council of State (which contains a number of present and former senior political and judicial office-holders; for details see articles 31.2 and 31.3), but the final decision rests with him or her alone. Finally, the President has the right to refuse a dissolution of the Dáil, and hence the holding of a general election, to a Taoiseach who, in the words of article 13.2.2, 'has ceased to retain the support of a majority in Dáil Éireann.'

Given the lack of excitement the office has aroused since 1937, it may seem remarkable that the Presidency caused perhaps more argument and unease among deputies than any other part of Bunreacht na hÉireann when the draft version was discussed by the Dáil. Opposition TDs appeared to suspect that the office might be a vehicle for the establishment of a de Valera dictatorship, either by his becoming President and being voted considerable power by a compliant government under article 13.10 (which reads, 'Subject to this Constitution, additional powers and functions may be conferred on the President by law'), or by his installing a 'yes-man' as President and enjoying unfettered power as Taoiseach.[5] Such misgivings were, perhaps, fostered by the fact that de Valera was already 'President' (of the Executive Council).

With the benefit of experience, these fears may seem absurd. However, given the similarity between the formal powers of the French and Irish presidents (see below), it is tempting to speculate on how the Irish presidency would have evolved if de Valera had become President in 1938 while remaining Fianna Fáil leader. While the office could clearly never have been used to establish a dictatorship, it might have become a much more politically active one, along the lines of the French presidency, had the élite of the day chosen to interpret it in that way, with important consequences for the whole of the political system.

Before discussing how presidents have used their discretionary powers, we shall first look at some further illustrations of the ambivalence in de Valera's mind about the Presidency, and particularly about how much autonomy the President should have. We find examples of this both in the way a President comes to be elected and in the restrictions placed on the holder of the office. The requirement that the President 'shall be elected by direct vote of the people' (article 12.2.1) is one of the more unusual features of the Irish presidency. When we look around western Europe today, we find that most heads of state are either hereditary monarchs or are elected indirectly, most commonly by the national parliament. The only other countries where the president is directly elected by the voters are Austria, Finland, France, Iceland and Portugal, and in three of these (Finland, France and Portugal) the president wields significant power, to the extent that these countries have been described as having 'semi-presidential' systems of government.[6]

In France, it should be said, the power of the President depends entirely upon the complexion of parliament. When the Presidency and the National Assembly are in the hands of the same party, the President is the most powerful political figure. When the President is confronted by an opposition majority in parliament, as was François Mitterand after the right's victory in 1986, his power dwindles to that explicitly provided by the constitution, which turns out to be, in normal circumstances, little more than that enjoyed by the Irish President.[7]

Giving the people the right to elect their President directly could be seen as being consistent with de Valera's professed conception of the President's role as the people's watchdog over the actions of the Government. However, no sooner was the right stated than it was heavily qualified. Any would-be President, other than a current or previous holder of the office, must be nominated by at least twenty members of the Oireachtas or by four county councils (article 12.4.2).[8] This ensures that no person can even reach the starting-post without the backing of one of the main parties or some combination of the smaller ones. It thereby makes it possible for the main parties to come up with an agreed candidate and so remove all choice from the voters. To date, presidential elections have been the exception rather than the norm: the position has become vacant on nine occasions, but there have been only four contested elections (in 1945, 1959, 1966 and 1973).

The present position is thus rather unsatisfactory, in that the theoretically open election process is effectively nullified by a restrictive nomination procedure. Over the years, some have recommended changing the election rules so that an electoral college (composed most probably of the members of the Oireachtas) rather than the entire electorate would choose the President.[9] An alternative idea, more in keeping with the idea of forging a direct link between President and people, would be to relax the nomination regulations so as to allow a certain number of citizens to nominate candidates themselves. The proposed new constitution published in January 1988 by the Progressive Democrats contained a suggestion along these lines (article 3.2): it would allow 10 members of the Dáil or 30,000 eligible voters to nominate candidates.

As well as this severe limitation on the people's right to choose the President, who is supposedly their constitutional guarantor, there are also some rather draconian restrictions placed on the President. First, he or she may not address a message either to the houses of the Oireachtas or to the nation unless the Government has approved its contents (article 13.7).

Second, the President may not leave the state 'save with the consent of the Government' (article 12.9). Although even the humblest among us is free to hop onto the boat to Liverpool at will, the foremost citizen of the state may not do so without first going to the Government to ask for permission. Once again we see the duality in the Constitution's conception of the President, who is venerated on the one hand and yet reduced to a rather demeaning dependence on the Government's grace and favour on the other.

So much for the Presidency in constitutional theory: how has the office developed in practice? Thus far, only six different people have held the post of President. Dr Douglas Hyde occupied the office from 1938 to 1945; Seán T. O'Kelly then served two seven-year terms, stepping down in 1959; Éamon de Valera also held the position for fourteen years, retiring in 1973. Since then there have been a further three Presidents: Erskine Childers was in office for only seventeen months before his death in 1974; Cearbhall Ó Dálaigh served for two years before resigning in 1976; and Dr Patrick Hillery has held the position since then. Apart from Dr Hyde, each President has been associated with Fianna Fáil. Four served for many years in Fianna Fáil governments; the fifth, Ó Dálaigh, stood twice (unsuccessfully) for the party in Dublin South-West, at the 1948 and 1951 general elections, as well as serving as Attorney General to the Government in 1946-8 and 1951-3.

It can be argued that the way the Presidency has evolved has depended not only on what the Constitution says but also on the way in which these six men, and the rest of the political élite, have chosen to interpret their role. Dr Hillery, at 53, was by some way the youngest President on accession to office. Cearbhall Ó Dálaigh was 62 when he became President, Seán T. O'Kelly 63, Erskine Childers 67, Éamon de Valera 76, and Douglas Hyde 78. While the Constitution prescribes that the President must be at least 35 years old (article 12.4.1), there is no upper age limit.[10] Being aged over 60 will not automatically induce an incumbent to neglect the political aspects of the role of the President. None the less, it would be little exaggeration to say that several occupants of the office, notably Presidents O'Kelly, de Valera and Hillery, appear to have retired from active politics to the Presidency. In 1973 Erskine Childers found to his disappointment that he had done the same, as his early attempts to widen the scope of the office were met with what have been described as 'warning growls' from politicians.[11]

We cannot, of course, be certain that the four former practising politicians who have gone on to become President disengaged entirely from party politics upon entering the office. In fact, in one case there is evidence to the contrary. Although Longford and O'Neill, in their very brief account of de Valera's fourteen years as President, state that he was now 'above politics' and was 'at all times... careful, even in private, to avoid any expression of a party political viewpoint'[12] the former Fianna Fáil minister Kevin Boland offers a different perspective. He relates that after he verbally resigned from the Government in August 1969, the President's secretary asked him to visit Áras an Uachtaráin. There, according to Boland, President de Valera appealed to him to reconsider, and employed an explicitly party political argument. He 'talked of the constitutional crisis that would be caused by my resignation,' and also 'foresaw a change to Fine Gael-controlled Government and pointed out the seriousness of this in the circumstances that existed.'[13]

In many ways, the mould was set by the first President, Douglas Hyde. Although he did exercise his right to refer bills to the Supreme Court (the Offences Against the State (Amendment) Bill in 1940 and one section of the School Attendance Bill, which the Supreme Court found unconstitutional, in February 1943), everything about him and his background fitted him ideally to be the head of state rather than a politically active figure. If ever a man was 'above politics', and especially above party politics, Dr Hyde was that man, and always had been. Back in 1915 he had resigned from the presidency of Conradh na Gaeilge when the rule requiring that it be 'non-political' was abolished.[14]

Of course, the main reason why Presidents have usually confined themselves to their ceremonial role as head of state is that few occasions have arisen on which they might have employed their discretionary political powers. In fact, opportunities have arisen to use only two: to refer bills to the

Supreme Court, and to refuse a dissolution to a Taoiseach who no longer has majority support in the Dáil.

The first of these has been used eight times to date. Four of the six Presidents, the exceptions being Seán T. O'Kelly and Erskine Childers, have referred at least one bill to the Supreme Court for a decision on its constitutionality. Usually this has been accepted by the Government of the day with a good grace, and on occasion has been positively welcomed, as when President Hillery referred the 1983 bill enfranchising British citizens, about whose constitutionality there was widespread uncertainty. But there have been occasions when governments have responded with less equanimity.

Most notably, President Ó Dálaigh's decision to refer the 1976 Emergency Powers Bill to the Supreme Court set in train the events that became known as the 'Donegan affair'. The President's relations with the Government were already poor; it later emerged that the Taoiseach, Liam Cosgrave, had paid him only four visits in the previous two years for the purpose of fulfilling his constitutional obligation (article 28.5.2) to 'keep the President generally informed on matters of domestic and international policy.'[15] It appears too that in 1975 the Government had refused to grant permission to Ó Dálaigh to travel to Belfast to deliver a lecture.[16]

The affair began on 18 October 1976 when Paddy Donegan, the Minister for Defence in the coalition government, reportedly described the President as a 'thundering disgrace' (some accounts are even more colourful), and seemed to imply that he did not fully 'stand behind the State'.[17] The Government insisted that this was merely an intemperate and deplorable remark by an individual minister, whose apology should have closed the matter. The opposition argued that Donegan was expressing a view shared by several ministers, and that his remarks, far from being uttered in the heat of the moment, had been 'premeditated, calculated and deliberate', in the words of Jack Lynch.[18] President Ó Dálaigh declared that Donegan's apology was, on its own, inadequate, and that the relationship between himself and the minister had been 'irreparably breached'. When the Government majority in the Dáil voted down an opposition motion calling for Donegan's dismissal, the President tendered his resignation and returned to private life.

The affair brought to the surface a seemingly widespread feeling that the President should be above criticism, even when exercising one of the discretionary powers pertaining to the office, although this conclusion cannot be stated with certainty given that Ó Dálaigh was the recipient not of reasoned criticism but of clearly unjustified abuse. If it is true, as has been suggested,[19] that other members of the Government shared the substance of Donegan's complaint, this would reinforce the impression that a President who tries to step too far beyond his or her ceremonial role will meet with resistance in high places.

It should also be noted that the President's power to refer bills to the Supreme Court is somewhat double-edged as far as protecting the citizens' rights is concerned. Under article 34.3.3, a bill cleared by the Supreme Court after referral by the President can never again be challenged on constitutional grounds, even though its subsequent operation may reveal possibilities unsuspected when the legislation was tested in the abstract, or if new and relevant information comes to light, or if subsequent interpretation of the Constitution means that a later Supreme Court would have reached a different decision. For these reasons, the President's ability to refer bills to the Supreme Court is suitable only for certain kinds of bill, in particular those raising, as Professor Casey puts it, 'a pure question of constitutional interpretation'. Indeed, in 1983 the Supreme Court implicitly urged the President to exercise this discretionary power more sparingly in future.[20] Of course, a bill signed into law by the President in the ordinary way then becomes open to challenge by any citizen, as occurred, for example, when John O'Donovan succeeded in having the 1959 Act that re-drew constituency boundaries declared unconstitutional in 1961. This being the case, there is much to commend the suggestion of the 1967 Oireachtas Committee on the Constitution that the validity of the Act should become open to challenge again after a period of, say, seven years.[21]

The power we now turn to is exclusive to the President. His right to refuse a dissolution to a Taoiseach who has ceased to retain the support of a majority in the Dáil would, if exercised, be far-reaching in its effects. The Constitution says: 'The President may in his absolute discretion refuse to dissolve Dáil Éireann on the advice of a Taoiseach who has ceased to retain the support of a majority in Dáil Éireann' (article 13.2.2). There is an obvious ambiguity here. What exactly does 'ceased to retain the support of a majority in Dáil Éireann' mean? Clearly, it covers a Taoiseach who has been defeated in a confidence vote. But does it cover a Taoiseach whose government has suffered defeat on a major item of legislation such as a budget, and if so, where exactly is the line to be drawn between 'major' and 'minor' items? It is interesting to note that de Valera himself clearly envisaged the President being able to refuse a request for a dissolution if it came from a Taoiseach who had been defeated 'on a matter of primary importance' but not actually in a confidence vote.[22] What, too, about a Taoiseach whose Dáil base has patently disappeared but who has not yet been defeated there; or a Taoiseach who, even though never defeated in the Dáil, has never actually commanded majority support there? Professor Casey suggests that the loss of majority support can be established only by a vote in the Dáil,[23] but Geoffrey Marshall observes that this criterion is inappropriate;[24] the mere fact that a doomed Taoiseach reaches Áras an Uachtaráin before a vote of censure can be taken should not enhance a request to dissolve.

The uncertainties are illustrated by several cases that have arisen in the 1980s. In January 1982 Dr Garret FitzGerald sought, and was granted, a dissolution after his government's proposed budget had been rejected by the Dáil. In November 1982 Charles Haughey unambiguously fell into the category described in article 13.2.2, seeking and being granted a dissolution after the Dáil had voted no confidence in his administration. In January 1987, when Labour pulled out of the coalition government, Dr FitzGerald, a Taoiseach who could now command only 68 votes out of 166 in the Dáil but had not been defeated there, was granted a dissolution. And it is debatable whether Charles Haughey has ever had the formal 'support of a majority' in the Dáil since re-entering office on 10 March 1987, since even including the casting vote of the Ceann Comhairle his supporters on that day numbered only 83, exactly half the membership of the Dáil. In fact, only six of the sixteen dissolutions since 1937 (those of 1943, 1948, 1961, 1969, 1977, and 1981) have taken place on the advice of a Taoiseach who indisputably commanded majority support in the Dáil.

The use of essentially the same phrase in article 28.10, which states that a Taoiseach shall resign from office 'upon his ceasing to retain the support of a majority in Dáil Éireann' unless the President agrees to his request for a dissolution, might seem to suggest that the intention is that only a Taoiseach who has actually lost a confidence vote comes within the scope of article 13.2.2, and that only such a Taoiseach can be denied a dissolution by a President. Even so, the absence of any fuller exposition of, or judicial comment on, the words, seems to give the President discretion, even if not absolute discretion, in identifying the circumstances in which article 13.2.2 may be invoked.

If President Hillery had chosen to deny the request for a dissolution made by a Taoiseach on any of the above occasions, his decision would have been at least defensible in terms of the letter of the Constitution, although of course it would have made no sense to deny Dr FitzGerald a dissolution in 1987, since an election had to be held within ten months in any case. Only the President's granting of Charles Haughey's request for a dissolution in November 1982 generated debate, but it is hard to criticise Dr Hillery's decision. It was clear that no alternative government with any prospects of survival could have been formed from within the existing Dáil, and given the succession of controversies in which the Fianna Fáil administration had been involved, a call for a grand coalition would have been inopportune. The President's action in acceding to the Taoiseach's request was vindicated further when the ensuing election produced a Government that lasted for over four years.

Whether, indeed, a President would ever be wise to decline a Taoiseach's request for a dissolution is an open question. One can envisage improbable scenarios—a request from a Taoiseach who has been ousted from his party, who no longer commands any support in the Dáil but has not yet been defeated there, and who now seeks to bring his party down with him; or, even more unlikely, from a Taoiseach whose party has just lost a general election but who has not yet been replaced by the Dáil[25]—in which the President might be generally regarded as justified in refusing to grant a dissolution, even though these cases would not be encompassed by a narrow interpretation of article 13.2.2. In more normal circumstances, the President would, in the words of the secretary to the first President, 'be slow to refuse a dissolution except for very adequate reasons.'[26]

A situation in which it seems a President might reasonably exercise his right to refuse a dissolution would arise if there had been several general elections in a short space of time, each producing roughly the same indecisive outcome and resulting in insecure minority governments. The point might be reached where the President felt entitled to insist that the people had made their wishes clear at the previous elections, and that it was for the Dáil collectively to accept the voters' repeated verdict and work within the situation it had created, even if this involved unfamiliar alliances or difficult compromises. This view, it should be said, goes further than the consensus among those who have discussed this question in the British context.[27] They conclude that a minority government, whether defeated or undefeated, may be refused a request to dissolve only, if at all, if an alternative government that has reasonable prospects of survival is possible. It is being suggested here that the President has a right to insist that further efforts be made to reach an alternative arrangement, even if the parties in the Dáil are disposed to maintain that no stable government is possible. Had President Hillery decided not to grant Mr Haughey a dissolution in November 1982, it would no doubt have been with this kind of consideration in mind.

There are two further points to make here. The first is that if a majority of TDs want an election, the President cannot stand in their way, for they then have the option of voting tactical support for a Taoiseach on the understanding that his or her first action will be to obtain a dissolution. The second is that any exercise by a President of his discretionary power in this area is fraught with hazard, might well lay the President open to the charge of displaying a partisan bias, and would be likely to evoke discontent and considerable unease among the political élite. It would hardly be surprising if Presidents were always to decide that the prudent course lay in agreeing to the Taoiseach's request, thereby referring the matter to the electorate.

This brings us to another question that has received some discussion in recent years, namely whether the President has any role in the process of government formation when there is a hung Dáil. Clearly, Bunreacht na hÉireann mentions no such role, and the President has not got the power, equivalent to that of the British monarch, to designate a TD as Taoiseach and invite that person to form a government. However, the idea has been mooted that the President could, in such a situation, take soundings among party leaders, and communicate privately to them his opinion as to who would have the best chance of forming a stable administration.[28] The President, it is suggested, would be able to wield some moral authority in such a situation despite not having any explicit constitutional power.

Although there is nothing to prevent the President, like any other citizen, attempting to help in the process of government formation, there is no reason to suppose that such efforts would meet with any success, unless of course the parties concerned were keen to allow themselves to be enticed off a hook of their own making in a manner that enabled them to avoid losing face. In normal circumstances, such presidential efforts would come into conflict with the far stronger pull of loyalty to the party. A suggestion from the President that, say, Fianna Fáil and Fine Gael form a coalition government, or that both join under the leadership of a member of one of the smaller parties, would count for not much more than a newspaper leader-writer's entreaty along the same lines. A call from President O'Kelly in 1952 for a merger or a coalition between Fianna Fáil and Fine Gael met with a complete lack of response from the parties.[29] Were the President to propose that a party might find broader support in the Dáil if it changed its leader, the response would probably be brusque. In March 1987, when it seemed that some (not including the President) were making such a suggestion to Fianna Fáil, Ray Burke declared: 'Nobody will decide on the leadership of Fianna Fáil except Fianna Fáil, and our leader is Charles J. Haughey.'[30] Any attempt by a President to intervene in a party's internal affairs would be much more likely to bring the Presidency into disrepute than to achieve the intended result. It might be more prudent for Presidents to walk before they try to run; to win acceptance of their right to exercise their constitutionally specified discretionary powers before trying to wield powers they do not possess.

What, then, is the current status of the office? On paper, there is a coherent case for arguing that there is something inherently unsatisfactory about the combination of the two hats the President is given to wear, the one ceremonial and the other political. On the other hand, Presidents have thus far donned their political hat so rarely that few have argued, or probably would argue, that the articles concerning the office are prime candidates for consideration in the context of a review of Bunreacht na hÉireann. It appears that there is a general consensus among people and politicians alike that a President should be very slow to step outside his ceremonial role.

There are, it seems, four changes that could be made to the office. The Presidency could be stripped of all political powers; it could be allocated additional ones; it could be allowed to become more active, though without any formal extension of its powers; or it could simply be abolished.

The first option, to turn the President into an entirely ceremonial figure, might be justified with the claim that this seems to have happened anyway. Many doubt whether it would ever be appropriate for the President to use his power to refuse a dissolution; the Supreme Court itself has voiced concern at the consequences of his using his power to refer bills to it. Even so, to take this option would surely be an over-reaction. The President's ability to refer bills to the Supreme Court has proved of value in some cases; his ability to refuse a dissolution to a Taoiseach who has ceased to retain the support of a majority in the Dáil could also prove so in the future.

The second option, to give the President additional discretionary powers, also has little to commend it. The only extra power anyone appears to have suggested would be that of designating a Taoiseach in a situation where no deputy can secure nomination by the Dáil.[31] While there might be some merit in endowing the President with a prescribed responsibility in these circumstances, it would also carry the danger that the Dáil's reduced responsibility would tempt it into irresponsibility, if the onus of selecting a Taoiseach were seen to rest ultimately on the shoulders of the President rather than the Dáil.

The third option, to widen the scope of the office, would, unlike the others, require a change in political culture rather than in Bunreacht na hÉireann. It would involve a higher profile by the President of the day; a willingness to speak out on controversial issues (such as environmental pollution or drug abuse), though without thereby becoming either identifiable with any particular party, or wearisome, by issuing excessively frequent homilies; and a preparedness on the part of politicians to accept such a role for the President. While it is true that Bunreacht na hÉireann states that any presidential 'message to the Nation' must have the prior approval of the Government (article 13.7.3), it is by no means certain that all public remarks by the President need be deemed a 'message to the Nation'. In any case, the remedy appears to lie in the President's own hands, as he could simply refrain from submitting his scripts for prior scrutiny to the Government (as, it has been alleged, President Ó Dálaigh did[32]). In this situation, the Government would be forced either to accept the position or to embark on the momentous and (in these circumstances) unpopular process of impeachment. Brian Doolan maintains that the issuing of a statement not previously vetted by the Government would amount to misbehaviour,[33] but the electorate might take a less severe view. It is more likely that a Government that tried to compel a President to confine himself to platitudes could expect little public sympathy, especially given the apparently lax regard that some past Taoisigh have had for their constitutional obligation to 'keep the President generally informed on matters of domestic and international policy.'[34]

Finally, should the Presidency be abolished? The 1967 Constitutional Review Committee considered the idea of allocating its ceremonial functions to the Taoiseach and dispensing altogether with its discretionary powers. The arguments they present suggest that more would be lost than gained by the idea.[35] An alternative idea would be again to transfer the ceremonial functions to the Taoiseach, but to charge a Presidential Commission with handling the discretionary powers. At present such a commission comes into operation when the Presidency is vacant (and on other occasions: see article 14.1) and consists of the Chief Justice, the Ceann Comhairle of the Dáil and the Cathaoirleach of the Seanad. Given that the last two posts are generally occupied by Government supporters, it may be doubted whether such a body would have sufficient independence of the Government to justify its being awarded the discretionary powers currently possessed by the President.

This difficulty could, it is true, be overcome by reversing the balance of the commission so that only one of its members is a politician, the other two being judges (perhaps the Chief Justice and the president of the High Court). But it would surely be an unhealthy development to involve the judiciary even more closely in the policy-making process than is already the case. To give judges the majority voice in settling the question of whether a bill should be referred to the Supreme Court for a decision on its constitutionality would give them two bites at the same cherry; to give them the power to decide whether a Taoiseach could or could not call a general election would be to confer on them an explicitly political responsibility that they would undoubtedly regard as a poisoned chalice.

But given the rather uninspiring record of the Presidency to date, it is difficult to think of many positive benefits the country has derived from the office. Political institutions must develop or die; and if Presidents continue to opt for the passive role adopted by most of the post's occupants, a future proposal to abolish the Presidency altogether may arouse only indifference.

NOTES

1. See John Kelly, *The Irish Constitution* (2nd ed.), Dublin: Jurist Publishing Company 1984, 57, for a discussion of this point.
2. Quoted in Michael McDunphy, *The President of Ireland*, Dublin: Browne and Nolan 1945, 4. For complete text, see Maurice Moynihan (ed.), *Speeches and Statements by Éamon de Valera*, Dublin: Gill and Macmillan 1980, 354.
3. *Dáil Debates*, vol. 67, cols. 40, 51, 11 May 1937.

4. *Dáil Debates*, vol. 67, col. 326, 13 May 1937.
5. See the speeches of John Marcus O'Sullivan and John A. Costello, *Dáil Debates*, vol. 67, cols. 229, 303, 12 May 1937, and Paddy McGilligan, *Dáil Debates*, vol. 67, col. 1007-9, 25 May 1937.
6. Maurice Duverger, 'A New Political System Model: Semi-presidential Government', in *European Journal of Political Research*, 8 (1980), 165-87. See also Arend Lijphart, *Democracies*, New Haven: Yale University Press 1984, 82-9, and Jan-Erik Lane and Svante Ersson, *Politics and Society in Western Europe*, London: Sage 1987, 233-41.
7. For a description see Jean Blondel, *The Government of France* (2nd ed.), London: Methuen 1974, 130-8.
8. Article 12.4.4 states that 'former or retiring Presidents may become candidates on their own nomination.' This could well be read as indicating that this is the *only* method by which such individuals can be validly nominated, particularly as article 12.4.2 seems to be restricted in its application to 'every candidate for election, not a former or retiring President'. However, in 1966 President de Valera's nomination by twenty members of the Fianna Fáil Oireachtas party was accepted, and the opposition of the day did not question its validity.
9. David Gwynn Morgan, *Constitutional Law of Ireland*, Dublin: Round Hall Press 1985, 52. Some pros and cons are discussed in *Report of the Committee on the Constitution*, Dublin: Stationery Office 1967 (Pr. 9817), 9-10.
10. Article 12.4.1 appears to be an example of a conflict between the Irish and English texts. The Irish text, which would take precedence in any case of a conflict, says that the President must have completed 35 years of age, but one reading of the English version, which requires a nominee only to have 'reached his thirty-fifth year of age', would allow a person of 34 to be eligible. See Kelly, *The Irish Constitution*, 143.
11. Basil Chubb, *The Constitution and Constitutional Change in Ireland*, Dublin: Institute of Public Administration 1978, 28-9. See also John Young, *Erskine H. Childers, President of Ireland: a Biography*, Gerrards Cross: Colin Smythe 1985, 169-92.
12. Earl of Longford and Thomas P. O'Neill, *Éamon de Valera*, London: Arrow 1974, 452.
13. Kevin Boland, *Up Dev!*, Rathcoole (Co. Dublin): Kevin Boland 1977, 13.
14. Longford and O'Neill, *Éamon de Valera*, 18.
15. *Dáil Debates*, vol. 294, col. 429-30, 23 November 1976. On the same occasion, Cosgrave stated that his predecessor, Jack Lynch, had visited President de Valera for this purpose on only four occasions in fifteen months. Subsequent Taoisigh have refused to be drawn on the number of visits they have paid to Áras an Uachtaráin. Longford and O'Neill (*Éamon de Valera*, 452) report that when de Valera was Taoiseach he visited President Hyde once a month, and that this practice was continued during de Valera's own presidency by Lemass and Lynch. President Childers' biographer writes that Cosgrave visited Childers about once a month, but that Cosgrave's briefings contained 'little more than could be gleaned from the newspapers' (Young, *Erskine H. Childers*, 190).

16. *Irish Times*, 3 December 1976, 14.
17. For a discussion of this incident see Michael Gallagher, 'The Presidency of the Republic of Ireland: Implications of the "Donegan Affair"', in *Parliamentary Affairs*, 30 (1977), 373-84, and David Gwynn Morgan, 'The Emergency Powers Bill reference: I', in *Irish Jurist* (new series), 13 (1978), 67-82.
18. *Dáil Debates*, vol. 293, col. 161, 21 October 1976.
19. Chubb, *The Constitution and Constitutional Change in Ireland*, 29-30.
20. James Casey, *Constitutional Law in Ireland*, London: Sweet and Maxwell 1987, 264-5.
21. *Report of the Committee on the Constitution*, 36. Mr Justice Walsh makes the same suggestion in his foreword to Casey's *Constitutional Law in Ireland*, xii.
22. *Dáil Debates*, vol. 67, col. 1212, 26 May 1937.
23. *Constitutional Law in Ireland*, 77.
24. Geoffrey Marshall, *Constitutional Conventions: the Rules and Forms of Political Accountability*, Oxford: Clarendon Press 1984, 41.
25. *Report of the Committee on the Constitution*, 13.
26. McDunphy, *The President of Ireland*, 52.
27. For example, B. S. Markesinis, *The Theory and Practice of Dissolution of Parliament*, Cambridge: Cambridge University Press 1972, 84-96; David Butler, *Governing Without a Majority* (2nd ed.), Basingstoke: Macmillan 1986, 122-34; Marshall, *Constitutional Conventions*, 35-44.
28. This question is raised by John Coakley, 'The General Election in Context', in Michael Laver, Peter Mair and Richard Sinnott (eds.), *How Ireland Voted*, Dublin: Poolbeg 1987, 166.
29. His speech was reported most fully in the *Limerick Leader*, 18 October 1952.
30. Shane Kenny and Fergus Keane, *Irish Politics Now*, Dingle: Brandon 1987, 59.
31. See the discussion in *Report of the Committee on the Constitution*, 11-13. An expanded role for the President in these circumstances is also envisaged in article 4.12 of the Progressive Democrats' proposed new constitution.
32. *Irish Times*, 3 December 1976, 14.
33. Brian Doolan, *Constitutional Law and Constitutional Rights in Ireland* (2nd ed.), Dublin: Gill and Macmillan 1988, 62.
34. See note 15.
35. *Report of the Committee on the Constitution*, 8.

PROFESSOR BASIL CHUBB

7. *Government and Dáil: Constitutional Myth and Political Practice*

Basil Chubb is Professor of Political Science at Trinity College, Dublin. His publications include *The Control of Public Expenditure* (1952), *The Government and Politics of Ireland* (2nd ed. 1982), *The Government: an Introduction to Cabinet Government in Ireland* (1974), *The Constitution and Constitutional Change in Ireland* (1978) and *A Source Book of Irish Government* (rev. ed. 1983).

'THE President has given the greater part of his time for the last three, four or five years to the drafting of the document now before us. He spent his time drafting a document for which there was no demand.'[1] The speaker was Deputy Daniel Morrissey, and the document he was talking about was Bunreacht na hÉireann. 'The President' was the President of the Executive Council, Éamon de Valera, who was piloting his brain-child through Dáil Éireann virtually single-handed. For this was *his* constitution. Deputy Morrissey might not have felt the need for it, but de Valera certainly did. Winning office in 1932 had given him the opportunity to justify his long campaign against the Treaty and to rewrite the fundamental law of the state to accommodate his version of Anglo-Irish relations. The very purpose of the new constitution was to destroy that settlement and thereby justify his opposition to it. That it also offered the opportunity to effect changes in the machinery of government and to introduce a new Catholic dimension, particularly in the statements of citizens' rights, was welcome but of secondary importance.

In general, the system of government within which de Valera had worked since 1927, when he came in out of the unconstitutional cold and assumed the leadership of the main opposition party in the Dáil, was not a matter for dispute. Far from it: it suited him and his party well. Originally, the Irish Free State Constitution had provided for a British-style cabinet government somewhat diluted by devices intended to limit the power of the government as against parliament and the people. These devices, which included provisions for the people to be involved directly in legislation and for so-called 'extern' ministers, i.e. ministers who would not be members of the cabinet or of the Oireachtas, were removed during the 1920s by the Cumann na nGaedheal government, and this trend towards consolidating the controlling, co-ordinating role of the cabinet was confirmed after Fianna Fáil won power. The system as it was then operating suited a strong prime minister bent on reform and supported by a loyal majority party that looked to their charismatic, messianic leader for initiative and direction.

Consequently Bunreacht na hÉireann to a large extent retained what had been in the Irish Free State Constitution or had evolved in practice in the tense, formative years of the state, when the circumstances had seemed to demand strong government, and the system had been put to the test. The only major exception was the arrangements for the senate. The Irish Free State Senate had been regarded by all parties in the 1920s as unsatisfactory. Abolished by the Fianna Fáil government in 1936, it was replaced only reluctantly by de Valera with a body that was both singular in its composition and circumscribed in its powers. Consequently the prestige of Seanad Éireann was, and remains, low. To most, it seems a leisurely body that is merely another selection of party politicians chosen in an unnecessarily complicated and not particularly democratic manner. Were it to disappear, it would not be missed.

This system of government can justly be described as 'British'; to be more precise, it should be labelled as the 'early-twentieth-century Westminster model'. As it happened, British practice at this time tended to emphasise the role and position of the cabinet at the expense of parliament, and it was this model, which the founders of the state adopted from the beginning, that received de Valera's *imprimatur*. It can appropriately be discussed in the present tense for the very good reason that it is still in operation, remarkably unchanged, after more than half a century.

The Government, which is the term used in the Constitution rather than 'cabinet', is the centrepiece of the whole system and has the dominant role. It consists of a group of parliamentary leaders of the party or coalition of parties that can command a majority in the Dáil, who meet as a committee to decide the major issues of public policy and the measures that they intend to put to the Oireachtas for approval; to co-ordinate the activities of the departments which, as ministers, they control; and generally to manage the public-sector business of the country. At present there are fifteen ministers, but there are in addition another fifteen junior ministers of one sort or another who are not members of the Government mentioned in the Constitution, i.e. the cabinet, but are otherwise part of what is commonly called 'the government'.

Governments usually emerge as a direct result of general elections at which the electorate choose leaders to govern them from rival groups of politicians, each consisting of a party leader and his most prominent colleagues and with one of which most candidates identify themselves. It is this process which, together with the continuous political competition that results from periodic elections, in theory at least makes political leaders responsive to the electorate.

The Government governs the country. It takes, or at least endorses, all those decisions that have to be made at the highest level. Because of their various leadership positions—as party leaders, as leaders of the majority in the Dáil, and as heads of Government departments—they are well placed to do so. In particular, they have at their disposal the resources of their departments and the advice of their senior civil servants, people of great experience and expertise. It is this combination of a group of people with political power and legitimacy and a group of professional experts with the influence that comes of knowledge and experience that both dominates and, we can almost say, monopolises, public policy-making and controls the administration of state business.

The Taoiseach is, as it is put in Bunreacht na hÉireann, 'the head of the Government'. This is another area where de Valera modified the provisions of the Irish Free State Constitution, for whereas that Constitution tended if anything to play down his role, Bunreacht na hÉireann pays considerable attention to him and specifically assigns duties and powers to him that were formerly assigned to the cabinet as a whole. To a large extent, however, these provisions only made formal what was in fact the practice, if not under the first prime minister, W. T. Cosgrave, before 1932, then certainly under de Valera, his successor. 'What is being done here', de Valera explained to the Dáil, 'has been to translate into practice what has been done in the past.' It was, he continued, 'only making explicit what was implicit all the time.'[2]

In any event, the Taoiseach is pre-eminent among his colleagues. He personifies the Government; and, since de Valera's time, the practice of building up the personal image of leaders by assiduous public relations activities has increased their potential to dominate. People speak of 'the FitzGerald government', 'the Haughey government', and so on. The precise degree of pre-eminence varies from Taoiseach to Taoiseach however. Personalities and political situations lead to differences between one and another. People are inclined to contrast de Valera, 'the Chief', or Haughey, 'the Boss', with allegedly less dominant, more 'chairman-like' Taoisigh: but W. T. Cosgrave was also in his time known as 'the Boss', and Jack Lynch, whose style was designedly intended to ensure that no-one called him 'boss', publicly fired two of his most senior colleagues, Haughey and Blaney, in May 1970. In coalitions it can be different, of course; but otherwise de Valera's chosen title for the office, 'Taoiseach', and his description, 'head of the Government', epitomise the facts of the situation.

A strong government under a strong leader, maintained in office by a majority of faithful supporters of one's own party—that is how de Valera envisaged the system, and this was his experience during most of his long tenure of office. He was not always in this position, though, and when that was the case he took an early opportunity to mend his hand by calling new elections, as in 1933, 1938, and 1944. This led him also, at the very end of his period of office, to seek to change the electoral system, which he believed was a major cause of the instability, as he saw it, of the late forties and fifties. He recognised that the divisions engendered by the Civil War, which produced two camps facing one another across a deep and unbridgeable divide in Dáil Éireann, were breaking down. His style of government required such a configuration. In his eyes, the presence of other parties endangered strong government, and coalitions were an evil to be avoided.

While de Valera's party has maintained its dislike of coalition—an attitude that is very cogent as long as it can continue to hope to win an overall majority—anti-Fianna Fáil coalitions became and remained the alternative. Irish people have become accustomed to coalition governments, but evidently for the politician, tradition dies hard. Few if any party leaders and almost no party activists have, or have ever had, a belief in coalition government as an inherently desirable form of government, even when involved in one. Nor do governments subscribe to the politics of compromise and transient parliamentary alliances to get agreement on particular policies. The tradition of strictly adversarial politics remains strong. Consequently, Alan Dukes's policy, announced in late 1987, of giving discriminating support to a minority Fianna Fáil government was viewed by most as a temporary tactic dictated by the political situation; some would say in the national interest, others that the interests of his party demanded it. In any case, there can be little doubt that most in both parties devoutly wished for changes in the political situation that would bring it to an end. Compromise and consensus politics will not easily replace adversarial politics in Ireland. The fact is though that the dichotomy of the de Valera epoch has disappeared, and Irish governmental and parliamentary practices need to be adjusted to this fact. For the politicians, this could be a long and painful process: in the eyes of an increasingly impatient and cynical public it is likely to be viewed as an overlong period of confusing and unsatisfactory government.

Ironically, one might think, the reason de Valera failed to get the election system changed was that in his Constitution he had deliberately given the final say in changing it, not to the Government, nor to the Oireachtas, but to the people by way of referendum. 'If there is one thing more than another that is clear and shining through this whole Constitution,' he declared to the Dáil, 'it is the fact that the people are the masters.'[3] And so they were: in 1959, when they rejected his proposal to amend the Constitution and alter the election system; in 1968, when they meted out the same treatment to the Lynch government on the same issue; and in 1986, when they turned down the FitzGerald government's proposal to allow for divorce. Clearly this is an important democratic device that works, and we owe it to de Valera.

The stark fact is, however, that the people can play only a very limited part in government. In traditional liberal theory the sovereignty of the people is made operational by the device of parliamentary representation. People elect representatives to parliament whose right and duty it is to make the law and watch over the government. In practice, for all the declaratory phrases of the Constitution, the Oireachtas has always had a modest role in policy-making, and has not proved itself a very efficient watchdog.

Although the Constitution declares that 'the sole and exclusive power of making laws for the state is . . . vested in the Oireachtas,' the fact is that the Oireachtas is rather a law-*declaring* than a law-*making* body. It is the Government that has a virtual monopoly on proposing legislation, and it is the Government's bills that the Oireachtas considers. Rarely is a bill presented by someone other than a minister, and none is likely to pass unless the Government in effect sponsors it. The Constitution itself bans the passage of any measure that might involve expenditure of public funds unless the Government recommends it. At most we might say that this is a system in which the Government makes the law with the advice and consent of the Oireachtas. If, as has usually been the case, the Government controls a loyal majority, that consent is virtually assured. Of course the Government's supporters in the Oireachtas expect to be consulted, but their views are only some of the opinions that the Government takes into account.

With an established tradition of adversarial politics the role of the parliamentary opposition is confined to criticism of what the Government is proposing to do or is doing. The leading idea upon which it is organised is not that the opposition is contributing positively to what is proposed but that it offers itself before the country, when the next election comes round, as an alternative government that could do better. Governments and their civil service advisers do not want the kind of contribution that the parliamentarians might make and, in truth, neither they nor the parliamentarians themselves see the role of the deputy as being that of a true legislator, in the style of the American congressman or senator or those in some continental European countries. The parliamentary procedures of these true legislatures include elaborate committee systems designed to give a much more positive role to the elected representative.

Until recently, few if any changes in this direction were made in Oireachtas procedures. In the last ten or fifteen years, however, there has been increasing dissatisfaction among deputies who have business or professional experience at the ineffectiveness of the Dáil and the low level of resources made available to them to do their jobs. Some changes have been made. Members have better secretarial and staff support. A number of specialist committees now enquire in detail into specific areas of government activity, such as the state-sponsored bodies; crime, lawlessness and vandalism; and, most important, Government expenditure. This development owes much to John Bruton and Fine Gael's 1980 policy document entitled *Reform of the Dáil*. Likewise the reforming zeal of Bruton and others, not least senior officers of that usually much-maligned organisation, the Department of Finance, led to the publication in 1981 of a Government policy document entitled *A Better Way to Plan the Nation's Finances* and to improvements in the amount and quality of information about state spending.

In principle, all this should have made it possible for deputies and senators to contribute more positively to policy formulation and have equipped them to criticise and comment more constructively, or at least more effectively. In fact, one or two of these committees occasionally do seem to make an impact, and perhaps the quality of debates has sometimes shown evidence of the higher level of information now available. As yet, however, there are few signs that what changes have been made are going to alter significantly the balance—or, to speak more accurately, to rectify the imbalance —between the Government and the Dáil.

The contrary might in fact be the case. The ineffectiveness, almost irrelevance, of Dáil Éireann has been made very obvious in some areas of economic policy-making where matters are decided by the Government and the so-called 'social partners'. Professor J. J. Lee has called attention to what he termed 'a subtle shift in the nature of public decision-making'[4] with the formulation of policy in bodies such as the National Economic and Social Council, with the National Wage Agreements of the 1970s and the National Understandings that followed them, and, more recently, the 'Programme for National Recovery'. These arrangements brought together employer bodies and the Irish Congress of Trade Unions with ministers and civil servants in hammering out agreements to which each of them is committed, and which involve both the Government and the 'social partners' incurring obligations to 'deliver', as the term is. The accommodations reached in this manner do not involve the Oireachtas in any way; in the past, even its formal approval of agreements already made has not always been sought. The elected representatives never were the makers of policy; at best, they were the declarers and legitimaters of policy. Even this role is now being cut back by developments such as these. The 'Programme for National Recovery', it might be argued, was legitimated more by its acceptance by a delegate conference of the Irish Congress of Trade Unions than by any action of Dáil Éireann.

Some matters have fallen outside the purview of the Dáil altogether. They are those that are now within the ambit of the European Communities. In the many important policy areas where the decisions are made in Brussels—and these include much more than agricultural prices and hand-outs—the Oireachtas has little or no say. No serious attempt has been made to devise arrangements to link the Euro-sector with the domestic sector or even to associate the Irish members of the European Parliament in some way with the domestic parliamentary system. A small number of ministers, civil servants, pressure-group spokesmen and members of the European Parliament shuttle back and forth to Brussels and elsewhere involved in a governmental system that is separate and distinct from the domestic system, and to the activities of which the Oireachtas gives minimal attention. Were it not for the coverage given to Community business by Radio Telefís Éireann and the newspapers, little or nothing about the Euro-sector would be known to most people. This no doubt suits ministers and their advisers, but it is not good enough.

Another example that seems to reveal who runs the show: one of the products of the period of reform of the seventies and early eighties, the creation of the office of Ombudsman, at first seemed to have markedly improved the redress of individual grievances. For the citizen with a complaint about official action or behaviour, there is now available an independent officer of the Oireachtas itself with real powers to investigate specific charges of administrative injustice or maladministration, and to seek remedies. He is appointed by and reports to the Oireachtas. But look what has happened. His office—the last one would think the Dáil would allow to be harmed—suffered particularly heavy staff reductions in the indiscriminate axing of public service personnel in 1987.

This survey of policy-making and administration under de Valera's Constitution makes clear that it is the Government and their civil service advisers who dominate the scene and are the principal architects of public policy. Although the Government must pay some attention to the Oireachtas and, in particular, to their party colleagues in the Dáil, their contribution is minimal, and Governments neither expect nor want a positive contribution. Thus the role of the elected representatives is a very limited one. This is not the case in some other democratic countries. Does this state of affairs have to be accepted in Ireland? The answer is probably 'yes, it does.' Ironically, it is only the Government itself that can promote the reforms that will alter the balance and create a more participative and democratic system. But to do this is to saddle itself with more effective controls and better-informed critics and to commit itself to a more give-and-take, consensus-seeking process of policy-making. Not surprisingly, such reforms are at best low down the priorities of all governments, however good the intentions of political leaders when they are in opposition.

NOTES

1. *Dáil Debates*, vol. 67, col. 100, 11 May 1937.
2. *Dáil Debates*, vol. 68, cols. 421, 423, 14 June 1937.
3. *Dáil Debates*, vol. 67, col. 40, 11 May 1937.
4. Joseph J. Lee (ed.), *Ireland 1945-70*, Dublin: Gill and Macmillan 1979, 20.

DR DERMOT KEOGH

8. *Church, State and Society*

Dermot Keogh is a lecturer in the Department of Modern History, University College, Cork. He is the author of *The Rise of the Irish Working Class: the Dublin Trade Union Movement and Labour Leadership, 1890-1914* (1982), *The Vatican, the Bishops and Irish Politics, 1919-1939* (1986), *Ireland and Europe, 1919-1948* (1988) and *Romero: El Salvador's Martyr* (1981), and has also published on church-state relations in Latin America.

WHEN Éamon de Valera died, in August 1975, he was buried in the habit of the Carmelite Third Order. That act was highly symbolic. It reflected—and was meant to reflect—de Valera's long-term association with members of the Carmelite order and with Carmelite spirituality.[1]

His gratitude to clerical friends who had been lifelong supporters was also reflected in another symbolic gesture: he left his personal papers to the Irish Franciscans at Killiney, an act illustrating the highest trust in the scholarship and integrity of the followers of the humble saint of Assisi. It was also, of course, a recognition of his confidence in their discretion.[2]

The Carmelites and the Franciscans were but two of the religious orders in which this distinguished Catholic nationalist found political support, friendship and intellectual stimulation throughout a public career characterised by revolutionary, slightly revolutionary and constitutional revolutionary phases.

Educated by the Christian Brothers and the Holy Ghost Fathers, de Valera retained a lifelong association with the latter order in particular, some of the priests of Blackrock College remaining his friends even during the Civil War period, when it was neither profitable nor popular to be seen in his company. Their lasting influence—personal, religious and intellectual—cannot be underestimated, particularly on a person who lost his father as an infant and who was raised away from his mother.[3] De Valera spent his early working years teaching in Rockwell, Carysfort and Maynooth, where he widened still further his circle of clerical friends.[4]

In Western European political terms, de Valera was a Christian Democrat who had much in common with Dom Luigi Sturzo, the leader of the Italian Popular Party. De Valera had little or nothing in common with the authoritarian Catholic leaders of the 1930s. He did not make a fetish out of religion like the 'monkish' Salazar of Portugal.[5] He was repelled by the extremism of General Francisco Franco's *cruzada*.[6] De Valera exhibited none of the demagoguery practised by the Central European Catholic dictators of the 1930s. Unlike some of his clerical friends, he was to transcend the narrowness, the limitations—some might say the sectarianism—of the tradition in which he was raised. If there is a parallel with any European statesman of his generation it is with General Charles de Gaulle. They were both patriotic and loyally Roman Catholic, but in a very independent way.

Paradoxically for a man who spent so many of his formative years nestling in the womb of the Catholic Church, de Valera found himself, during the 1920s in particular, in conflict with the pastoral guidance of the Catholic bishops over his rejection of the Treaty. Such a bruising historical experience as the Civil War does not appear to have altered substantially his attitude towards religion or his loyalty to the Catholic Church. In de Valera's view, the bishops had simply made an error of political judgment and, in time, they would come to see the error of their ways.[7]

De Valera always had the closest relations with members of the Catholic clergy at all levels of the ecclesiastical power structure. Throughout his public career he developed a national and international network of clerical friends and contacts, religious and diocesan, male and female, who formed a nexus that served many useful purposes. This network was of great practical political assistance. Firstly, he was made aware of tensions and personality conflicts in the higher clergy; secondly, he knew of the policy differences between bishops in the most intimate detail; thirdly, he received scholarly theological advice on how to deal with complex questions of church and state. Many of his friends were clerical dissidents who were free and unburdened in volunteering their opinions because they had long given up entertaining desires of 'upward mobility'.

In the 1920s, de Valera had his own 'parallel magisterium'—let me call it that loosely—made up of men like John Hagan, Rector of the Irish College in Rome, and Peter Magennis, once Superior-General of the Carmelites, in the robes of whose Third Order de Valera was buried. These are but two of the high-level contacts who helped de Valera navigate his way back to political 'respectability' after the Civil War. (Of course, Hagan and Magennis would have said that he never lost respectability.)

It is of some importance to stress these clerico-political connections before dealing with the interaction between church and state during the framing of the constitution. De Valera proved himself to be an astute—not to say courageous—manager of church-state relations in the period 1932-6. He had successfully discouraged any idea of the bishops—individually or collectively—playing an activist role in Irish politics. Like a stern schoolmaster, he complained directly to the Vatican on one occasion about the political behaviour of two bishops. It was his way of warning any others on the bench who might have been imprudent enough to entertain similar ambitions.

The central role of Catholicism in the political life of the new state must be kept to the fore. The influence of individual clergymen in the drafting of the 1937 Constitution must be set in that context. By the 1930s, Catholicism had become the central characteristic of Irish nationalism. The Anglo-Protestant and Scots-Presbyterian traditions did not exercise a major influence on the political leadership of the new state. As regards the Gaelic-Catholic tradition, the historical emphasis must be placed upon the latter half of that equation, notwithstanding the nostalgia of 'race memory'. The Eucharistic Congress in 1932 demonstrated the central importance of Catholicism in the celebration of national identity. On that occasion, Faith and Fatherland were as one.

But it does not follow that because Catholicism played such a central role in the cultural and political life of the state, the Irish shared a single Catholic world view. Contrary to the more recent perceptions of the 1930s, the good historian would be hard pressed to arrive at the conclusion that, at the time, Irish Catholicism was politically and socially homogeneous. Some find it fashionable to regard the 1930s as a decade of darkness. Undoubtedly there existed a vibrant and extreme ultramontane religious current. Calls for censorship were frequent, and some of the country's best short-story writers suffered quite unfairly at the hands of bigots. The Ethiopian and Spanish Civil Wars revealed an authoritarianism that was associated with professedly crusading 'church' groups. The Irish Christian Front, led by Paddy Belton, was a most prejudiced and intolerant group. It furnishes a good example of the rawer side of Irish political culture.

However, at no time was de Valera ever associated with such confessional, right-wing authoritarianism. Many of the personalities in the civil service who were closest to de Valera during the drafting process were Catholic, but of a liberal disposition. Maurice Moynihan, Secretary to the Department of the President, was a mild-mannered man of measured views. John Hearne, Legal Adviser in the Department of External (now Foreign) Affairs, was reserved, highly intelligent and professional in his diplomatic career.[8] De Valera, Moynihan and Hearne were all people of wide culture. They were wholly free of the stridency associated with certain vociferous elements in the Irish Catholic Church in the 1930s. All three had broad intellectual horizons. None were the victims of then fashionable ideological phobias.

In this context, other names could be mentioned as having provided de Valera with highly professional administrative judgment during the protracted drafting process. Philip O'Donoghue, legal assistant in the Attorney General's office, was most centrally involved. Michael McDunphy played an important role, as did Arthur Matheson of the Parliamentary Draftsman's office. The Secretary of the Department of Finance, J. J. McElligott, also contributed with acerbity. It is difficult to associate any of these men with the stridency of

street politics in the 1930s. They formed—in t
majority—part of a more liberal Catholic culture that shunne
the excesses of many of their crusading co-religionists.[9] De
Valera's style of government lent itself to rule by the inner circle—a principle that excluded many cabinet ministers in the case of the drafting of the Constitution and included a meritocratic administrative élite who had proved individually their competence and capability to 'the Chief'. He required only two things from his hand-picked civil servants: efficiency, and strict secrecy.

De Valera was, therefore, fortunate to have the administrative assistance of a group of very able, highly professional civil servants. But the idea of introducing a new constitution was particularly difficult in the highly volatile world of Irish politics during the mid-1930s. The bipolar political world of Treaty and anti-Treaty was never characterised by a wealth of ideological diversity. But the range of political ideas in the mid-1930s offered choices of vocationalism and corporatism to the electorate. The Fianna Fáil economic 'miracle' had been reduced in stature by a trade war with England. It was not the ideal political moment to begin to comtemplate providing the country with a new constitution.

The role of the Catholic Church in any major redefinition of Irish identity—as the introduction of a new constitution was undoubtedly to be—was likely to prove of major importance. The range of largely Mediterranean Catholic political ideas on offer in the 1930s was a complicating factor. Corporatism and vocationalism were seen as the third way, the *via media*, between capitalism and communism. But the attachment of leading members of the Catholic Church to that new political vision may be exaggerated. In fact very few bishops or prominent members of the clergy supported vocationalism. Of far greater importance was the view, held strongly in Irish Catholic circles, that the 1922 Constitution was in some way not a wholly Irish document. It was an 'imposed' document. (The supporters of vocationalism certainly viewed it as a flawed charter, based on the false principles of European liberalism.) Other members of the higher clergy had developed sufficient confidence in de Valera's orthodoxy and Christian leadership new constitution not to be a major threat. going to try to influence the content. Any servations about de Valera's handling of d questions had been removed between 1932 and he d

Valera enlisted clerical support in the writing of the Constitution for a number of obvious reasons. He needed to draw upon the resources of the Irish intellectual élite. That was all the more necessary because he had not chosen to draft the document in full committee. There were experts he could have turned to in an ideal world devoid of political partisanship. Patrick McGilligan was a distinguished constitutional lawyer. Daniel Binchy was also a man of international reputation in the area of jurisprudence. But both were identified with the opposition. Many of de Valera's academic friends were members of the clergy. He needed clerical expertise if for no other reason than that he could not risk writing his document in an administrative and political vacuum.[11]

Two clergymen in particular are identified with the writing of the Constitution. The Jesuit Edward Cahill and the Holy Ghost priest John Charles McQuaid were among his advisers outside the civil service. The latter was much more important than the former. Cahill was a founding member of Irish Catholic Action, An Ríoghacht, which never really became popular in Ireland.[12] He was also the scourge of international freemasonry.[13] An active cultural nationalist, he had been friendly with the de Valera family. But he was never very close to de Valera.

Cahill was a strong political partisan of Fianna Fáil. For example, on 22 March 1932 he wrote to de Valera:

> I thank God from my heart that the ten year 'nightmare' is over and I thank God too that you have been spared to take charge of the helm again. I have great hopes that the good God will utilise you to do great things for His glory in building the destinies of the country you love so well and have served so faithfully. You have suffered calumny as few men have; and, as far as I know, have borne it with remarkable Christian patience. All this I look upon as an

> earnest of the blessings with which God will crown the work which is now before you.[14]

Cahill, who did not enjoy very good health, remained in contact with de Valera by letter between 1932 and 1936. The President did not develop a close friendship with him; but he had an affection for the man, and visited him when he was ill in hospital. It is not surprising, therefore, that Cahill would have been privileged to hear of de Valera's plans to write a new constitution. He wrote to de Valera on 4 September 1936, enclosing a long submission. He also volunteered to 'get the opinion of some few others of the fathers who are interested in these matters and revise the present draft.'[15] In his submission, Cahill had encouraged de Valera to 'make a definite break with the Liberal and non-Christian type of state.' The latter had been 'forced upon us by a foreign, non-Catholic power.' Such an imposition was 'exotic, unnatural and quite foreign to the native tradition.' Moreover it tended to 'cramp and paralyse the free development of the people's Catholic life and culture.' Cahill wanted a new Irish constitution to be 'if not confessedly Catholic, then definitely confessedly Christian.'[16]

De Valera thought sufficiently of the material to have it typed, and he replied on 19 September 1936, taking up the invitation: 'If you could find time to put into the form of draft Articles, with perhaps a draft preamble, what you think should be formally written into the Constitution, it will be helpful. I could then arrange, when I had seen your draft, to have a chat with you about it.'[17]

When Cahill brought the matter to the attention of his superiors, they decided to set up a committee of some of the best minds in the Jesuit province to comply with de Valera's request. On 21 October 1936, Cahill wrote to de Valera enclosing a draft preamble and constitution. It was a short document, with articles on religion, marriage, the family, education, private property and liberty of speech. The content drew heavily upon papal encyclicals, the Code of Social Principles from Malines, and the Austrian, Portuguese and Polish constitutions.

The Jesuit submission (which I may have played down too

much in my book) was important in a number of respects. It was a draft on which de Valera, Hearne and others undoubtedly worked. It may not be an accident that the topics on which the Jesuits wrote became articles 41 to 45 of the new constitution—even if the content was radically altered.

The Jesuit article on religion is of particular interest. It was certainly influential at a later stage in the drafting process. The relevant part read:

> The Catholic Faith, which is the faith of the vast majority of the nation, and which is inseparably bound up with the nation's history, tradition and culture, occupies among religions in our country a unique and preponderant position.

That was undoubtedly where de Valera derived his inspiration for the final wording of what was to become article 44.[18] In essence, Jesuit influence on de Valera was more indirect than direct in that the Milltown draft may have set the agenda for further discussion.

John Charles McQuaid was much more centrally involved in the drafting process than either Cahill or the Jesuits. He was later to become, in 1940, the Archbishop of Dublin with the Taoiseach's support. It is necessary to view McQuaid's relationship with de Valera at three distinct levels. Firstly, he was a friend of de Valera's family and teacher of his children. He was also a great source of consolation to the entire family when Brian de Valera died following a riding accident in 1936. Secondly, he was an unofficial adviser to de Valera in drafting certain sections of the Constitution. Thirdly, he was an ideologue, raised in the border county of Cavan and schooled in French conservative theology, who wished to see his own interpretaion of Catholic orthodoxy reflected in the Constitution. As friend, adviser and ideologue, McQuaid worked very hard to supply de Valera with material in late 1936 and early 1937, when the document was taking final shape. So great is the volume of actual documentation that other members of the Holy Ghost Order must also have been recruited by McQuaid to help with the research and preparation of the submissions. The influence of the Holy Ghost Order can be found particularly in articles 41 to 45.[19]

Overwhelmed by the size and importance of the work, de Valera may have taken on more than he could cope with efficiently. He had to run the government at the same time as writing the Constitution. The result of 'overload' can be best seen in the wording of the first draft of the article on religion, church and state. The wording was strongly confessional, recognising as it did that 'the Church of Christ is the Catholic Church.'[20] Perhaps de Valera was so preoccupied with trying to ensure that the draft would not provoke a backlash from a variegated and volatile Catholic constituency that he failed to anticipate the reaction from some members of his own front bench and, most importantly, from the other churches. The explanation may lie in the fact that de Valera accepted the ultramontane formula as conforming most closely to his own personal views. But when the political ramifications of such a formula were pointed out to him, he immediately saw the public danger to his own personal position and to the Fianna Fáil government.

It proved much more difficult to retrieve the situation once the formula had gone into print.[21] At least de Valera salvaged some ground by restricting the circulation of the draft article to a handful of people.[22] When he distributed the first draft of the Constitution on 16 March to the Executive Council and departmental secretaries, there was a blank space where the religious article had been only days previously.[23]

Thus began one of the most instructive political consensus-building manoeuvres in the history of the state. De Valera, having partially created the problem himself, had to be at his most balletic to tiptoe his way to a successful solution without alerting his political opponents to his vulnerability. By the end of March 1936 no obvious solution was in sight to the problem of formulating a religious article that would satisfy various conflicting interest groups. It had become quite apparent, however, that the original wording had to be replaced with a formula that satisfied all the churches—a difficult task in a pre-ecumenical age. It was like trying to tattoo bubbles.

With the assistance of the urbane Franciscan Paschal Robinson, who had been Papal Nuncio in Ireland since 1930, de Valera set out to consult dignitaries of the Catholic Church, the Church of Ireland, the Presbyterians, the Methodists, the Society of Friends, and the Jewish congregations. This happened mainly in the first two weeks of April 1937. The 'shuttle diplomacy' was important in two respects. Firstly, consultation tended to be a way of winning the leaders of the different churches over to his side. Secondly, the information gathered in those meetings would enable him to frame an article that would go a long way towards meeting all sides of the religious divide. Moreover, de Valera was genuinely seeking a way out of the dilemma that he had not been shrewd enough to anticipate and avoid. He needed guidance to clarify his mind.

The following is a copy of de Valera's own record of his talks with various church leaders. He had a crowded agenda in the first two weeks of April 1937. The people he consulted were the Nuncio; Cardinal Joseph MacRory of Armagh; Dr Edward Byrne, Archbishop of Dublin; Dr Irwin of the Presbyterians; Dr Gregg, Church of Ireland Archbishop of Dublin; and W. H. Massey, head of the Methodist Church in Ireland.

April		
3rd,	Called on the Nuncio	(Saturday)
5th,	Saw the Cardinal at the Nunciature	(Monday)
,,	Called on Archbishop Byrne	,,
10th,	Saw the Nuncio, who promised to see Cardinal	(Saturday)
,,	Saw Archbishop Byrne?	,,
,,	Saw Dr. Irwin	,,
11th,	Saw the Nuncio at Seán T's	(Sunday)
12th,	Called on Archbishop Gregg	(Monday)
,,	Called on the Nuncio	,,
,,	Saw Dr. Irwin	,,
13th,	Phoned the Nuncio	(Tuesday)
,,	Saw the Rev. W. H. Massey, head of the Methodist Church in Ireland	,,
14th,	Saw Dr. Irwin	(Wednesday)
16th,	Saw Dr. Irwin, the Moderator, and the Moderator Designate, who travelled from Belfast.	(Friday)
16th,	Saw the Nuncio at Seán T's	,,
,,	J. P. W. went to Rome	,,
22nd,	Called on the Nuncio	(Thursday)

23rd,	Nuncio phoned to say Cardinal approved Christian Churches	(Friday)
24th,	Saw Nuncio and Cardinal	(Saturday)
26th,	Mr. Moynihan saw Arch. Gregg, and Dr. Robinson got letter from Gregg to D'Arcy	(Sunday)
27th,	Robinson goes to see D'Arcy[24]	(Monday)

Although the Jewish congregations do not appear on the list, de Valera almost certainly consulted members of that group. The inclusion of the Jews in the article on religion was particularly important in view of the fact that anti-Semitism throughout Europe was growing in strength and destruction.[25]

By 14 April, de Valera had satisfied himself that his new formula—which had been pieced together slowly—would suffice. It was virtually identical with what subsequently emerged as article 44. The relevant sections are as follows:

> The State recognises the special position of the Holy Catholic Apostolic and Roman Church as the guardian of the Faith professed by the great majority of the citizens. The State also recognises the Church of Ireland, the Presbyterian Church in Ireland, the Methodist Church in Ireland, the Religious Society of Friends in Ireland, as well as the Jewish Congregations and the other religious denominations existing in Ireland at the date of the coming into operation of this Constitution.

All other churches consulted were positive about both the religious article and the wording of the preamble. De Valera only encountered difficulties with the Catholic Church. The Archbishop of Dublin, Edward Byrne, proved to be most helpful and encouraging. The Archbishop of Armagh, Cardinal Joseph MacRory, was less compliant. He sought what would have been considered by Rome to be the 'orthodox' position: recognition in the Constitution that the Catholic Church was the 'one true church'. As leader of the Irish Catholic Church he may have felt compelled to take the official line; but it also seems that it was the position with which he personally felt most comfortable.

The Papal Nuncio, Paschal Robinson, was very helpful to de

Valera in those difficult weeks. MacRory was not actively obstructive; but his silence was not sufficient guarantee for de Valera that there would not be difficulties from certain like-minded churchmen when the document was made public. It was certain that the article on religion would not be acceptable to ultra-canonical Catholics. Only a statement that 'the Church of Christ is the Catholic Church' would suffice in those circles. Neither was the phrase acceptable that began, in the draft (this did not remain in the final version), 'The State also recognises the other Christian Churches, namely...' It is probable that the latter sentence had been the subject of a significant difference of opinion between de Valera and McQuaid on the night of 15 April 1937. The Holy Ghost priest could not agree that it was theologically acceptable to refer to the other 'bodies' as 'churches'. Secondly, he did not approve of the use of the phrase 'Church of Ireland'. The fact that de Valera had instructed the Secretary of the Department of External Affairs, Joseph Walshe, to bring the matter to the Vatican may have further added to the short-lived personal friction between the two friends.[26] The necessity of sending a senior diplomat to Rome to solicit the views of the Vatican may have been regarded as a slight by McQuaid on his judgment and ability to interpret the teaching of the Catholic Church.

It was somewhat out of political character for de Valera to risk sending Walshe to Rome. But it was the measure of his difficulties at the time that he took that course of action. Perhaps he saw it as the only way to neutralise potentially dangerous Catholic episcopal opposition to the religious clause of the constitution. He was *not* 'running to Rome'. De Valera—unlike other political leaders—was economical in his contacts with bishops and cardinals. It was a bold stroke to try to outmanoeuvre local episcopal opposition by taking the matter beyond the court of the national lords of the church. It is likely that he sent Walshe to Rome in the near-certain knowledge, based on the advice of Paschal Robinson, that the Vatican would not want to intervene in domestic Irish politics. Of all institutions, the centuries had taught the Vatican the art of compromise and *raison d'état*. De Valera was gambling on its record of *savoir-faire*.

Walshe had explicit instructions from de Valera when he left Ireland on 16 April for Rome:

> (1) General approval for religious part
> (2) To get the official name of the Catholic Church
> (3) To get permission to phrase ARTICLE 3 so as to include the phrase 'The State also recognises the other Christian Churches, namely, Church of Ireland, etc., as well as the Jewish Congregations and the other religious bodies existing in Éire at the time of the coming into operation of this constitution.'[27]

Walshe also went to the Vatican armed with a memorandum and a copy of the preamble. He had been in Rome before on a number of important diplomatic missions in the 1920s, and knew his way around quite well. However, this former Jesuit scholastic had his task made all the easier by the presence in Rome of an experienced Irish envoy to the Vatican, W. J. B. Macaulay, who was married to the Duchess Genevieve Garvan Brady. Both were very friendly with the Secretary of State, Cardinal Eugenio Pacelli. That is possibly why the Irish question received such prompt attention. Walshe had extensive talks with Pacelli on 20 April and on two subsequent occasions.[28]

Pacelli proved to be very well briefed on Ireland. Paschal Robinson had not been inactive. To Walshe's surprise, the cardinal referred on two separate occasions to the 'heretical' aspects of the Irish constitution. Referring to the 'one true church', Pacelli told Walshe that, 'quite truthfully, according to the strict teaching of the church, we were heretics to recognize any church but the one true church of Christ.'

Walshe was relieved when the cardinal said that 'the church would not take our heresy too seriously.' On another occasion, Pacelli held that the Irish state was heretical on the question of marriage. But the cardinal was only engaging in gentle leg-pulling of an ultra-serious and pious Irish civil servant. He knew perfectly well from the Nuncio's reports the background to Walshe's trip to Italy.[29]

Decoding Pacelli's diplomatic language, the cardinal was telling Walshe the following: We know what has been happening in your country; we are aware of the tensions between de Valera and the cardinal; we know the issues of conflict. Cardinal Pacelli, when asked an opinion as Secretary of State, could only state the official position of the church. However, it was really up to de Valera to do what he felt the Irish had to do in their unique political situation.

When the cardinal had an opportunity to speak to the Pope on the matter, the response was not unhelpful to de Valera's position. On the issue of the phraseology of the description of the Catholic Church, the Pope said: '*Nè approvo nè non disapprovo; taceremo* [I do not approve, neither do I disapprove; we shall maintain silence].' Pacelli interpreted the Pope's position in a positive light, from the Irish point of view. The Pope had taken a middle position, of neutrality, on the crucial political question of the description of the Catholic Church. This was more than de Valera could have expected. It was certainly a highly desirable outcome to the Walshe mission.

Pacelli had shown himself very pleased at the official title chosen for the Catholic Church in the Constitution. He was less helpful on the question of the use of the phrase 'other Christian Churches'. He preferred 'Christian bodies'. Walshe, in summing up his mission, was a little hard on himself:

> I want to express my great regret at not having been able to do what I was sent out to do. But I have learned a great deal about the attitude of the Holy See to such matters—and I can assure you, most confidently, that at the back of their adherence to rigid forms and dogmas there is very sincere respect, and even gratitude for the extent to which you have been able to go in making our Const. Catholic; notwithstanding the very great difficulties which they understood better than they pretended to understand them. I will of course amplify this report viva voce on my return.

The position of 'friendly and sympathetic silence', as Walshe described it, was very much the attitude that de Valera had hoped for from the Vatican. He was in a strong position to outmanoeuvre his local clerical opponents. If the Pope had taken up a position of strict neutrality, then the Irish bishops were obliged to follow his lead.

There was one remaining area, however, where de Valera was still on very slender ground: the reference to 'other Christian churches'. As the Walshe mission ended in Rome around 22 April 1937, de Valera undertook another round of discussions with the Papal Nuncio, the Cardinal, the Church of Ireland Archbishop of Dublin, Dr Gregg, and McQuaid. The 'friendly and sympathetic silence' of the Vatican had completely altered the political situation in his favour. The Cardinal was compliant. It appears that he was prepared to accept the use of the phrase 'other Christian churches'. However, de Valera finally decided to drop the phrase, which he may have considered both superfluous and potentially contentious.

Against considerable opposition, de Valera left the phrase 'Church of Ireland' in the final draft of the Constitution. This drew considerable criticism from MacRory, and two Jesuits, P. J. Gannon and Edward Cahill. The latter called the use of 'Church of Ireland' nothing less than 'authoritative approval of a piece of lying propaganda.' But de Valera was not persuaded to change his mind.

He had to consolidate the support that he had managed to acquire from the Church of Ireland. He sent Maurice Moynihan to Gregg on 26 April 1937 with the final text of the religious article. De Valera subsequently clarified by phone whatever lingering doubts the Archbishop may have had about the article on religion. Gregg may have been anxious to know what legal status was given to the Catholic Church by the use of the phrase 'recognises the special position'. His fears were quickly assuaged by de Valera: 'Gregg satisfied' reads a minute in de Valera's hand.[30] Gregg sent word of his agreement by letter to the Church of Ireland Primate in Armagh.

All the religious denominations were satisfied, with the exception of the disaffected elements in the Catholic Church. The other Christian churches and the Jewish congregations had not seen anything other than a draft article on religion, and the preamble. Yet there appeared to be general approval of the full text of the Constitution. The trip to Rome had neutralised the most dangerous Catholic opponents of the Constitution. Had not de Valera succeeded in tattooing bubbles?

There is a danger of underestimating the gravity of the

church-state crisis in 1937 because it did not end in public confrontation. But it could easily have done so. That it did not was a tribute to de Valera's personal political skills and his sense of religious tolerance, which was so much at variance with the thrust of some of the theological advice he was receiving at the time.

The sharp church-state divisions over the religious article may deflect attention from the degree to which Catholic culture influenced the articles on personal rights, the family, education, private property and directive social principles. In a sense, the cluster of articles 41 to 45 is a petrified image of positions particular to a certain current of Irish Catholicism in 1937. A senior civil servant once heard Seán Lemass say to de Valera during the drafting: 'But you can't put the papal encyclicals into the Constitution.' However, he did do so, and that has resulted in certain difficulties as Irish society and Catholic social teaching have changed in the meantime. Pope Leo XIII's *Rerum Novarum* is quite distinct from Paul VI's *Populorum Progressio* and John Paul II's *Sollicitudo Rei Socialis*. Now, over fifty years later, the Constitution remains, with certain amendments. Paradoxically, the one article that had won the active approval of all the churches in Ireland in 1937 was amended in 1972. The sections that de Valera had worked so hard to formulate were dropped from the text. How he would have voted in that particular referendum will never be known; but one could speculate that he would have found it very difficult to vote for deletion.

In the age of de Valera, social legislation was predicated on the principles of the Roman Catholic Church. De Valera may have adopted a more advanced theological position than the bishops preferred; but it was his personal familiarity with contemporary Catholic theology—and his knowledge of ecclesiastical politics—that enabled him to outflank the bishops on more than one occasion in his political career. Nonetheless, de Valera always worked within a Catholic philosophical context.

In the late 1980s, the Ireland dreamed of by de Valera is nothing more than another piece of nostalgia. There are deep divisions within the Catholic Church over the role that religion should play in civil society. Many Catholics differ on the question of the relationship between law and morality. There are substantial differences between churches on the same question. The alienation of large numbers of people from their churches and from religion itself has already taken place. The secularisation of society has grown.

The Catholic Church, in this changed social situation, can follow one of two distinct paths. It can seek 'only the freedom to proclaim the Gospel,' as Cahal Daly told the New Ireland Forum, or it can adopt a much more defensive role.[31] The Catholic church can try to 'conserve' what ground it holds, like a general under siege, summoning all the power at its disposal to repel 'the enemy'. The latter is a very depressing prospect; it is also the most likely path to be followed, and can only lead to the institutionalisation of church-state conflict to the ultimate advantage of neither. Even de Valera's consummate ability to 'tattoo bubbles' would not, in those circumstances, prevent unnecessary and rancorous confrontations. If de Valera left an example of political adroitness to be emulated by his successors, certain articles of his constitution will help keep Irish society divided.

NOTES

1. Peter Magennis was one of de Valera's staunchest political allies. As a priest working in New York, Magennis had immersed himself in Sinn Féin politics. The Carmelite house in that city was a contact address for prominent Sinn Féin politicians. Those who stayed in the house at one time or another included Éamon de Valera, Harry Boland and Liam Mellows. Other leading Irish nationalists were also given refuge there. Magennis was transferred to Rome as superior-general of the order and remained there until he returned to Dublin, where he died in the 1930s. He was a close friend of John Hagan, rector of the Irish College. Together they acted almost as unofficial envoys from 1919 until 1922. Both remained friends with de Valera during the Civil War and throughout the 1920s. De Valera remained very much in their debt. He visited members of the order throughout his political life. See Dermot Keogh, *The Vatican, the Bishops and Irish Politics, 1919-1939*, Cambridge: Cambridge University Press 1986, chapters I-III.
2. The de Valera Papers are housed in the Franciscan Institute of Celtic Studies and Historical Research, Killiney, Co. Dublin, where they are being prepared for access to historians by Breandán Mac Giolla Choille. The opening of the papers relevant to the framing of the 1937 Constitution is an auspicious beginning. But it cannot be gainsaid that de Valera's reputation has been distorted, virtually of necessity, by the

fact that historians have had to use the personal papers of his political opponents or the diplomatic archives of England and the United States to evaluate his contribution to the building of modern Ireland. It is desirable that the archives be opened as quickly as possible.

3. I would not like to make too much of this psychological argument. But it does seem likely that de Valera built firmer friendships with members of that order by virtue of the fact that he did not have strong family support. The relationship between de Valera and the Holy Ghost Order is presented with great detail in Seán Farragher's *Dev and his Alma Mater: Éamon de Valera's Lifelong Association with Blackrock College, 1898-1975*, Dublin: Paraclete Press 1984.
4. The intellectual formation and political career of 'the young de Valera' has not yet received adequate treatment by the historian. The forthcoming biography by Deirdre McMahon will certainly address the issue and advance the debate. Her *Republicans and Imperialists: Anglo-Irish Relations in the 1930s*, New Haven: Yale University Press 1984, is a substantial scholarly contribution to the area.
5. I have developed this argument in *Ireland and Europe, 1919-1948*, Dublin: Gill and Macmillan 1988, chapters II and VI.
6. ibid., chapter III.
7. The robust handling of Republicans during the Civil War by certain members of the hierarchy did not result in alienation from the institutional church for de Valera and some of his close associates. The former Tánaiste and Minister for Foreign Affairs, Frank Aiken, once told me quite simply that they knew that the bishops were wrong. There was no self-doubt. But what the politico-episcopal friction did succeed in doing was to make de Valera much more independent in his theological judgment and appreciative of dissident theological opinion.
8. As far as is known, there are no Hearne papers, which is something of a historical tragedy. His role in the drafting process was central. As a former clerical student he may have had an additional insight into the sensitive world of church-state relations. However, his role in the process is obvious. This has been confirmed for me by Mgr John Tracy Ellis, the distinguished American church historian, who was a personal friend of Hearne.
9. At least one recent study appears to be wholly unaware of this. It certainly could not be argued—although this has been attempted—that the first generation of senior Irish civil servants were British in outlook. This view is wholly innocent of the most rudimentary knowledge of the administrative history of the 1920s and 1930s.
10. See *The Vatican, the Bishops and Irish Politics*, chapter VII.
11. For a man who had developed the reputation of living in a world of abstractions, de Valera usually made sure to keep his feet planted firmly in urban and rural Ireland. He tried to keep in touch with happenings in the country by talking to back-benchers, with whom he displayed endless patience. This side of de Valera's character has been confirmed to me in a number of interviews with leading members of Fianna Fáil.
12. Organised in the 1920s, An Ríoghacht failed to develop a popular base. Unlike the situation in many countries in continental Europe, Catholic

Action in Ireland did not have an appeal. See Cahill Papers.

13. Cahill was a prolific author. He wrote on a large number of topics and contributed to many journals. See *Ireland's Peril*, An Ríoghacht pamphlet 1930, and *Framework of a Christian State*, Dublin 1932. Following the receipt of that book, de Valera wrote to Cahill on 2 August 1932 thanking him for the volume: 'Is fiú é a léigheamh agus a aith-léigheamh, agus is minic, dar liom, a raghfar chuige chum comhairle agus treorú 'fhagháil as ins na blianta atá le teacht [It is worth reading and re-reading, and I believe it will be consulted frequently for advice and guidance in the years ahead]' (Cahill Papers).
14. De Valera Papers (1095/1).
15. De Valera Papers (1095/2B).
16. ibid.
17. ibid. (1095/1).
18. For Jesuit constitution and correspondence see de Valera Papers (1095/2B). Cahill followed his letter of 21 October, in which he submitted the draft articles, with another letter on 13 November, in which he included many of his personal ideas. He first had to submit these to two Jesuits who acted as censors. The Cahill submission of November was not influential.
19. It is unfortunate that we have no record of John Hearne's reaction to the flood of documentation from Blackrock Castle. One is tempted to speculate that he may have developed, as a consequence, a lifelong aversion to certain papal encyclicals.
20. A detailed examination of the drafting of the religious article can be found in Dermot Keogh, 'The Irish Constitutional Revolution: an Analysis of the Making of the Constitution', in *Administration*, January 1988, 4-84.
21. He did not burden his political colleagues with the fine details of the religious article. He got, however, from the Executive Council a free hand to conduct negotiations on the content of the religious article, provided the result did not establish any particular church. (Interview with Seán MacEntee.)
22. The text of the first draft of the religious article can be found in *The Vatican, the Bishops and Irish Politics*, 236-7.
23. Exactly who saw the privately circulated draft by de Valera is difficult to say, but the number of people would have been very small. There is no evidence at this time to indicate who voiced opposition to the religious article as it was first worded.
24. De Valera Papers (1995/1B).
25. De Valera may have gone indirectly to the Jewish community in Dublin through Robert Briscoe, a back-bench member of Fianna Fáil. However, de Valera had been on close personal terms with a number of prominent members of the Jewish community. He was a friend of Dr Herzog, who had left Ireland to become Chief Rabbi of Palestine.
26. 'The Irish Constitutional Revolution', 39-43.
27. De Valera Papers (1995/2F).
28. Walshe paid tribute to the help he had received from Minister Macaulay and his wife at the end of his confidential report to de Valera. De Valera Papers (1995/1D).

29. ibid.
30. De Valera Papers (1995/1B).
31. Irish Episcopal Conference delegation, report of proceedings (public session), New Ireland Forum, 9 February 1984, 2.

DR YVONNE SCANNELL

9. *The Constitution and the Role of Women*

Yvonne Scannell lectures in law in the Law School, Trinity College, Dublin. She is a former chairwoman of the Women's Political Association and of the Environment Awareness Bureau. She has written articles on environmental law and women's rights, and is the author of *The Law and Practice Relating to Pollution Control in Ireland* (2nd ed., 1982).

WOMEN had no part in framing Bunreacht na hÉireann. Not one woman took part in drafting it. Of the 152 TDs who had an opportunity to comment on the draft, only three were women. These three, known sorrowfully as the 'Silent Sisters', made no meaningful contribution whatever to the debate on the draft. Outside the Dáil, a number of women's organisations protested in vain against certain articles—so much so that de Valera admitted knowing that he had a 'bad reputation with women'.[1]

Why, therefore, did some women object to de Valera's Constitution? There are, after all, at least six articles that can be used, directly or indirectly, to vindicate women's rights. The answer to this question lies in the assumptions made in the Constitution—and by de Valera in piloting it through the Dáil—concerning the legal rights, the role and the status of women in Irish society.

It is clear from reading the Dáil debates that de Valera was no feminist. Neither, however, was he consciously anti-women. His views on women's rights reflected those of most people in Irish society at the time. They certainly accorded with those of nearly all of the deputies who spoke in the Dáil,[2] and indeed they still accord with those of a diminishing number of Irish people today.

The Constitution expressly states that women are entitled to vote, to become TDs, and to become citizens on the same basis as men.[3] These rights had been granted under the 1922 Constitution.[4] There was nothing revolutionary about re-enacting them in 1937.

But if de Valera was prepared to give women full political rights, that was as far as he would go. He deleted the words 'without distinction of sex' from the draft of article 40.1, which now reads:

> All citizens shall, as human persons, be held equal before the law.
> This shall not be held to mean that the State shall not in its enactments have due regard to differences of capacity, physical and moral, and of social function.

The words 'without distinction of sex' were deleted because de Valera considered them 'altogether unnecessary'.[5] It is clear, however, from reading his justification for the deletion that he intended equal rights for women to be confined, initially at least, to the political sphere. Three times in his short justification he speaks, not of women's rights but of women's *political rights*.[6] The subtle qualification went unnoticed by his opponents.

The article in the Constitution that attracted the fiercest opposition from women at the time was article 41.2. This article reads:

> 1° In particular the State recognises that by her life within the home, woman gives to the State a support without which the common good cannot be achieved.
> 2° The State shall, therefore, endeavour to ensure that *mothers* shall not be obliged by economic necessity to engage in labour to the neglect of their duties in the home. [Emphasis added.]

There are two ways of looking at this article. The first is to take de Valera at his word and to regard the first paragraph as a tribute to the work that is done by women in the home as mothers.[7] The second paragraph, if it is to be regarded as anything other than a paternalistic declaration, can be read as a constitutional guarantee that no *mother* is to be *forced* by economic necessity to work outside the home to the neglect of her duties there. The mothers covered by this guarantee would include widows, unmarried mothers, mothers whose husbands are unable or unwilling to support their families, even relatively rich mothers with heavy expenses such as those necessitated by caring for ill or handicapped children.

The second way of looking at article 41.2 is different. To some, it is grossly offensive to the dignity and freedoms of womanhood. It speaks of woman's *life* within the home (not just her work there), implying that the natural vocation of woman (the generic is used, so it means *all* women) is in the home. It is the grossest form of sexual stereotyping. It can be regarded as an implicit denial of freedom of choice to women in personal matters, a freedom taken for granted by men. It speaks of *mothers* neglecting their duties, but omits to mention the duties of fathers. It fails to recognise that a woman's place is a woman's choice.

Despite the protests about article 41.2, de Valera refused to delete it. His reasons for refusing show that his vision of the role of woman in Irish society was that of a full-time wife and mother in an indissoluble marriage, having 'a preference for home duties' and 'natural duties' as a mother.[8] This protected creature is to be supported by 'a breadwinner who is normally and naturally in these cases when he is alive, the father of the family... able by his work to bring in enough to maintain the whole household.'[9]

De Valera's defence of article 41.2 can be rationalised by an attitude of romantic paternalism, which, as a famous American judge has said, 'in practical effect puts women, not on a pedestal, but in a cage.'[10]

Constitutional history shows that it is the second and less positive interpretation of article 41.2 that de Valera's successors in office have almost invariably adopted. Lawyers for the state tried to rely on article 41.2 to justify tax discriminations against married women in the Murphy case,[11] and social welfare discriminations against women in the recent Hyland case.[12] They successfully relied on it to justify social welfare discriminations against deserted husbands obliged to assume full-time child care duties in *Dennehy* v. *Minister for Social Welfare.*[13]

The Oireachtas in its legislation continued to assume that the normal vocation of women was in marriage, motherhood and the home. In particular, the social welfare system until very recently was founded on the philosophy that women are dependent on men and that society must only support them when this dependence (for one reason or another) ceases. The women of 1937 were right to fear that the state would give article 41.2 the most restrictive interpretation of their rights.

Consistent with his vision of women's role, de Valera, to his credit, did provide (in article 42) that the right to educate children was to rest primarily with parents. This was to prove a significant enhancement of the rights of mothers, because at common law the right to the custody of legitimate children, even small children, automatically belonged to the father unless he was demonstrably unfit.[14]

Other direct and indirect references to women's rights are contained in article 45. This article contains directive principles of social policy for the guidance of the Oireachtas, 'ideals, aims and objectives'[15] to be achieved when, and if, the Oireachtas thinks fit. Women's rights implied in this article are not fundamental rights: they are rights that may be granted to them by their political representatives.

Article 45 deals, *inter alia*, with certain social and economic rights for women. It obliges the state to strive 'to promote the welfare of the whole people by securing and protecting as effectively as it may a social order in which justice and charity shall inform all the institutions of the national life.' It specifically and particularly obliges the state to direct its policy towards securing that 'men and women equally' have 'the right to an adequate means of livelihood.' In the article, the state pledges to safeguard with special care the *economic* interests of the weaker sections of the community and, where necessary, to contribute to the support of the infirm, the widow, the orphan and the aged. It should be noted that the responsibility for caring for the infirm, the orphan and the aged in Irish society almost invariably lies with women. Lastly, article 45 states that the state will endeavour to ensure that the strength and health of workers, men and women, and of children, shall not be abused, and that citizens shall not be forced by economic necessity to enter avocations unsuited to their sex, age or strength.

De Valera intended article 45 to be a 'constant reminder to the legislature of the direction in which it should work.'[16]

These then were the provisions dealing with women in de Valera's Constitution. Taken at face value, women were guaranteed equality before the law, tempered with regard to differences of capacity. Indeed, the Constitution seemed to contemplate, as three judges have since held, some *preferential* treatment for women citizens.[17]

The remainder of this paper will deal with how women fared under the Constitution since 1937.

For almost thirty years after the Constitution was adopted, the position of women in Irish society hardly changed at all. The common law relegation of women to domesticity and powerlessness continued. Laws based on the premise that women's rights were inferior to those of men survived in, and indeed even appeared on, the statute books. Despite the constitutional adulation of marriage and motherhood, the legislature preferred to keep women in the home by foul rather than fair means. Contraception was effectively illegal.[18] The economically powerless home-maker was denied access to free legal aid. No financial aid was available as of right to unmarried mothers, deserted wives or prisoners' wives, even when they were fulfilling their 'duties' in the home. The battered wife and mother could not exclude her violent husband from the home (which was almost invariably his) except by resort to the most cumbersome procedures. If she fled the home, her husband had a right to damages from anyone who enticed her away, or who harboured her or committed adultery with her.

The married woman by her work in the home might give the state 'a support without which the common good cannot be achieved', but until the Succession Act, 1965, came into force in 1967, her husband could legally disinherit her and leave her homeless in his will. Even now, a woman's work in the home does not of itself entitle her to any share in the ownership of it. For that, she must either contribute towards the purchase of the home in money or money's worth or ensure that her name appears as owner or joint owner on the title deeds. The courts have consistently refused to recognise that the contribution a woman makes in managing the home is very often as important to the family's economic advancement as the work of a husband as breadwinner.[19]

In *De Búrca and Anderson* v. *Attorney General*[20] it was recognised that 'some preferential treatment of women citizens seems to be contemplated by the Constitution,' and it was noted that article 41.2 'makes special provision for the economic protection of mothers who have home duties.' It is open to the courts, by relying on this article, on the constitutional guarantee to 'protect the family', and on the words of the marriage contract itself (under which the husband endows his wife with his worldly goods), to recognise that the woman by her work in the home acquires some beneficial or proprietary interest in it.[21] Although Mrs Tilson succeeded in asserting the equal rights of a mother to custody of her children in 1951, it took the Oireachtas a further thirteen years to enshrine this right in the Guardianship of Infants Act, 1964.

Work outside the home for married women was regarded as a selfish distraction from home duties. The Civil Service Regulation Act, 1956, provided that women employed in the civil service, other than those employed in certain excluded non-pensionable posts, were required to resign on marriage. The Civil Service Commissioners Act, 1956, enabled the Commissioners, in making regulations in relation to a competition for a civil service position, to require that a female candidate be unmarried or a widow. The Local Government Act, 1941, enabled the Minister for Local Government to declare as a qualification for a specified office that any woman holding that office be unmarried or a widow. A small number of married women were employed in the civil service and local authorities until these discriminations were abolished, but they were employed in positions where recruitment difficulties were experienced and in temporary (non-pensionable) capacities or on a fee-paid basis.[22]

Women working in many other jobs had no legal redress when obliged to resign on marriage. Women were not entitled to unemployment allowances, because it was assumed that some man would provide for them. The income of a married woman was deemed to be her husband's for tax purposes.[23] Women were grossly underrepresented in politics and in public life despite having equal political rights with men since the foundation of the state.

These instances, of course, describe the legal position of women, not necessarily their actual position. Laws are frequently far worse than the people who execute them, and most men did not inflict, nor did all women suffer, all the misery that could legally be inflicted or suffered. But we are not entitled to judge any system solely by its best instances.

In 1970 the Government appointed a Commission for the Status of Women. The report of this Commission (on which women and men were equally represented) contained forty-nine eminently reasonable recommendations for improving women's rights in a number of areas.[24] The Government was in no rush to implement them. Indeed, some of them have not yet been implemented.[25]

Nevertheless, in spite of legislative inertia and political indifference to the injustices women suffered, the laws began to change.

From about 1970, three main factors combined to bring about a considerable improvement in the position of women in Irish society. The first was the flowering of judicial review. People began to seek redress in the courts for grievances that the Oireachtas had chosen to ignore.[26] The courts by their interpretation of the Constitution created an awareness of the citizen's constitutional rights and of the role the courts could play in protecting and vindicating these rights. Most importantly, in a case taken by a woman, Gladys Ryan,[27] the courts declared that the constitutional rights of the citizen included rights that were not specifically named in the fundamental rights articles, and that other constitutional rights could be implied under article 40.3. These rights are to be implied by a consideration of the fundamental nature of society envisaged by the Constitution itself.[28]

The second factor that influenced improvements in the legal status of women was the re-emergence of the feminist movement in the late sixties and early seventies. The peaceful revolution by black Americans that began after the Second

World War and gained momentum in the fifties provided a model for American women, who began to agitate for equal rights for women in the sixties. The American women in turn provided a model for Irish women. In 1970 the Irish Women's Liberation Movement was launched. The founders included a number of journalists who were to disseminate its message to the media. A manifesto, *Chains or Change*, was agreed and delivered to the people of Ireland on the 'Late Late Show' of 6 March 1971. It contained five demands: equal pay, equality before the law, equal education, contraception, and justice for deserted wives, unmarried mothers and widows. It sent shock waves through Irish society. Women's issues became news on radio and television. The *Irish Press*, the *Irish Times* and the *Irish Independent*, in response to the chord that the movement struck, all started feminist 'women's pages'.

The unlikely coalition of economically socialist and conservative women that had formed the movement was not to last. It splintered; but many of the women in it went on to found, or become prominent in, a number of pressure groups for women's rights. From 1970 to 1980 the number of women's organisations in Ireland increased from 17 to over 55. They were a telling indictment of, and a manifestation of disillusionment with, the political system that had proved, and continued, to be so unresponsive to demands for equal rights for women. The women's movement was significant in bringing to public attention the extent to which women, and particularly women in their capacities as wives and mothers, were discriminated against.

The third factor, which was to provide the main impetus for the achievement of equal economic rights for women, was Ireland's accession to the European Economic Community in 1973. Article 119 of the Treaty of Rome obliges member-states to ensure and subsequently maintain the application of the principle that men and women should receive equal pay for equal work. This article's requirements are amplified by EC Directive 75/117 on equal pay and by EC Directive 76/207 on equal treatment, which calls on member-states to end all sex discrimination in social security schemes that are work-related. This law is now part of our Constitution, and rights granted under it may not be challenged as unconstitutional.

In the 1970s, individual Irish women began to challenge the constitutionality of laws that discriminated against them. In this brave and expensive endeavour they frequently employed a young woman barrister, Senator Mary Robinson, who was counsel in most of the constitutional cases where women's rights were vindicated.

In 1970 the High Court, in *Murtagh Properties* v. *Clery*, declared that women had a right to earn a livelihood under article 40.3 and that sex discriminations in employment recruitment policies were unconstitutional.[29] In 1973 the Supreme Court, again relying on article 40.3, upheld the right to marital privacy and the right of married women to use contraceptives, in the McGee case.[30] Shortly afterwards, in *De Búrca and Anderson* v. *Attorney General*, the Supreme Court declared the Juries Act, 1927, unconstitutional under article 38.5 in so far as it provided that women were exempt from jury service but entitled to serve on application.[31] Until 1973, only three women had ever served on juries. At common law, women were regarded as unqualified for jury service by reason of the doctrine of *propter defectum sexus*. Some of the discriminations against married women in the income tax code were held to violate article 41, which protects the institution of marriage, in the Murphy[32] and Muckley[33] cases in 1980 and 1985, respectively.

Although the courts were prepared to strike down laws that discriminated against women, they were sometimes reluctant and always cautious when doing this.[34] Despite the efforts of Murtagh, de Búrca and Anderson, and the Murphys, it proved impossible to persuade the courts to strike down sex discriminations under the equal rights clause in article 40.1. In all of these cases, the plaintiffs' rights were held to derive from other articles in the Constitution. The courts preferred to limit the scope of article 40.1 ('All citizens shall, as human persons, be held equal before the law') by reading the words 'as human persons' as a restriction on the potential of the article, although individual judges did rely on it to disapprove of sex discriminations.[35]

The assumptions of some judges in these cases about the role of women would leave contemporary liberals more than a little uncomfortable. Their failure to outlaw sex discriminations by relying on article 40.1 has been heavily criticised by nearly all who have written on this article.[36] If the courts had outlawed discriminations against women under article 40.1 in the early seventies, they would have provided the women's movement in its heyday with the encouragement to undertake a systematic challenge to all unjustifiable sex discriminations.

While the courts in their interpretation of the Constitution were prepared, when given the opportunity, to respond fairly positively in favour of women's rights, the same cannot be said of the legislature. There has admittedly been a great deal of legislation on family law and equal rights for women since 1970, but apart from the Succession Act, 1965, it is difficult to identify any major piece of legislation relevant to the rights of women that was not forced on our representatives by the courts, the women's movement or the EC.

In the seventies, after vigorous and sustained campaigns by women's groups such as AIM, 'Cherish', and 'Adapt', legislation was passed entitling unmarried mothers, deserted wives and prisoners' wives to social welfare allowances.[37] Contraception facilities were made available, to some at least.[38] Improved arrangements were made for the recovery of maintenance from errant husbands.[39] Better provision was made for the exclusion of violent spouses from the family home.[40] Married women were given the right to prevent the sale of the family home without their consent.[41]

In the eighties, the oppressive court actions for criminal conversation, enticement, and harbouring a spouse—actions based on the notion that a woman was the property of her husband—were abolished.[42] Married women were given the right to a separate domicile from their husbands.[43] Discriminations against the children of unmarried mothers were removed.[44] A restricted right to free legal aid in family law cases was conceded after Josie Airey's courageous journey to assert it in the European Court of Human Rights.[45] Eventually, in *O'G* v. *Attorney General*,[46] the High Court invalidated a sex discrimination for being in violation of article 40.1 by declaring section 5 of the Adoption Act, 1974 (which prevented widowers, but not widows, from adopting in certain circumstances), unconstitutional because it was 'founded on an idea of difference in capacity between men and women which has no foundation in fact.' And on 12 February 1988, in *McA.* v. *McA.*,[47] the High Court held that the dependent domicile rule, 'like all other appendages of female servitude', did not survive the enactment of the Constitution.

If the Oireachtas could be persuaded by the courts and the women's movement to improve the laws applicable to women as wives and mothers, nothing less than the European Economic Community could persuade it to give women equal economic rights, and in consequence to fulfil the objectives of article 45. Imaginative tactics were employed by legislators, trade unions and employers to deny or delay women's rights to equal pay, equal opportunities, equal taxation and equal social welfare benefits. Wedges were driven between the working and what used to be called the non-working married woman, and between married and single women. Women campaigning for equal taxation were contemptuously dismissed by George Colley, the Minister for Finance, as 'well-heeled and articulate', as if they had no right to speak about the injustices they were subjected to, or to be well-heeled. The spectre of undeserving women holding down 'men's jobs', or of married women selfishly depriving young and single people of their right to work, was constantly raised.

The rights of women to work after marriage, to equal pay and to equal opportunities, to pregnancy leave and to equal social welfare allowances, were only granted by the Oireachtas when, and sometimes long after, it was obliged to grant these rights in order to comply with obligations arising out of our membership of the European Communities. Any advances in women's rights that could cost money were always vigorously resisted by the legislature—even in the relatively affluent past. Many of the above-mentioned rights might have been won by women without the intervention of the EC had they had the resources and the energy to fight for them in the courts.

In 1983 a reactionary backlash against the achievements of the women's movement here and abroad was instrumental in persuading the legislature to countenance what may prove to be a constitutional erosion of women's rights.[48] In that year, legislative fools rushed in where angels feared to tread and commended to the people the Eighth Amendment of the Constitution. This so-called 'pro-life' amendment of article 40.3 ensures that the right to life of an Irish mother is in no way superior to, or deserving of more respect than, the right of life of the unborn. Soldiers are permitted to kill in war; any person violently attacked may kill in self-defence in certain circumstances; the Constitution itself, in article 13.6, overtly accepts capital punishment—but a mother's right to life must be balanced against that of a foetus.[49]

De Valera's Constitution was not consciously designed to advance the cause of women's rights. Nevertheless, the judges have shown that it has the capacity to do just that. Under it, Irish women now have many rights unavailable to, and even superior to, those of their English and indeed their American sisters. Our legislators must know that, should they fail in their duty to vindicate women's rights, the Constitution will be invoked even more frequently to compel them. Ironically, then, the Constitution, though rooted in a patronising and stereotyped view of womanhood, may yet justify the claim that it is truly ours.

NOTES

1. *Dáil Debates*, vols. 67–8, col. 63.
2. The exceptions were John A. Costello, Professor John M. O'Sullivan and Cecil Lavery, all members of the opposition. Helena Concannon, the only woman TD who made a contribution, displayed great confidence in the *bona fides* of her leader.
3. Articles 16.1.1, 16.1.2 and 9.1.3, respectively. The Proclamation of the Irish Republic, 1916, specifically called on 'Irishmen and Irishwomen', and promised the franchise to men and women.
4. Constitution of the Irish Free State, articles 3, 14, 15.
5. *Dáil Debates*, vols. 67–8, col. 64.
6. ibid., cols. 64–5.
7. ibid., col. 67. 'Is it not a tribute to the work that is done by women in the home as mothers?' asked de Valera.
8. ibid., col. 68.
9. ibid., col. 67.
10. Justice Brennan of the US Supreme Court, in *Frontiero* v. *Richardson*, 411 US 677, 93 S. Ct 1764, said that 'Traditionally sex discrimination was rationalised by an attitude of romantic paternalism which, in practical effect, put women not on a pedestal, but in a cage.'

11. *Murphy* v. *Attorney General*, [1982] IR 241.
12. *Hyland* v. *Minister for Social Welfare*, High Court, unreported, 18 January 1988.
13. *Dennehy* v. *Minister for Social Welfare*, High Court, unreported, 26 July 1984.
14. The common law rule of paternal supremacy was replaced by the right of both parents jointly to educate and to have custody of their children in *Re Tilson*, [1951] IR 1.
15. *Dáil Debates*, vols. 67-8, col. 69.
16. ibid., col. 71.
17. In *De Búrca* v. *Anderson*, [1976] IR 385, Chief Justice O'Higgins said that 'some preferential treatment of women citizens seems to be contemplated by the Constitution,' and Justice Walsh in the same case said that article 41.2 'makes special provision for the economic protection of mothers who have duties.' Justice McCarthy in *Weir* v. *Somers*, [1983] IR 112, stated that 'the judicial branch of the Government of the State must . . . recognise its duty under Article 41 and seek to achieve the objectives as set out in that Article.'
18. The Criminal Law (Amendment) Act, 1935, made it a criminal offence for any person to sell or to import for sale any contraceptive.
19. In *Conway* v. *Conway*, [1975] IR 257, Justice Kenny held that 'when the matrimonial home is purchased in the name of the husband either before or after marriage, the wife does not as wife become entitled to any share in its ownership either because she occupies the status of wife or because she carries out household duties.' See Alan Shatter, *Family Law in the Republic of Ireland* (3rd ed.), Dublin 1986, 492-513.
20. See note 17 above.
21. See Shatter, *Family Law*, 511.
22. See *Commission on the Status of Women: Report to the Minister for Finance*, Dublin: Stationery Office 1972 (Prl. 2760), 110.
23. Income Tax Act, 1967, section 192.
24. *Commission on the Status of Women: Report to the Minister for Finance.*
25. Some of the remaining discriminations against women are described in *Irish Women: Agenda for Practical Action*, Dublin: Stationery Office 1985 (Pl. 3126).
26. Between 1937 and 1970, a period of thirty-three years, there were only thirteen major constitutional challenges to post-1937 statutes. Between 1971 and 1987, a period of sixteen years, there were forty-five major challenges. See T. A. Finlay, *The Constitution: Fifty Years On*, Dublin 1988, 12.
27. *Ryan* v. *Attorney General*, [1965] IR 294.
28. See Finlay, *The Constitution*, 12.
29. [1972] IR 330.
30. *McGee* v. *Attorney General*, [1974] IR 284.
31. [1976] IR 38.
32. [1982] IR 241.
33. [1986] ILRM 364.
34. See Yvonne Scannell, 'Changing Times for Women's Rights', in Eiléan

Ní Chuilleanáin (ed.), *Irish Women: Image and Achievement*, Dublin 1985, 64-5.

35. Justice Walsh, in *De Búrca and Anderson* v. *Attorney General*, [1976] IR 385, said that in his view 'it was not open to the State to discriminate in its enactments between persons who are subject to its laws solely on the grounds of the sex of those persons.' Justice Hamilton, in *Murphy* v. *Attorney General*, [1982] IR 241, held that section 192 of the Income Tax Act, 1967, violated article 40.1, because 'it discriminated invidiously against married couples and the husband in particular.'
36. See John Kelly, *The Irish Constitution* (2nd ed.), 1987, 451; Michael Forde, *Constitutional Law of Ireland*, 1987, 427; James Casey, *Constitutional Law in Ireland*, 1987, 354; Yvonne Scannell, 'Changing Times for Women's Rights', in *Irish Women: Image and Achievement*', 63-5; Francis X. Beytagh, 'Equality under the Irish and American Constitutions: a Comparative Analysis', in *Irish Jurist* (new series), vol. 18 (1983), 56.
37. Social Welfare Act, 1970 (deserted wives' allowances), Social Welfare Act, 1973 (unmarried mothers' allowances), Social Welfare (No. 2) Act, 1974 (prisoners' wives' allowances).
38. Health (Family Planning) Act, 1979. See also the Health (Family Planning) (Amendment) Act, 1986.
39. Family Law (Maintenance of Spouses and Children) Act, 1976, and Maintenance Orders Act, 1974.
40. Family Law (Maintenance of Spouses and Children) Act, 1976, and Family Law (Protection of Spouses and Children) Act, 1981.
41. Family Home Protection Act, 1976.
42. Family Law Act, 1981.
43. Domicile and Recognition of Foreign Divorces Act, 1986.
44. Status of Children Act, 1987.
45. After the judgment in *Airey* v. *Ireland*, [1979] 2 European Human Rights Reports 305, the Government established a non-statutory scheme of legal aid and advice, to be administered through law centres. The scheme is very defective. See Shatter, *Family Law*, 60-70.
46. [1985] ILRM 61.
47. High Court, unreported, 12 February 1988.
48. In *Attorney General (Society for the Protection of the Unborn Child (Ireland) Ltd.)* v. *Open Door Counselling Ltd*, [1987] ILRM 477, Justice Hamilton, president of the High Court, relied on this amendment to deny Irish women the right to information on abortion facilities available outside the jurisdiction. On appeal to the Supreme Court, this decision was upheld; the process of erosion may have begun.
49. The author's objections, as a lawyer, to this amendment relate to the very grave legal and ethical difficulties it presents for people (including the sick mother) involved in decision-making when pregnancy threatens a woman's life.

The author thanks her colleagues William Duncan, Gerard Hogan and Gerry Whyte for their many helpful suggestions for this paper.

MR JUSTICE RONAN KEANE

10. Property in the Constitution and in the Courts

Ronan Keane was called to the Bar in 1954, to the Inner Bar in 1970 and became a Barrister of Lincoln's Inn in 1979. He was appointed a Judge of the High Court in 1979. In 1986 he succeeded Mr Justice Brian Walsh as President of the Law Reform Commission. He is the author of *The Law of Local Government in the Republic of Ireland* (1982), *Company Law in the Republic of Ireland* (1985), *Equity and the Law of Trusts in the Republic of Ireland* (1988) and edited the 2nd edition of *Walsh's Planning and Development Law* (1984).

THE Constitution of the Irish Free State referred only in passing to any rights of private property. The state was prohibited from expropriating the property of religious or educational institutions except for what were called 'works of public utility', and then only on payment of compensation.[1] It was very different in 1937: there was indeed a similarly worded provision, but in addition the state undertook, in article 40, 'by its laws [to] protect as best it may from unjust attack and, in the case of injustice done, [to] vindicate the . . . property rights of every citizen.' And that was not all. In the cluster of articles headed 'Fundamental Rights', an entire article (article 43) was devoted to 'Private Property'. This reads:

> 1. 1° The State acknowledges that man, in virtue of his rational being, has the natural right, antecedent to positive law, to the private ownership of external goods.
>   2° The State accordingly guarantees to pass no law attempting to abolish the right of private ownership or the general right to transfer, bequeath, and inherit property.

2. 1° The State recognises, however, that the exercise of the rights mentioned in the foregoing provisions of this article ought, in civil society, to be regulated by the principles of social justice.
2° The State, accordingly, may as occasion requires delimit by law the exercise of the said rights with a view to reconciling their exercise with the exigencies of the common good.

At first reading, this article would seem to have two objects, the first being to prohibit the state from abolishing private property as an institution. It would be fanciful to suppose that there was the remotest prospect in 1937 that an Irish parliament would seek to create either a utopian society in which all property was owned in common or some form of Marxist-Leninist polity in which all property was vested in the state. If those were the dangers intended to be avoided, the practical consequences of article 43 would have been small indeed. But the view seems to have been taken at the time that the first part of the article might be read more restrictively so as to prohibit *any* interference by the state with private property, and hence its second limb.

Both the state and its colonial predecessor had, of course, been interfering with property rights for generations: the citizen's income was taxed since the Napoleonic wars, and his land could be taken away from him for many purposes. Indeed, the mightiest social revolution ever to take place in Ireland, the end of landlordism as the dominant form of ownership of agricultural land, had been fuelled by the vast powers of expropriation vested in the Irish Land Commission. De Valera and those who framed the Constitution with him had no intention of allowing these major social changes to be rolled back, or similar reforms to be impeded in the future, and hence the second section of the article, permitting such inroads on private property rights where they were justified by the requirements of 'social justice' and 'the common good'.

The question immediately arises as to why it was thought necessary to have any such article in the Constitution, since the absence of corresponding provisions in the Irish Free State

Constitution had not apparently given rise to any controversy or difficulty. The answer is probably to be found in the fact that the article appeared in a section of the Constitution where the influence of contemporary Catholic teaching was particularly marked. Those doctrines were reflected not only in the Preamble, but also in the adjoining articles dealing with fundamental rights under the headings of 'The Family', 'Education' and—more guardedly—'Religion'. Mr Justice Gavan Duffy, indeed, described articles 41 and 42 as being 'redolent . . . of the great papal encyclicals . . . '[2]

The year 1936, in which work on the drafting of the Constitution started in earnest, was also the year in which the Spanish Civil War began. Communism, rather than fascism, was seen in Catholic terms—at least in Irish Catholic terms—as the most dangerous of political systems, and this is reflected in the first section of article 43. But the church had also accepted the right of the state to restrain the excesses of free-market economies. Thus, the rights conceded to the state in the second part of the article to delimit rights of private property, where what was called (with no doubt deliberate vagueness) 'social justice' so required, mirrored both Catholic orthodoxy and the prevailing political realities. Viewed in this light, the article might be thought to belong to what Mr Justice Barrington in his paper, adopting an expression of Walter Bagehot, called the 'confessional' rather than the 'efficient' part of the Constitution.

The first reported judicial comment on article 43 seemed to confirm that it would be of little significance in practical terms. An attempt to rely on it as rendering unconstitutional legislation that sought to regulate the bacon industry, on the ground that it was contrary to 'social justice', was rejected by Mr Justice Hanna, who said that he found it impossible to define that expression as a matter of law, describing it as 'a nebulous phrase involving no question of law for the courts, but questions of ethics, morals, economics and sociology'.[3] But this was not to be the final consignment of article 45 to the attic of the Constitution, so to speak, where it could keep company with the other principles of social policy proclaimed in article 45 but expressly withdrawn from the ambit of the courts. The judgment of the Supreme Court in the Sinn Féin funds case[4] in 1948 seemed to make this clear.

That decision arose out of an attempt by the Oireachtas to prevent the High Court from entertaining an action brought to determine the ownership of funds belonging to the old pre-1922 Sinn Féin organisation and to have the application of the funds administered by a board, thereby, as it was hoped, preventing the funds from being swallowed up in legal costs. This invasion of the judicial sphere was sharply rejected both in the High Court and the Supreme Court, but in the latter court the argument was also advanced that it violated article 43. It was contended for the state that the article did no more than simply prohibit the total abolition of the right of private property and that, subject to that overriding constraint, it was entirely for the Oireachtas to decide what was necessitated in any particular case by social justice or the requirements of the common good. This was not so, the court ruled: the article was intended to enshrine the property rights of individual citizens, and while those rights could be regulated by the Oireachtas in the interests of the common good, any decision by the Oireachtas as to what the common good might require could be reviewed by the courts.

While declining to become entangled in the philosophical problems that underlay article 43, Mr Justice O'Byrne made it clear that it might indeed be availed of to repel a particular attack on property rights:

> It was contended by Counsel for the Attorney General that the intendment and effect of Article 43.1.2 was merely to prevent the total abolition of private property in the State, and that, consistently with the clause, it is quite competent for the Oireachtas to take away the property rights of any individual citizen or citizens. We are unable to accept that proposition. It seems to us that the article was intended to enshrine and protect the property rights of the individual citizen of the State and that the rights of the individual *are* thereby protected, subject to the right of the State, as declared in Clause 2, to regulate the exercise of such rights in accordance with the principles of social

> justice and to delimit the exercise of such rights so as to reconcile the exercise with the exigencies of the common good...In particular cases this may give rise to great difficulties. It is claimed that the question of the exigencies of the common good is peculiarly a matter for the Legislature and that the decision of the Legislature on such a question is absolute and not subject to, or capable of being reviewed by, the courts. We are unable to give our assent to this far-reaching proposition...

In that case, the legislation was held to violate the property rights of individual citizens in a manner not necessitated by the common good.[5]

Yet despite this apparently uncompromising assertion of the citizen's right to question in the courts the judgment of the Oireachtas on matters of social policy and the common good, unease similar to that voiced by Mr Justice Hanna at the courts becoming involved in such questions seemed to persist. True, in *Foley* v. *Irish Land Commission*[6] the Supreme Court, while rejecting a challenge to the constitutionality of the Land Purchase Acts based on article 32, made it clear that they were not receding from the position adopted in the Sinn Féin funds case: the abridgment of property rights effected by that code was, in their view, reconcilable with the exigencies of the common good. But in *Attorney General* v. *Southern Industrial Trust Ltd*[7] a more ambivalent posture was adopted. That case arose out of the forfeiture of a motor car owned by a hire purchase company in respect of which a customs offence had been committed. The company were innocent of the offence, but no compensation was payable to them in respect of the seizure of their property. Their claim that this was in breach of the constitutional guarantees as to private property was rejected, and in the Supreme Court Mr Justice Lavery made clear his reluctance to give article 43 anything more than a strictly limited operation, stating that the delimitation of private property rights and the assessment of what the common good required were 'matters primarily for the consideration of the Oireachtas'.[8]

This was obviously difficult to reconcile with the approach

adopted in the Sinn Féin funds case; and in *Central Dublin Development Association* v. *Attorney General*[9] Mr Justice Kenny, confronted with this embarrassing divergence of opinion at the Supreme Court level, made clear his preference for the approach adopted in the Sinn Féin funds case. Adopting an analysis of the relevant articles by Mr Justice Davitt, President of the High Court, at first instance in the Southern Industrial Trust case, he held that if any of the rights that constituted ownership were abolished or restricted, the absence of compensation for the restriction or abolition would make the legislation invalid if it was an 'unjust attack', within the meaning of article 40, on those property rights. In arriving at a decision on the propriety of such legislation, the court was entitled to enquire into whether the restriction or abolition was in accordance with the principles of social justice and whether the relevant legislation was necessitated by the common good.

In a later Supreme Court decision a clearer pattern emerged. It was said in *Blake* v. *Attorney General*,[10] where the Rent Restrictions Act, 1960, was under challenge, that it is article 40, under which the state undertakes to protect the property rights of the citizen against unjust attack, that guarantees a citizen's right to a *particular* item of property. Article 43, by contrast, is a *general* injunction to the state not to abolish the institution of private property, but permitting its regulation in the interests of social justice and the common good. If the citizen's right to a particular property is significantly interfered with by legislation, that legislation will be unconstitutional as being an unjust attack under article 40 unless it is justified under article 43 because of the requirements of social justice and the common good. Conversely, it would seem, if it is justified by those requirements it cannot be regarded as an unjust attack on the citizen's rights.[11]

This at least is the theoretical framework within which the courts have sought to define the property rights of the citizen. In practice, as one might expect, the controversy in particular cases has tended to focus on the question of compensation. It is one thing to admit the right of the state to abridge the property rights of the citizen in the interest of society as a whole, but quite another to allow this to happen without compensation.

That would seem to be a classic example of what article 40 calls an 'unjust attack'. Yet the position is not quite as simple as that. There are many instances in which the citizen's property rights are seriously affected without payment of compensation and which have been held to be constitutional. Thus, as we have seen, a motor car could be forfeited without compensation because of a customs offence of which the true owner—a hire-purchase company—was innocent. The value of property could be affected by the decisions of a planning authority concerning the area in which it was situated and no compensation be payable to the owners.[12] An employee in a particular business could be deprived without compensation of a salary that his or her employer was willing to pay, because of pay policy legislation.[13] The owners of land on which a prehistoric fort was situated could be prevented from using it for normal agricultural purposes and yet not be entitled to compensation.[14] In all these cases, the view of the Oireachtas that the common good required the curtailment of the particular property right without compensation was upheld by the courts; all of which serves to emphasise that an abridgment of property rights that may at first sight seem to be unjust within article 40 may yet be held to be constitutionally pure by reference to article 43. And where compensation is payable, while the normal measure in legislation is to pay the owner the market value of the property taken, the fact that he gets less than that—as where the compensation for a holding acquired by the Land Commission is paid in land bonds—will not necessarily render the acquisition constitutionally invalid.[15]

Those are all instances where the challenge to the constitutional validity of the particular legislation failed. On the other side of the line there are important instances where it succeeded. Thus in the Blake case, the rent control legislation that froze the rents payable to some landlords in what was found to be an arbitrary manner and without compensation was found to be unconstitutional. Similarly, the power of the ESB to lay electric lines across people's land without compensation failed to survive such a challenge.[16] It is again the question of compensation that tends to dominate: is the legislature unjustly forcing particular sections of the community to subsidise a desirable social object that should be the responsibility of society as a whole? The difficulty is in determining where the line should be drawn: when can such legislation be saved because of the demands of social justice or the common good?

The actual language of article 43 has also given rise to some difficulty. Like some other articles in the Constitution, it indicates an acceptance of what can be broadly called a theory of natural law, which represents one of the solutions legal philosophers have offered over the centuries to the problem of how legal rights arise. Are they, as John Austin argued in the nineteenth century, simply what the sovereign power of the state allows? Or is there some framework of values or norms that exists independently of human laws? If so, where does the framework come from, and how do we identify the rights that can be derived from it?

Article 43 undoubtedly rejects the positivist philosophy of Austin and his disciples, and defines the right of private property as one that derives from natural law rather than positive law. A consideration of the difficulties involved in securing agreement as to what in any context constitutes the natural law would take us too far afield: it is enough to say that it is a noteworthy feature of codes that seek to articulate such concepts, whether founded on the natural law or some other philosophy, that they are no sooner enunciated than the qualifications to the rights start to appear. To this, article 43 is no exception. What is of more immediate interest is the actual wording used and the problems to which it has given rise.

Whatever the actual right declared in article 43 may be (and there is a surprising divergence between the Irish text, which, literally translated, refers to a person's right to 'his own private share of worldly wealth', and the English version, which refers to his right to 'the private ownership of external goods'[17]) the right is described as belonging to man 'in virtue of his rational being'. This curious qualification has caused some problems, since there obviously exist in society combinations, such as companies, that are recognised by the law as legal entities capable of owning property just as human beings are. Are such groupings deprived of the protection of article 43? It would seem that they are, although a solution has been proposed in the case of companies by permitting the shareholders to invoke rights protected under article 43 when the interests of their company are unjustly attacked.[18] Yet this is not without its complications, since shareholders in companies may notoriously differ as to what the interests of the company may require. One cannot help wondering what the words 'in virtue of his rational being' are doing in the article in the first place, or what the necessary relationship is between man's rational capacity and his 'right' to own property.

Then there was the problem of what property rights were protected. If one were confined to article 43, it would seem that only the 'natural right . . . to the private ownership of external goods' and 'the general right to transfer, bequeath, and inherit property' were protected. In the earlier cases, it was said that these were indeed the *only* property rights protected under the Constitution and were the rights that the state undertook in article 40 to protect and vindicate.[19] It would seem to follow from this that rights that simply arose under a contract, for example, or a right to bring legal proceedings, could not attract the protection of the Constitution. But, as we have seen, the Supreme Court ultimately rejected this view and held that the citizen's rights to individual items of property—and not merely the general rights acknowledged by article 43—were protected. Thus, while the point remains to be decided, it would seem that a right to sue is a constitutionally guaranteed property right and that an arbitrary or unreasonable interference with it by legislation would be struck down as an unjust attack on the citizen's property rights.[20]

It will be seen that the constitutional safeguards for private property have led to decisions that offer an uncertain guide as to what legislation may survive challenge in the courts. But it is also true that very few enactments of any significance have been struck down. The most conspicuous casualty was the rent control legislation, but it is important to remember that it was not the principle of rent control that the courts rejected in those cases: it was the unjust and arbitrary manner in which it was applied by the Oireachtas. Indeed, one could reasonably say that the first challenge to the Rent Acts would never have emerged had the Oireachtas fulfilled its proper role of keeping such legislation under review so as to ensure that, with the passage of time, measures that were wholly acceptable in principle were not producing indefensible anomalies. There has never in the history of these articles of the Constitution been anything remotely approaching the conflicts that in the United States have been the result of a President and Congress at grips with a Supreme Court of a different ideological bent.[21]

Is there then no substance in the charge frequently levelled against these articles that, by unduly stressing the sanctity of property rights, they in some sense impede the passage of socially desirable legislation? The history of the Kenny Report on building land might be seen as lending support to such criticisms. That report was the result of the considerable increase in the price of building land in the 1970s, the effect of which on the cost of housing led the Government to appoint a committee to enquire into the problem. The chairman of the committee was Mr Justice Kenny, who, in *Central Dublin Development Association* v. *Attorney General*, had considered exhaustively the constitutionality of the Local Government (Planning and Development) Act, 1963.

The majority recommendation in the report,[22] to which Mr Justice Kenny subscribed, proposed a 'designated area' scheme, under which the High Court would have power to declare that certain areas would probably be used during a ten-year period for development and would be increased in value by works carried out by the local authority. Local authorities were to be entitled to acquire land in such areas compulsorily at its existing use value, with an addition of 25 per cent, but without regard to its development potential. Compensation was not to be payable for the refusal of planning permission in such areas. The possible constitutional frailty of such a proposal was carefully addressed by the majority, but they came to the conclusion that, while it would be desirable for any legislation implementing their proposals to be referred to the Supreme Court for a decision on its constitutionality, the legislation they envisaged did not appear to constitute an unjust attack on the property rights of the citizen. They were of the view that the legislation would be treated by the courts as being a necessary regulation of private property rights by the principles of social justice.

The minority were distinctly less happy with the constitutionality of this scheme. They questioned whether such a radical departure from the normal method of assessing compensation for expropriation, based on market value, could survive a challenge in the courts. They also saw the scheme as necessarily involving a dual price system, under which some people would get market value for their land while others, whose land was taken by local authorities, would have to accept the fixed price level. In their view, such legislation would almost certainly be held by the courts to be invidiously discriminatory and, as such, repugnant, having regard both to article 40.3.2 and article 40.1, which provides that 'all citizens shall, as human persons, be held equal before the law.'

The majority recommendation was never implemented, and the weight to be attached to it was somewhat weakened by this passage:

> The Constitution does not give to each citizen the right to get the full market price for any of his property which he decides to sell. If it did, then all price controls would be repugnant to the Constitution and we are convinced that this is not the law. Moreover, if each citizen has the right to get the full market price for any part of his property which he decides to sell, each owner of house property must have the right to get the full market rent for it when he lets it. But if this is the law, the Rent Restrictions Acts and the Landlord and Tenant Acts, both of which regulate the amount of rent which a landlord may lawfully get for some types of property and which, in effect, prevent him from realising the full market price on sale of the property by giving privileges to tenants, are repugnant to the Constitution. *Nobody has ever suggested this in the thousands of cases under those Acts which have come before the Courts.* [Emphasis added.][23]

As we have seen, the Rent Restrictions Act, 1960, was subsequently held unconstitutional, precisely because it deprived the landlords of the market rent from their property without compensation. A similar fate befell the Housing (Private Rented Dwellings) Bill, 1981, which was intended to replace it.[24] It must be at least doubtful, in these circumstances, whether a bill implementing the majority recommendations of the Kenny Committee would surivive a constitutional challenge.[25]

Yet it is also the case that rent control *as such* was not stigmatised as an unconstitutional violation of property rights in either of these decisions. It was the arbitrary and unjust manner in which the control was applied that was the decisive consideration. This is of considerable relevance when one turns to the particular case of planning decisions, which have caused some controversy in recent times: it is simply not the case that legislation that restricts the owner's use of his property without compensation is necessarily unconstitutional. The planning code prescribes a vast range of circumstances in which planning decisions can be made that do not attract compensation, and these have so far withstood constitutional challenge.[26] If existing legislation is tilting the balance unfairly in favour of the private speculator and against the public interest, then it should be perfectly possible for the legislature to design a scheme that further delimits the property rights of the people concerned, in the interests of the common good. This would probably be a more rewarding approach to the problem than judicial creativity: recent suggestions that substantial awards of compensation may themselves be constitutionally frail, as being an unwarranted diversion of public funds into the pockets of speculators, while they have an attractively rhetorical ring may not withstand closer scrutiny.[27]

It is of the nature of a society that favours the promotion of private enterprise—and, under the directive principles of social policy, the state is required to favour such enterprise[28]—that it will occasionally award windfalls to some. The legislature should be capable of deciding at what point social justice or the common good requires that individuals should sacrifice the gains they have made from their shrewdness, foresight, hard work or good fortune to the greater welfare of the community. Provided the statutory framework they establish for so doing is not flawed by a basic unfairness, there hardly seems occasion for the courts to intervene. It is an unhappy fact, however, that there will always be ministers, legislators and civil servants who prefer leaving things as they are on the basis that this will cause them less trouble in the long run. And it is unfortunately the case that the tangled undergrowth of the constitutional provisions on private property has given the apostles of inertia a plausible excuse for their restful attitudes.

Article 43, as we have seen, probably owes its appearance in the Constitution to the influence of Catholic social teaching. In its rejection of communist or utopian visions of a propertyless society on the one hand and unbridled *laissez-faire* on the other, it reflected, then as now, the broad political consensus in Irish society. The framers of the Constitution, I suspect, would have been surprised to find that article 43 had in fact been so frequently invoked in litigation and, had they foreseen that development, might have been happier to see it tucked away among the social policy directives, which are not within the ambit of the courts, rather than be the subject of painstaking judicial exegesis. Had they contented themselves with the forthright protection of the citizen against unjust attacks on property rights contained in article 40, there might have been a less tangled history to unfold. At least the damaging impression could not have taken so firm a hold that the Constitution imposes unnecessary barriers against progress to social justice.

NOTES

1. Article 8. The wording closely followed that of section 5 of the Government of Ireland Act, 1920.
2. *In re Tilson, Infants*, [1951] IR 1, 14.
3. *Pigs Marketing Board* v. *Donnelly (Dublin) Limited*, [1939] IR 413, 418.
4. *Buckley and Others* v. *Attorney General and Another*, [1950] IR 67.
5. The court, however, might well have taken the view in that case that the legislation was in truth reconcilable with the exigencies of the common good, since the latter might have been seen as requiring that funds voluntarily subscribed for a particular object were not dissipated in legal costs. A similar problem arose in the case of funds belonging to the Royal Hospital, Kilmainham: here, however, the draftsman of the relevant legislation, obviously with the Sinn Féin funds case in mind, was at pains to respect the jurisdiction of the High Court, which eventually decided the application of the funds under the *cy près* jurisdiction. See Royal

Hospital Kilmainham Act, 1962: *Re Royal Hospital, Kilmainham*, [1965] IR 451.

6. [1952] IR 118.
7. (1960) 94 ILTR 161.
8. ibid., 176.
9. (1973) 109 ILTR 69.
10. [1982] IR 117.
11. Per Mr Justice Walsh in *Dreher* v. *Irish Land Commission*, [1984] ILRM 94.
12. Per Mr Justice Kenny in *Central Dublin Development Association* v. *Attorney General*, [1974] ILRM 90.
13. *Condon* v. *Minister for Labour*, [1981] IR 62.
14. *O'Callaghan* v. *Commissioners of Public works*, [1983] ILRM 391.
15. *Dreher* v. *Irish Land Commission*.
16. *E.S.B.* v. *Gormley*, [1985] IR 129.
17. See *Central Dublin Development Association* v. *Attorney General*, 83, per Mr Justice Kenny.
18. *P.M.P.S. Limited and Moore* v. *Attorney General*, [1983] IR 339.
19. *Foley* v. *Irish Land Commission; Attorney General* v. *Southern Industrial Trust*.
20. In *O'Brien* v. *Keogh*, [1972] IR 144, and *O'Brien* v. *Manufacturing Engineering Company Limited*, [1973] IR 334, the Supreme Court held that a right to sue was a property right, protected by article 40.3.2. In *Moynihan* v. *Greensmyth*, [1977] IR 55, Chief Justice O'Higgins, delivering the judgment of the court, noted that neither Foley nor Southern Industrial Trust had been cited to the court in those cases and that, accordingly, the court expressly reserved the question as to whether the cases were properly decided. In view, however, of the subsequent disapproval by the court in Blake's case of the approach adopted in Southern Industrial Trust, it would seem that the decisions in *O'Brien* v. *Keogh* and *O'Brien* v. *Manufacturing Engineering Company Limited* can now be regarded as correctly stating the law.
21. Reaching its height in the attempts by Franklin D. Roosevelt to 'pack' what was regarded as a hostile Supreme Court during the New Deal era in the 1930s.
22. *Report of the Committee on the Price of Building Land*, Dublin: Stationery Office 1973 (Prl. 3632).
23. ibid., 46-7.
24. *Re Housing (Private Rented Dwellings) Bill, 1981*, [1983] IR 181.
25. See Ronan Keane, 'Land Use, Compensation and the Community', in *Irish Jurist* (new series), vol. 18 (1983), 23. The Joint Oireachtas Committee on Building Land was, however, advised by counsel that the principle of market value could be modified in cases of compulsory acquisition without offending the Constitution. See *Report of the Joint Oireachtas Committee on Building Land*, Dublin: Stationery Office 1985 (Pl. 3232), 5.
26. See *Central Dublin Development Association* v. *Attorney General*.
27. For example, in *Re XJS Investments Limited* v. *Dún Laoghaire Corporation*, [1987] ILRM 659.

28. Article 45.3.1: 'The State shall favour and, where necessary, supplement private initiative in industry and commerce.' While the application of the principles set out in this article is stated not to be 'cognisable by any Court', it has been held that they may provide guidance in a number of contexts, for example in clarifying the expression 'the exigencies of the common good' in article 43. See *Landers* v. *Attorney General*, (1973) 109 ILTR 1.

PROFESSOR JAMES CASEY

11. Changing the Constitution: Amendment and Judicial Review

James Casey is Professor of Law at University College, Dublin. He is the author of *The Office of the Attorney General in Ireland* (1980) and *Constitutional Law in Ireland* (1987).

THE theme of this paper instantly provokes thought. One can well see how the Constitution may be changed by amendment—but how can it be changed by judicial review? Has this happened? If so is it not undemocratic, and subversive of the whole constitutional structure? To examine these questions it is first necessary to stress some differences between Bunreacht na hÉireann and its predecessor, the Irish Free State Constitution of 1922.

We know that Mr de Valera's concern in preparing a new constitution was mainly to re-write the Treaty settlement.[1] He was not dissatisfied with the main elements of the governmental system. Hence, the institutional arrangements of Bunreacht na hÉireann are broadly similar to those under the earlier constitution, and in many instances the language used is identical. For, as Mr de Valera told the Dáil on 11 May 1937, 'I was anxious . . . that the things that we were satisfied with should remain; that we should not have change simply for change's sake.'[2] But he provided for two changes in the matters that concern us here. Firstly, the new constitution was to be much less easy to amend. Secondly, judicial review—the power of the courts to declare laws unconstitutional—was put on a firmer foundation than before.

Perhaps the most marked contrast between Bunreacht na hÉireann and the 1922 Constitution lies in the matter of amendment. Originally it was intended that the 1922 Constitution could be amended by ordinary legislation for eight years only; thereafter a referendum would be required. But that eight-year period was extended—by ordinary legislation—to sixteen years, and in 1934 that extension was ruled constitutionally valid by the Supreme Court.[3] It follows that for the whole of its lifetime the Constitution was flexible, in the sense that its provisions were subject to alteration by the will of a parliamentary majority. So, necessarily, were the rights declared by the Constitution.

This development robbed the 1922 Constitution of its potential as a check upon the executive and a protection for the citizen. For the view could be—and was—taken that *any* statute conflicting with the Constitution operated to amend it; and this even if the statute was not described as a constitutional amendment, or failed to say just which articles were amended.[4] The power the Constitution gave the courts to hold legislation unconstitutional could not be expected to operate properly when the foundations were so insecure and shifting.

The framers of the 1937 Constitution avoided this by stipulating that it could be amended by ordinary legislation for three years after the first President took up office.[5] Thereafter a referendum was necessary. And it was specifically provided that the three-year period itself could not be prolonged.[6] So, since 25 June 1941 the Constitution has been a rigid one: amendments to the text require the passage of a bill by the Oireachtas and its subsequent approval by the people in a referendum.[7] There is no other process of amendment; and it should perhaps be emphasised that our Constitution—unlike, say, those of Italy or West Germany—contains no provisions that are beyond amendment.[8]

Since 1937 there have been ten Amendment of the Constitution Acts. Two of these were passed before 25 June 1941 and so did not require, or receive, popular approval. These two amending Acts made several important alterations in the text approved by the electorate. Two in particular may be mentioned. Article 34 was amended to provide that where the President had referred a bill to the Supreme Court under article 26, and that court had upheld the bill as valid, its constitutionality could never thereafter be questioned.[9] In addition, articles 26 and 34 were amended to provide that when the Supreme Court ruled on the validity of a bill or an Act, there could be only one opinion of the court: that is, no judge was allowed to voice his own conclusions, whether he disagreed entirely with his colleagues or agreed in the result but for different reasons.[10]

The inspiration for the latter change lay in the fact that when President Hyde referred the first bill under article 26—the Offences Against the State (Amendment) Bill, 1940—Chief Justice Sullivan, announcing the result, said: 'The decision now announced is the decision of the majority of the judges . . . '[11] In fact, there were no separate opinions, dissenting or otherwise; nonetheless, the amendments were designed to foreclose any such possibility for the future. Mr de Valera told the Dáil that 'from the point of view of the public interest, it is better to have a single judgment pronounced and no indication given that other judges held a different view.'[12]

But this 'one-opinion rule' is an unusual provision, which can make it very difficult for the Supreme Court to produce a judgment; and a number of judges, past and present, have indicated their dislike of it. Mr Justice Walsh, indeed, has recently suggested that the fiftieth anniversary of the Constitution would be fittingly marked by getting rid of it.[13]

It was thirty-one years before the next amendments were effected. This does not mean that no problems had been discerned nor suggestions for alteration mooted. In 1959, and again in 1969, Fianna Fáil governments secured the passage of bills to amend the electoral system by abolishing proportional representation; but on both occasions these proposals were rejected in referenda. In December 1967 an all-party committee had recommended a number of changes: for example, replacing article 3 with a more conciliatory formula; altering article 5 to describe the state as a republic; modifying the provisions of article 38 on special criminal courts; and including in the directive principles of social policy of article 45 the principle of equal pay for men and women for work of equal value.[14] However, no action was taken on any of the committee's recommendations.

In 1972 there were three amendments. One lowered the

voting age in Dáil elections to 18;[15] the second cleared away any constitutional barriers to membership of the European Community;[16] and the third altered article 44 by deleting the provisions on the recognition of named churches.[17] In 1979 came the Sixth and Seventh Amendments. The first of these inserted what is now article 37.2, designed to protect adoption orders against possible constitutional challenge on separation of powers grounds.[18] The second allowed the Oireachtas to widen the representation of institutions of higher education in the Seanad (it has not yet been implemented).[19] The Eighth Amendment, in 1983, was the famous 'pro-life' amendment, the implications of which remain to be worked out.[20] In 1984 the Ninth Amendment permitted the passage of legislation giving non-citizens the right to vote in Dáil elections.[21] Finally, the Tenth Amendment, passed in 1987 in the wake of Raymond Crotty's case,[22] allowed the state to ratify the Single European Act.[23]

The one overall conclusion that can be drawn from this survey is that the basic structures and principles laid down in 1937 remain in place. The institutions of the state—presidency, executive, legislature, courts—remain unaltered, and the same is true of the catalogue of rights declared in 1937. The changes have been in matters of detail, not in fundamentals. And some are, of course, much more significant than others. From the point of view of political, social, economic and legal consequences, the most important is undoubtedly that of 1972, permitting our entry to the European Community. An incidental consequence of that entry was to enshrine in our law the principle of equal pay for equal work. Though this is still not stated in the Constitution (contrary to the all-party committee's 1967 recommendation) it *is* contained in article 119 of the EC Treaty. And it is consequently as binding upon Government and Oireachtas—and as much beyond their power to change—as if it featured in Bunreacht na hÉireann itself.

So much, then, for the formal processes of amendment. But before turning to judicial review I must refer to the emergency powers provisions. Under article 28 of the Constitution, the Oireachtas may pass resolutions declaring the existence of a national emergency, and in fact such resolutions have been in force continuously since 1939. Under cover of these the

Oireachtas has power to pass virtually any legislation it wishes; all constitutional restrictions are relaxed.[24] Had legislation, say, abolishing PR been passed in this way (without a referendum), it is difficult to see how it could successfully have been challenged in the courts. That nothing of this kind has been attempted seems a tribute to the wish of successive governments not merely to play by the rules but by the spirit of the rules.

What we have considered so far are changes in the actual text of the Constitution. But the Constitution of 1988 is much more than the text of 1937. It can be fully understood only in the light of the judicial decisions interpreting it; and in the last twenty-five years the number of those decisions has increased enormously. This is not to suggest that from 1937 until 1962 the Constitution was never invoked before the courts—indeed, some very important cases were decided in that period[25]—but the pace accelerated in the 1960s; due, I think, to a multiplicity of factors, all impinging on each other. Irish society was changing. There was the stimulus of economic development; the opening to the outside world caused by that and by the advent of television. There was plainly also a heightened awareness of, and concern for, rights, stimulated perhaps by the civil rights campaigns in the United States and in Northern Ireland. And as well as this, legal practitioners, and a new generation of judges, had become more conscious of the Constitution's potential for safeguarding—and indeed extending—existing rights. As a consequence, challenges to legislative, executive and administrative decisions, invoking the Constitution's provisions, are now quite common, with effects that are very significant indeed.

In a way it is strange that this should have happened. Mr de Valera was no admirer of lawyers, and he had reason to look with disfavour on judicial review: a 1934 Supreme Court decision had cast a shadow over some of his legislation dismantling the Treaty settlement.[26] Nonetheless he clearly and unequivocally provided for judicial review in Bunreacht na hÉireann.[27] In part this may have been due to a wish to preserve existing arrangements; but Mr de Valera clearly appreciated that under this more rigid constitution, with its more emphatic statement of rights, judicial review might prove more significant than under its predecessor. When introducing the draft constitution he told the Dáil that ultimately the Supreme Court would be the body to decide on its interpretation; indeed he said that determining the constitutionality of Acts would be one of that court's 'principal functions'.[28] Nonetheless, it is unlikely that he really envisaged for the courts the role they have actually come to play under the Constitution. I think that by 'principal functions' he meant 'most symbolically significant functions', and not 'most frequently exercised functions'.

The effects of judicial review may be summarised under three headings: (1) the protection of individual rights; (2) the recognition of 'unenumerated' rights; (3) insistence upon constitutional restrictions.

Since the first and second are dealt with in other papers, I shall say little about them. But I may point out that in several instances the courts have interpreted the Constitution as abolishing antiquated rules that the Oireachtas intended to change but somehow never found time to.

The prime example is the 1971 case of *Byrne* v. *Ireland*.[29] The plaintiff here was walking along a footpath in Bray when it suddenly subsided, as a consequence of which she sustained severe injuries. She claimed that the subsidence was due to the negligence of Department of Posts and Telegraphs workers in filling in a trench they had dug. Her argument was that their employer was the state—Ireland—and that it, like any other employer, was liable in law for the faults of its employees. But the defence argued in essence that the state was not so liable, that before independence no such liability was recognised, and that the 1922 and 1937 Constitutions had continued this rule of state immunity in force. In the High Court this defence argument succeeded, but on appeal the Supreme Court rejected it completely. There was nothing in Bunreacht na hÉireann to indicate that the state enjoyed any such immunity from liability: indeed, the indications were all to the contrary, for the Constitution specifically made the President immune from suit[30] and also conferred a limited immunity on members of the Oireachtas,[31] but it extended no such privilege to the state.

The result of that case is that the state is now liable on the same basis as any other employer. Irish law on this matter is now in line with that of most other states. Other common law countries had originally accepted the state immunity rule but had later abolished it by legislation.[32] However, despite a 1961 promise by the Minister for Justice, no such legislation has been enacted here. Thus the decision in the Byrne case shows the courts invoking the Constitution to modernise the law—and protect individual rights—by extirpating an outdated and unjust rule.

The importance of the Constitution's unenumerated rights may be illustrated by reference to the right of privacy. Though the text makes no mention of this right, the courts have held it to be one implicitly guaranteed. So, although it is not necessarily unconstitutional to tap telephones or intercept mail, to do these things deliberately, consciously and unjustifiably is an interference with a constitutional right.[33] For that the courts will provide a remedy by way of damages and, if necessary, an injunction. And those remedies, be it noted, would be available whether the interference stemmed from state or private action. This, again, is something the Oireachtas could have legislated for but as yet has not done so. Those who disparage the significance of the Constitution as a source of rights should observe how the English High Court, with no written constitution to depend upon, handled the phone-tapping question. In the Malone case[34] in 1979 the Vice-Chancellor, Sir Robert Megarry, concluded that it was quite lawful; but he deplored the absence of any safeguards, and said this was not a subject on which it was possible to feel any pride in English law[35]—an unusual statement for an English judge to make!

As to insistence upon constitutional restrictions, what the courts have done here is to emphasise and re-emphasise that the Constitution is the basic, fundamental law of the state. If necessary it can be amended—but only by following the proper procedure. Modification by stealth is out. This is illustrated by the decisions on electoral matters, than which there can hardly be anything more fundamental. The courts have emphasised that the Constitution requires broad equality of representation; a situation where in one constituency there was one deputy per 20,000 people while in another it was one per 30,000 is not permissible.[36] Likewise, when article 16 says that voting in Dáil elections shall be by secret ballot, that means fully secret; and any system that could lead to discovery of how someone voted must be outlawed.[37] The same article laid down the broad principle that all citizens over 18 could vote in Dáil elections. In 1983 the Oireachtas passed a bill which, if enacted, would have given the vote to British citizens resident in the state. There was general agreement that this should be done, and successive governments had indicated an intention of changing the system. But doubts were expressed in the Dáil about whether such a change could be effected merely by statute, and President Hillery referred the bill to the Supreme Court for a ruling on its constitutionality. The court held it invalid, saying that the whole structure of the Constitution indicated that when article 16 gave citizens the vote it meant that *only* citizens could vote.[38] The result, as already mentioned, was the Ninth Amendment of the Constitution Act, 1984, and subsequently legislation to implement it.[39] This gave voting rights in Dáil elections to British citizens, and established machinery for extending those rights to citizens of other EC states on a reciprocal basis.

The judicial enforcement of constitutional restrictions is often inconvenient. It was doubtless disagreeable for the Government to have to change the tax regime for married couples after the decision in the Murphy case,[40] or to have to devise a new rent subsidy scheme following the invalidation of the Rent Restrictions Acts.[41] The executive was clearly shocked to find the Ireland-US extradition arrangements invalidated because the agreement had not been approved by the Dáil, as article 29.5.2 requires.[42] Most recently, politicians have deplored the result of the Crotty case,[43] which they think unduly restrictive of the executive's power to conduct foreign affairs. Private individuals and groups may also complain about particular decisions: the famous McGee case[44] on access to contraceptives provoked the fury of some people, while others were disappointed by the Norris decision[45] on homosexuality.

Has judicial review then *changed* the Constitution? In a sense it has. Bunreacht na hÉireann now protects many more rights than the text, read literally, suggests.[46] The courts now apply the Constitution's separation of powers provisions more restrictively than they once did.[47] And the Crotty decision[48] certainly poses problems for the state's power to enter into certain kinds of international agreement. Judicial review has thus altered our understanding of the Constitution. In particular, the Government and Oireachtas now have to ponder much more carefully the possible constitutional implications of their decisions.

All this, however, flows from specific constitutional dispositions. Judicial review is built into Bunreacht na hÉireann in the plainest terms; it has not, as in the United States, been *inferred* from the Constitution's provisions. Its operation in practice may have produced some controversial results, but those results are based upon principles stated or implicit in the text. So it can hardly be said that judicial review is undemocratic. Nor has its operation subverted the constitutional structure: that remains intact, save where the electorate has chosen to alter it. But we now have a more balanced constitution; if Government and Oireachtas adopt policies arguably at variance with the Constitution, their decisions may be challenged and overturned. There is nothing surprising or unusual about this. The same applies in many other countries, specifically in the majority of EC member-states.

It follows that in some situations the courts will effectively have a veto on the implementation of policies. However, it would be quite wrong to suppose that we now have a system of 'government by judges'. The courts can adjudicate only if someone brings a case before them; and they will pronounce on a constitutional issue only if the plaintiff has a proper interest to raise it,[49] it is still a live question,[50] and there is no other ground on which the case may be decided.[51] They presume statutes to be constitutional, so that the plaintiff has the burden of proving otherwise, and if possible they will interpret statutes to conform with the Constitution.[52] And, of course, they decide only after hearing argument from both sides in open court.

Though the courts play a significant role under the Constitution they are far from being the ultimate policy-makers in our society. There are obvious limits on their powers, especially since so many policy choices involve public expenditure priorities. The courts have no power to decree a new social welfare or health service scheme, a more progressive taxation system, or a new policy for full employment. Such policy choices remain the prerogative of Government and Oireachtas. The electorate, of course, retains the ultimate policy choice of whether to keep judicial review or abolish it. It is noteworthy that no government—no matter how irritated by a particular decision—has proposed its abolition. This suggests that judicial review, as it has now developed, has come to be accepted—indeed to be prized—as a valuable constitutional safeguard.

NOTES

1. See Ronan Fanning, 'Mr de Valera drafts a Constitution', page 33 above.
2. *Dáil Debates*, vol. 67, col. 40.
3. *State (Ryan)* v. *Lennon*, [1935] IR 170.
4. See *Att. Gen.* v. *McBride*, [1928] IR 451, and *R. (Cooney)* v. *Clinton*, [1935] IR 245.
5. See article 51, one of the transitory provisions not now printed in texts of the Constitution.
6. Article 52.3.
7. Article 46.
8. The Italian Constitution places the state's republican status beyond amendment (article 139), while the Federal Republic of Germany's Basic Law makes inadmissible amendments affecting the federal principle or the basic principles laid down in articles 1 and 20 (article 79 (3)).
9. Article 34.3.3.
10. Articles 26.2.2 and 34.4.5.
11. *In re Article 26 and the Offences Against the State (Amendment) Bill, 1940*, [1940] IR 470, 475.
12. *Dáil Debates*, vol. 82, col. 1854, 2 April 1941.
13. In his foreword to James Casey, *Constitutional Law in Ireland*, London 1987, xiii.
14. *Report of the Committee on the Constitution*, Dublin: Stationery Office 1967 (Pr. 9817).
15. Third Amendment of the Constitution Act, 1972.
16. Fourth Amendment of the Constitution Act, 1972.
17. Fifth Amendment of the Constitution Act, 1972.
18. Sixth Amendment of the Constitution (Adoption) Act, 1979.
19. Seventh Amendment of the Constitution (Election of Members of Seanad Éireann by Institutions of Higher Education) Act, 1979.
20. Eighth Amendment of the Constitution Act, 1983.
21. Ninth Amendment of the Constitution Act, 1984.
22. *Crotty* v. *An Taoiseach*, [1987] ILRM 400.

23. Tenth Amendment of the Constitution Act, 1987.
24. Article 28.3.3.
25. e.g. *N.U.R.* v. *Sullivan*, [1947] IR 77; *Buckley* v. *Att. Gen.*, [1950] IR 67; *In re Irish Employers' Mutual Insurance Association Ltd*, [1955] IR 176.
26. *State (Ryan)* v. *Lennon*, [1935] IR 170. See also Casey, *Constitutional Law in Ireland*, 22-4.
27. See articles 34.3.2 and 34.4.4.
28. *Dáil Debates*, vol. 67, col. 54, 11 May 1937.
29. [1972] IR 241.
30. Article 13.8.1.
31. Article 15.13.
32. See Peter Hogg, *Liability of the Crown*, Melbourne 1971.
33. *Kennedy and others* v. *Ireland*, (High Court, Hamilton P., 12 January 1987).
34. *Malone* v. *Metropolitan Police Commissioner*, [1979] 1 All ER 620.
35. ibid., 648.
36. *O'Donovan* v. *Att. Gen.*, [1961] IR 114; *In re Article 26 and the Electoral (Amendment) Bill, 1961*, [1961] IR 169.
37. *McMahon* v. *Att. Gen.*, [1972] IR 69.
38. *In re Article 26 and the Electoral (Amendment) Bill, 1983*, [1984] IR 268.
39. Electoral (Amendment) Act, 1985.
40. *Murphy* v. *Att. Gen.*, [1982] IR 241.
41. See *Blake* v. *Att. Gen.*, [1982] IR 117, and *In re Article 26 and the Housing (Private Rented Dwellings) Bill, 1981*, [1983] IR 181.
42. *State (Gilliland)* v. *Governor, Mountjoy Prison*, [1987] ILRM 278.
43. *Crotty* v. *An Taoiseach*, [1987] ILRM 400.
44. *McGee* v. *Att. Gen.*, [1974] IR 284.
45. *Norris* v. *Att. Gen.*, [1984] IR 36.
46. See Casey, *Constitutional Law in Ireland*, chapter 12.
47. ibid., chapter 9.
48. [1987] ILRM 400.
49. *Cahill* v. *Sutton*, [1980] IR 269.
50. *Condon* v. *Minister for Labour*, [1981] IR 62.
51. *Cooke* v. *Walsh*, [1984] ILRM 208; *O'Brien*. v. *S.*, [1984] IR 326.
52. *East Donegal Co-op. Ltd* v. *Att. Gen.*, [1970] IR 317; *Re Haughey*, [1971] IR 217.

JOHN KELLY, TD

12. Fundamental Rights and the Constitution

John Kelly is a member of the Dáil for Dublin South, and is Professor of Jurisprudence and Roman Law at University College, Dublin. He is the author of several books on legal topics, most recently *The Irish Constitution* (2nd edition, 1984; with Supplement, 1987). He is a former Minister for Industry, Commerce and Tourism and former Attorney General.

WHEN the Irish Free State was set up in 1922, its Constitution provided for a structure fairly closely modelled on the familiar British pattern: a parliament, of which the popularly elected 'lower house', the Dáil, was the most important element; an executive Government substantially appointed from within that lower house and responsible to it; and an independent judiciary. The Constitution of 1937 essentially continued that same basic structure; so that today, sixty-six years after the British administration left this part of the country, we still have a system of government recognisably of the British type.

In only one truly important respect does our Constitution diverge from the British model; and that is in the fact that it incorporates what is sometimes called a 'bill of rights', in other words a set of statements about citizens' fundamental rights and liberties, which the parliament is not entitled to cut down by ordinary legislation, and which the High Court is empowered to uphold, through its general jurisdiction to declare laws void if they should infringe the Constitution. This is a very un-British element, since the central doctrine of the unwritten British constitution is the sovereignty of Parliament (or more correctly, of the Queen in Parliament); although even in Britain voices have been heard advocating the establishment of this kind of bill of rights, whether for Northern Ireland or for the United Kingdom generally.[1]

The fact that this very un-British institution was adopted here is certainly due to the example of the United States, where the Supreme Court, ever since the early nineteenth century, has exercised a jurisdiction to 'strike down' laws (as Americans call it) for infringing the Constitution, and in particular for infringing some part of the 'Bill of Rights', which it incorporates. This American example was followed in 1922 by the men who drafted the Irish Free State Constitution. This contained statements of the right to personal liberty; to inviolability of the dwelling; to freedom of conscience and practice of religion; to free expression of opinion; and to freedom of assembly and association.[2]

The enforcement of these rights through the courts as against Acts of the Oireachtas was, however, frustrated during the years of the Irish Free State because of a clause permitting the Constitution itself to be amended by an ordinary Act, in other words without a referendum, for the first eight years.[3] This eight years was then extended to sixteen;[4] and, on top of that, the judges held that in order to amend the Constitution, an Act did not even need to say that it was so intended.[5] What this boiled down to then was that from 1922 until 1937 any ordinary Act took precedence over the Constitution in the sense that, even if it conflicted with it, it was taken to be in fact an amendment of it and so to override it. Accordingly, while I suppose in practice during those years there was as much freedom here for the ordinary citizen in ordinary circumstances as a British citizen would have enjoyed in his or her own country, the statements of fundamental rights contained in the Constitution were powerless to invalidate an Act of the Oireachtas that failed to respect them; and a very elaborate Act passed in 1931 actually incorporated within the Constitution itself, as a new article 2A, a formidable set of powers, including the establishment of a military court, for the repression of subversion.[6]

In 1937, however, a new start was made. Mr de Valera's party, which saw the old Constitution as tainted by the Treaty, wanted a completely new one, this time enacted directly by the people in a plebiscite[7] so that there could be no doubt that the Irish people's sovereignty was the source of the state's legitimacy. (The old Constitution had been enacted by the Dáil alone and had been constrained to keep to the terms of the Treaty.) In most substantial respects the 1937 Constitution, as I have already said, was much the same as its predecessor; indeed large tracts of Mr de Valera's document were copied pretty well word-for-word from that of 1922.

Nevertheless there were some striking new elements. One was a much more elaborate statement of fundamental rights, this time augmented by statements of the right to private property (and of the limitations on that right[8]) as well as of the rights of the family and of marriage,[9] and of parents in regard to their children's upbringing and education.[10] These items had not figured in the 1922 Constitution, no doubt because they were thought sufficiently well protected already by the conservative instincts of the people and their representatives. In the drafting period of the 1937 Constitution, however, it appears that the influence of the Catholic Church—which Mr de Valera could not ignore, for fear that its opposition might torpedo his whole scheme—secured the statement, in articles 41 to 43, of principles relating to the family and to property that had been set out in papal encyclicals of modern times. A further concession that Mr de Valera made to the same interests—though a far smaller one than those that were being demanded of him by some of them—was the statement, in article 44, of the 'special position' of the Catholic Church; this 'special position' was removed by referendum in 1972, by a huge majority, without any protest or opposition from the church, which the experience of thirty-five years had made much more relaxed and much less anxious about its external dignity.

But the 1937 Constitution differed from its predecessors in an even more important respect, namely that the period of transitional amendment of the Constitution by ordinary legislation—which had virtually nullified the 1922 Constitution, as we saw—was much shorter, only in effect three and a half years. It could not itself be extended beyond that time; and even while the period was running, no court took the point—nor was it even argued—that an ordinary Act could operate to override the Constitution.[11] Accordingly, the express fundamental rights provisions of the Constitution, together with other constitutional rules important to civil liberty—such as the rules requiring all criminal trials to be conducted in due course of law, and in serious cases with a jury—add up to a genuine and effective Irish bill of rights, which the courts will enforce even as against a law enacted by the Oireachtas.

All the same, this bill of rights was slow in making itself felt. This perhaps was partly due to the fact that the older generation of judges, those who sat in the High Court and Supreme Court in the 1940s, were men educated in the old, British tradition, which regarded the parliament as sovereign and which considered that civil liberties and decent standards of government were sufficiently protected by the moderation and good sense of the members of that parliament, who would not be likely to pass an arbitrary or tyrannous law or to support an arbitrary or tyrannous government. Even Mr de Valera, though he entrenched this elaborate bill of rights in his constitution, intended it to be primarily a set of 'headlines to the legislature' rather than a hurdle on which that legislature would frequently stumble and fall; his contributions to the Dáil debate on the draft constitution seem to me to show that he did not see himself as calling into existence a sort of legal shredding-machine, which a later generation of lawyers and judges would use with devastating effect on the Acts of the sovereign Irish people's own parliament.[12]

However, in the early years after 1937 none of this yet showed itself. The Constitution was occasionally, not very often, pleaded in one sort of case or another between 1937 and about 1960; but the total number of cases in which it had any decisive effect on the outcome was tiny. Indeed if we take the shorter period 1937 to 1950 or thereabouts, it almost seems as if only one judge, the late Mr Justice Gavan Duffy, was taking the Constitution seriously. It was he who, in 1939, declared the internment provisions of the Offences Against the State Act, 1939, unconstitutional;[13] it was he who, in 1945, declared unconstitutional the old rule that refused to regard communications made to a priest by one of his flock as privileged from disclosure in court;[14] it was he who, in 1947, held invalid the Sinn Féin Funds Act, which purported to tell the High Court to dismiss an action over the ownership of the funds that had already been begun;[15] and it was he who, in 1950, held invalid, as being contrary to the rights of the family declared in articles 41 and 42, the old rule that made the father at all times the dictator of his children's upbringing, including their religious upbringing, and even in defiance of an antenuptial promise on the matter made to his wife.[16]

In singling out Mr Justice Gavan Duffy I am perhaps not being fair to the Supreme Court, which in fact upheld his judgments in the Sinn Féin funds case and in the case about children's religious upbringing, and which had in addition in 1942 struck down part of a School Attendance Bill that looked like authorising the state to prescribe to parents what sort of education their children should receive;[17] but he was unquestionably, as an individual judge, far ahead of his colleagues in pioneering the acceptance in Ireland of a constitutional bill of rights as an effective check on the operations of parliament and of the executive.

In the 1950s, after the death of Mr Justice Gavan Duffy in 1951, there were a few notable cases in which constitutional fundamental rights were successfully asserted in the courts. But the Constitution's fundamental rights articles, and the articles protecting the integrity of the courts themselves, really began to 'take off' only in the 1960s. While the High Court and Supreme Court of the 1960s still contained one or two judges who had already made a mark in the application of the Constitution, notably Mr Justice Budd and Mr Justice Kingsmill Moore, the very active period that now set in was, I think, due to the attitude of the new Chief Justice, Cearbhall Ó Dálaigh, who was appointed in 1961, and two other judges newly appointed to the Supreme Court and High Court, respectively, Mr Justice Brian Walsh (who is still a member of the Supreme Court) and the late Mr Justice John Kenny.

This new judicial generation at the top led nothing less than a revolution in constitutional jurisprudence, most particularly in the area of fundamental rights. The most spectacular conquest of this revolution was the recognition—which an earlier generation of judges would have thought fantastic—that the Constitution implicitly protected an indefinite range of citizens' rights over and above those specifically enumerated in one or other article, and that the courts were entitled to identify such latent rights, whenever the occasion arose, by reference to their understanding of a standard such as 'the Christian and democratic nature of the state'.[18]

This development came about in this way. In 1963 Mrs Gladys Ryan, who belonged to a group opposed to the new practice of adding to the public water supply a trace of sodium fluoride (which was known to reduce the incidence of tooth decay), brought an action against the state claiming that the Act that authorised this treatment of the water supply was unconstitutional. It was, she said, an infringement of what she claimed was her right, and her children's right, to what she called 'bodily integrity', inasmuch as she and her children would now in practice be obliged to consume water containing a substance that she believed to be poisonous. Now the Constitution says nothing about 'bodily integrity'. But it does, in article 40.3, undertake to defend and vindicate what it calls the 'personal rights of the citizen'; and Mrs Ryan's counsel argued that the expression 'personal rights' should be understood as going far beyond the handful of traditional civil liberties such as freedom from arbitrary arrest, freedom of speech and of the press, freedom of conscience, and so on. Personal rights, they argued, ought in any case to include the right not to have poisonous water forced upon you by the state.

The late Mr Justice John Kenny, in a landmark judgment, agreed with her. He also went on to hold that the water fluoridation being proposed was completely harmless and indeed beneficial; but the principle for which she was contending, namely that the citizen's personal rights are not exhausted by the specific recitals in special constitutional articles, he fully admitted; and he said it would be a matter for the High Court, according as appropriate cases presented themselves, to identify and enforce such latent and unspecified rights, even as against an Act of the Oireachtas. Cearbhall Ó Dálaigh's Supreme Court, although it too held that fluoridation was harmless, agreed with him on the point of principle, thus making Mrs Ryan's case into a sort of floodgate for assertions of personal rights claimed to be latent in the Constitution.

Since that time, now twenty-five years ago, a large list of further personal rights has been declared to be latent in the guarantee of article 40.3 and thus enforceable by the courts, although none of them is specifically mentioned anywhere in the Constitution. Thus—to take as an example a case that many people will recall—the Supreme Court upheld in 1973 the right of a married woman, Mrs McGee, to import contraceptive material for her own use, on the ground that the law that prohibited this was an infringement of what the court recognised as her personal right of 'marital privacy'.[19] In other cases, the courts have upheld, even against Acts of the Oireachtas, a whole string of further personal rights: the right to earn a livelihood (though this does not amount to a right to any particular employment),[20] the right to litigate,[21] the right to fair procedures,[22] the right to travel outside the state and consequently the right to a passport,[23] and the right to get married.[24] In addition, although the Constitution recognises as a 'family' only that based on marriage, the courts have also, via the same article 40.3, recognised that both the mother of an illegitimate child and the illegitimate child itself have personal rights that go a long way towards making up their lack of standing under article 41, which deals only with the marital family.[25]

This list, I must emphasise, is not closed: any citizen who feels he or she has a particular personal right that is under attack or under threat, even though such a right is not mentioned anywhere in the black-and-white text of the Constitution, may still succeed in getting the courts to enforce it if they are persuaded that it is something inherent in, something necessarily implied by, what Mr Justice Kenny called 'the Christian and democratic nature of the State', or even—to use a term of venerable antiquity that expresses an eternal value and standard—something implied by 'natural law'.[26]

Of course there have been failures among the efforts to mobilise the 'personal rights' provision in article 40. For example, in the case in 1983 in which the legislation penalising male homosexual acts was challenged on the ground that it invaded the right of individual personal privacy of consenting adults, the Supreme Court held—though only by a margin of three to two—that although a right of individual privacy could be asserted, it could not be absolute, and, in particular, could not prevail over what the then Chief Justice, Tom O'Higgins, called 'the State's interest in the general moral well-being of the community' and its right 'to discourage conduct which is morally wrong and harmful to a way of life and to values which the State wishes to protect.'[27] Nevertheless, the generally very open-minded approach of the modern High Court and Supreme Court to the claims advanced in favour of people's 'personal rights' as against the state seems to promise further extensions of our constitutional rights, in areas undreamt of back in 1937.

Another feature of the Constitution that I must not forget to mention is the emergency provision of article 28.3.3. This clause exempts completely from constitutional control by the courts any Act, or anything done under any Act, that is expressed to be 'for the purpose of securing the public safety and the preservation of the State in time of war or armed rebellion'; and the latter expression is so defined as to allow the Dáil and Seanad to declare a national emergency under cover of this article even when the emergency arises from a conflict that is not taking place within the state. On the strength of such a resolution of both houses in 1939, very far-reaching laws were in force during the Second World War; the resolution was rescinded only in 1976, to be immediately replaced with a similar one relating to the emergency caused by the Northern Ireland troubles.[28] No actual measure is in force at the moment in reliance on this national emergency, but it is important to remember that this residual and very drastic power potentially exists all the time; and probably every other country has also, in one form or another, a similar weapon for dealing with national emergency even if at the expense of what in normal conditions are people's fundamental rights.

In interpreting the Constitution, including the fundamental rights articles, the methods adopted by the courts are not all above criticism. For example, I think the Supreme Court has in some cases gone much too far in its over-literal interpretation of a document not originally intended to be so minutely parsed and scrutinised. Indeed, in one case the court put itself in the really unsustainable position of deciding a point on the ground that the Irish verb used to render an English phrase was in the future rather than in the present tense, while the English phrase was open to either a present or a future construction, and that the future sense of the Irish must therefore prevail, although plenty of other examples showed that the present construction was the one that accorded with actual known practice.[29] The unreality of this seems clear, particularly when it is remembered that the Irish version of the text arrived later in the Dáil than the original English draft, and was scarcely debated at all there, let alone properly analysed by people who knew Irish; nor were the possibly divergent implications of Irish usage examined. It is true that, in case of conflict, the Irish text must prevail, but one ought not to look for conflicts needlessly; one should, I think, bend over backwards to reconcile what may be apparent conflicts by looking at what common sense and practice suggest the drafters and the Dáil intended.

It is true also that the extreme case I have mentioned arose in a context that was not one of fundamental rights; I mention it only in order to suggest that constitutional interpretation generally, including interpretation of the fundamental rights articles, should bear in mind that the Constitution, back in 1937, was not intended by anyone to become a sort of machine lathe, engineered to minute tolerances, which could shear away whole strips of legal timber on the strength of a linguistic usage which, at that time, no-one thought it necessary to scrutinise closely or indeed at all.

Finally, there remain some grey areas within the fundamental rights clauses, quite apart from the open-ended status of article 40.3. The most important of these, certainly the most sensitive one politically, is the status of private property rights in article 43, to which article 40.3 is also relevant. The decided cases up to now have tended to establish that the state cannot expropriate somebody's property without compensation, or unjustly reduce their property interests. It was, for example, on this basis that the old Rent Restrictions Act was held unconstitutional, because landlords of controlled property were not allowed under that law to charge the going market level in rent. This was, if you like, a piece of well-intended social legislation, but the cost of achieving the social objective of cheap housing was being borne, not by society at large but by the landlords, who might be, and often were, much less well off than their tenants. The Supreme Court held this to be unjust.[30] But does this then mean that, in every case, if the state interferes with property rights it must compensate the legal owner, up to the last penny of the market value of his interest? To take the most topical instance, is the state obliged to pay compensation, at full market rates, to the landowner whose acres have suddenly multiplied in value through being rezoned for housing, or have appreciated because of the proximity of publicly paid-for roads, sewers and water pipes, should it wish to preserve the land as an amenity or to acquire it for some public purpose?

These questions have not yet been fully answered in a concrete case; but there has been, in recent years, an increasing accumulation of judicial opinion to the effect that the Constitution, which recognises in article 43 not only private property but also the counterbalancing value of the common good, does not, in fact, require full market-value compensation in every such case, but only such treatment as is necessary to ensure that the owner is not unjustly treated; and this, when expressed in pound notes, may amount to something very much less.[31] But the matter is still undecided, and promises, when an appropriate case squarely arises, to give us perhaps the legally most revolutionary case of the century.

Let me end with a caution. Often enough in recent years we hear politicians or journalists, or people with some special enthusiasm to which the structure of the state is not especially favourable, calling for a new constitution. It is a theme that frequently takes up newspaper space in slack periods of the year. But there is no point—as the 1986 divorce referendum showed—in drafting a shiny new constitution, or new articles, if the people are not yet ready to support the change, since any amendment, even the tiniest, requires the Yes vote of the majority who go to the polls. This awkward necessity causes impatience among social reformers; but it is also the guarantee for ordinary people that their rather old-fashioned set of fundamental rights will not be rashly reduced, nor rashly enlarged, in response to the pressures of a passing moment.

NOTES

1. See Colin R. Munro, *Studies in Constitutional Law*, 1987, 105-6; Colin Campbell (ed.), *Do We Need a Bill of Rights?*, 1980; Kevin Boyle and Tom Hadden, *Ireland: a Positive Proposal*, 1985; *Standing Advisory Commission on Human Rights* (Cmnd. 7009), 1978.
2. Articles 6-9.
3. Article 50.
4. Constitution (Amendment No. 16) Act, 1929.
5. *R. (Cooney)* v. *Clinton*, [1935] IR 245. See also John Kelly, *The Irish Constitution* (2nd ed.), 1984, 718-9.
6. Constitution (Amendment No. 17) Act, 1931.
7. Kelly, *The Irish Constitution*, 2-4.
8. Article 43.
9. Article 41.
10. Article 42.
11. Article 51.1; Kelly, *The Irish Constitution*, 717.
12. See *Dáil Debates*, vol. 67, col. 1747, 1784-6, and vol. 68, col. 216-7.
13. *The State (Burke)* v. *Lennon*, [1940] IR 136.
14. *Cook* v. *Carroll*, [1945] IR 515.
15. *Buckley* v. *Attorney General*, [1950] IR 67.
16. *In re Tilson, Infants*, [1951] IR 1.
17. *In re Article 26 and the School Attendance Bill, 1942*, [1943] IR 334.
18. *Ryan* v. *Attorney General*, [1965] IR 294.
19. *McGee* v. *Attorney General*, [1974] IR 284.
20. *Landers* v. *Attorney General*, 109 ILTR 1.
21. *Macauley* v. *Minister for Posts and Telegraphs*, [1966] IR 345.
22. *The State (Healy)* v. *Donoghue*, [1976] IR 325.
23. *The State (M.)* v. *Attorney General*, [1979] IR 73.
24. *Ryan* v. *Attorney General*, [1965] IR 294.
25. *G.* v. *An Bord Uchtála*, [1980] IR 32.
26. On the latent personal rights generally, see Kelly, *The Irish Constitution*, 475 ff.
27. *Norris* v. *Attorney General*, [1984] IR 36.
28. See Kelly, *The Irish Constitution*, 163 ff.
29. *The State (Ennis)* v. *Farrell*, [1966] IR 107; Kelly, *The Irish Constitution*, 140-1.
30. *Madigan* v. *Attorney General*, [1986] ILRM 136; *In re Article 26 and the Housing (Private Rented Dwellings) Bill*, [1983] ILRM 246.
31. *Dreher* v. *Irish Land Commission*, [1984] ILRM 94; *O'Callaghan* v. *Commissioners of Public Works*, [1985] ILRM 364. See also Kelly, *The Irish Constitution (Supplement)*, 1987, 189 ff.

PETER SUTHERLAND, SC

13. *Twin Perspectives: an Attorney General Views Political and European Dimensions*

Peter Sutherland was called to the Bar in 1968 and to the Inner Bar in 1980. He is barrister-at-law, Middle Temple, London, and as Attorney, New York Bar, admitted to practise before the Supreme Court of the United States. He is a former Attorney General and a member of the Commission of the European Communities with responsibility for competition policy and relations with the European Parliament.

THE fundamental contribution made by the Constitution of 1937 is that it has provided a certain sense of underlying stability and coherence to society, based upon the rule of law. The fact that over fifty years have passed since it was enacted inspires in itself a certain respect and an understandable reluctance to change it. This should not blind us, however, to its inadequacies.

Ultimately, a written constitution is concerned with the process of legitimate decision-making in society. Whilst there is a great deal to be said in regard to the provisions in the Constitution that are not central to the process of decision-making (but which have influenced the politics of the whole of Ireland, for both good and ill), these go beyond the subject of this essay. As Professor Kelly has written, 'the Constitution was conceived in part as a manifesto rather than as bare law.'[1]

My concern here is with the law, not the manifesto. More specifically, it is to deal with the difficult issue of judicial influence, through the Constitution, on policy-making in the state. It is in a sense the political view of a former Attorney General, a constitutional officer who is placed at the interface between the Government and the courts. During my period as

Attorney General I became aware of a lack of clarity amongst those concerned with government about the nature and extent of the judicial role in policy-making. This situation is less than satisfactory. For one thing, as Mr Justice Keane recently pointed out, the Constitution can sometimes provide an easy excuse for not tackling seriously needed reform.[2]

The Constitution, of course, expresses our societal commitment to democracy both in general and specific terms. The general statement of this commitment is to be found in article 5. The details of the structure, ensuring the practical implementation of the commitment, are set out in various other articles. Thus, article 15.2.1 states that 'the sole and exclusive power of making laws for the State is hereby vested in the Oireachtas.' This unambiguous statement, however, presents something less than the full picture, having regard to the extent to which the courts have become involved in the process of policy-making.

As Disraeli said, 'all power is a trust . . . we are accountable for its exercise . . . from the people, and for the people, all springs and all must exist.'[3] The provision of absolute powers to the representatives of the people to decide policy as they might think fit from time to time appears to some to be the most perfect manifestation of these democratic principles in action. The first Lord Birkenhead, sitting as Lord Chancellor in a Canadian case, described the unwritten constitution of the United Kingdom as being 'uncontrolled'. By the word 'uncontrolled' he meant that there was no limit to what legislation Parliament might enact. Even if the statement is no longer strictly true, having regard to the accepted principle of the supremacy of the Community law throughout the European Communities, it is still widely believed in the United Kingdom that Parliament should remain effectively unfettered in its exercise of power, at least in domestic matters.

It was Abraham Lincoln, in his memorable Gettysburg Address, who dedicated his nation to government 'of the people, by the people and for the people',[4] and he did so after the power of judicial review had been established. As the experience of the United States had then and has since testified, it can be argued that a societal commitment to democracy can coexist with an ultimate judicial authority to review legislation under certain circumstances.

The rejection of the principle of absolute parliamentary sovereignty in Ireland represented, however, a radical departure from the governmental system that preceded independence. The process of rejecting absolute parliamentary sovereignty was begun earlier than 1937, however imperfectly, by the 1922 Constitution, but the second attempt took the process very much further. How much further has only become evident as the judiciary defined in an increasingly activist manner the meaning of the Constitution, particularly during the period from 1960 onwards.

The framers of the Irish Constitution had considerable advantages from the point of view of historical precedent. Even though the American Constitution, whilst clearly intended to create a supreme law, did not specifically authorise the judiciary to review federal action, the courts themselves had developed their powers throughout the period following the famous judgment of Chief Justice Marshall in *Marbury* v. *Madison* in 1803.[5] They did so in a radical manner, going beyond mere interpretative review; in other words they did not confine the review process to testing legislation and acts against expressed provisions in the Constitution: they also looked to implied rights.

The Irish Constitution makes clear that there are limits to what the elected representatives of the people may do, and that these limits are to be enforced by the courts. The Oireachtas is expressly precluded, in article 15, from enacting laws that are repugnant to the Constitution. Furthermore, article 34 makes it clear that there is a power of review vested in the courts, permitting them to intervene in order to obstruct the realisation of the legislative intent of the Oireachtas when this is required. Article 34.3, for example, indicates that the jurisdiction of the High Court shall extend to the question of the validity of any law having regard to the provisions of the Constitution. As an additional safeguard it is provided that the powers of the Supreme Court and the High Court to review the consistency of legislation with constitutional provisions cannot be removed by simple laws, as had been the case under the 1922 Constitution.

The fact that the Constitution requires the judiciary to intervene to protect constitutional values, and that the people adopted the Constitution by plebiscite, creates the necessary nexus between the power of judicial review and democracy itself. The people in effect have required the judiciary to intervene in the protection of constitutional values. Their intention was not merely to deal with Jefferson's 'elective despotism'—the power of a majority in parliament once elected to disregard the opinions of the majority whom they represent—but also with the potential problem of moderating and sometimes prohibiting the implementation of oppressive policies desired by popular majorities. This authentication of judicial review is incorrectly believed to be a common characteristic of written constitutions, but of course it is not. As Michael Forde has pointed out, the Constitutions of the French Third and Fourth Republics and the Italian Constitution of 1848, for example, do not provide this power.[6]

It was and is of central importance that the judicial review of executive and legislative acts should follow a principled and clear line that remains faithful to the mandate for intervention provided by the text. After all, as Alexander Hamilton pointed out in the Federalist Papers, the courts 'have neither force nor will but merely judgment.' They rely upon their inherent authority. If they seek to impose values that are beyond those legitimated by their mandate, then ultimately that authority will be damaged.

The Supreme Court has been anxious in some ways to circumscribe the circumstances and manner of its interventions. Mr Justice Henchy, in *State (Woods)* v. *Attorney General*,[7] stated two principles of construction that in this regard are important and have often been expressed. The first is that there exists in Ireland a presumption in favour of the constitutionality of Acts of parliament based upon the deference properly paid by the courts to the fact that the people have invested the parliament with the sole law-making function. This presumption of constitutionality and the limitation of power that it implies is of course applied also in the United States.[8] Further, the courts have determined that when there are two possible constructions of the statute, one constitutional and the other unconstitutional, a court should presume that parliament intended the constitutional construction, and will uphold that construction. This constitutes a further attempt to minimise possible conflict between the courts and the legislature.

These rules of construction, however, do not go to the essence of the authority claimed by the courts. The real issue relates to determining how far the courts can go in their review function. What are the values that they can protect? How closely are they bound by the text?

The fact that the people intended to endow the courts with the power to strike down legislation repugnant to *expressed* provisions in the Constitution is not, as we have seen, open to question. Thus, for example, any attempt by a Government to remove a judge of the Supreme Court or High Court for a reason other than stated misbehaviour or incapacity and in the manner prescribed (by Dáil and Seanad votes) would be clearly repugnant to the Constitution, and the courts would not merely be entitled but would be obliged to strike it down. The simplest example therefore of a clearly legitimate form of judicial review is provided by cases where no interpretative function is really involved. The text of the Constitution itself is plain.

A second type of judicial review, which can be described as interpretative review,[9] arises where the courts take up specific values clearly expressed in the Constitution but which are open to various constructions, and then proceed to interpret them. The first question, before one even gets to the stage of construing a particular value expressed in the text, is to enquire whether it was intended to be justiciable: in this regard I refer particularly to the values set out in the 'Fundamental Rights' articles.

There is some evidence that suggests that Mr de Valera did not intend these articles to be justiciable. Certainly the Dáil reports are not terribly helpful in this regard (the great bulk of debate seems to have centred on issues far removed from those that have become central in subsequent discussion on judicial interpretation), but however imperfect our knowledge may be of the intentions of the framers, it can nonetheless be said that the people clearly intended that the expression of these rights would guide and influence the development of the state. Functionally, this intention could only be given effect by the courts, otherwise they would amount to little more than rhetoric. Furthermore, the preamble to article 45—the 'Directive Principles of Social Policy'—provides that the principles 'are not cognisable by any Court'. No such phrase is included in articles 40 to 44.

The questions that give rise to greatest difficulty regarding the permissible limits of judicial intervention are related to what may be described as non-interpretative review. By this I mean the elaborating and enforcing by the courts of various values not expressly included in the Constitution. A justification for such intervention might be provided either on a historical or textual basis. I am aware of no adequate historical evidence of an intention to provide for non-interpretative review. The courts have not in fact relied on historical material but on the text of the Constitution itself, and in particular on the reference to 'personal rights of the citizen' contained in article 40. Since *Ryan* v. *Attorney General* in 1965[10] they have developed a theory that has permitted them to constitutionalise rights that are not specifically contained in the text. Whatever the arguments may be against this significant extension of the power of judicial review, on the basis of lack of democratic intent, the resulting interventions have been generally considered to be of real benefit to society. The necessity to establish and enforce additional rights in order to maintain a just society has not been substantially questioned, and the functional justification, combined with the prestige of the courts that have defined them, has resulted in the comparatively smooth integration of this extended authority into our legal order. Increasingly, however, the methods used to determine these rights have been questioned, as they may result in the future in further unforeseen interventions that could be more contentious than those of the past.

Mr Justice Kenny, in the Ryan case, defined the unspecified rights that the courts might uphold as being those that 'result from the Christian and democratic nature of the State'. One commentator has suggested that while Mr Justice Kenny's judgment 'gave a much needed impetus to constitutional development, the highly subjective method of constitutional interpretation which he espoused seems questionable'.[11] Whatever about the method being subjective, the results of such interpretation have not always been foreseeable. Since that time various broad approaches to the methods of definition of these rights can be discerned in Supreme Court judgments. One strongly held view is that recourse to the natural law in defining the nature and extent of these rights is the correct method, and that it is justified by the text of the Constitution. This view is articulated clearly in the landmark decision of *McGee* v. *Attorney General*,[12] delivered by Mr Justice Walsh.

It is no denial of the intellectual legitimacy of a theory of natural law in regard to human behaviour to question the adequacy of using natural law as the source from which one is to derive knowledge of the definition of legally enforceable rights. The theological nature of the concept of natural law renders it difficult to transpose into a constitutional framework. Apart from the complicated question as to the difference between absolute and qualified rights in natural law theory, the overall uncertainties introduced by this concept are not helpful in providing clarity to our legislators. Mr Justice Walsh himself said, in the McGee judgment, 'what exactly natural law is and what precisely it imports is a question which has exercised the minds of theologians for many centuries and on which they are not yet fully agreed.' He went on: 'The Judges must, therefore, as best they can from their training and their experience interpret these rights in accordance with their ideas of prudence, justice and charity.'

Another view articulated from time to time about how the courts are to define the unspecified rights has been to seek guidance merely from the Constitution itself. Thus, in the case of *State (Healy)* v. *Donoghue*,[13] Mr Justice Henchy pointed out that for a right to come within the constitutional guarantee[14] it must be shown that it is a right that inheres in the citizen in question by virtue of his human personality, and assistance in determining whether the right asserted comes within the constitutional guarantee is to be derived by looking at the matter in the light of the Constitution as a whole.

More recently Mr Justice Costello, in an informative and interesting essay,[15] has suggested that one should rely upon the natural law in defining the unspecified rights but should do so in the context of the Constitution as a whole. He made the point there that, in the last analysis, natural law is 'a body of precepts established by reason'.

It can surely be argued that the uncertainties of this situation are unsatisfactory. It would be preferable if the Constitution contained a list of the rights actually protected. Of course a mere statement of all rights would itself leave considerable scope for defining their application in particular cases, but at least a textual basis would be a clearer foundation for interpretation. There must, in the absence of a clearer statement of the limits of judicial authority, be a greater likelihood that situations of conflict could arise in the future between the various organs of the state. If the nature and scope of rights are to be defined by what amounts to little more than a judicial view, formed without any obvious external source, of what is 'fair'—unrelated even to a statement of the rights protected—then interventions in areas such as taxation or social policy could create serious constitutional tensions, with the potential to weaken the courts themselves.

I do not advocate the position that, unless and until the Constitution is amended, the courts should recoil from the activism that has been so much admired since the 1960s in the area of unspecified rights. What one might argue is that rights of this kind, to be protected, should be only those necessarily implied from the overall text of the Constitution. In this context, the nature of the state as defined is such that in establishing the extent of these rights, regard could be paid to the reasoning of others concerned with defining human rights in democratic countries. Recourse might be had for example to the reasoning of the Commission and Court of Human Rights established under the European Convention. One would not, of course, be bound to follow their conclusions, but they should be of significant influence and would provide an objective intellectual basis for dealing with unlisted rights that would be more foreseeable than is currently the case.

Whether the rights are defined more explicitly in the future or not, one principle now generally recognised and accepted is that the courts have to interpret the Constitution in a manner that reflects 'prevailing circumstances and ideas'. There can be little real objection to the courts, in defining the application of stated constitutional principles, having regard to current thinking rather than that which prevailed in 1937 or at any other particular time. As Mr Justice McCarthy put it in *Norris v. Attorney General*,[16] 'it would plainly be impossible to identify with the necessary degree of accuracy of description the standards or mores of the Irish people in 1937—indeed, it is no easy task to do so today... In my view, it passes from the realm of legal fiction into the world of unreality if the test sought to be applied is one based on some question such as "did the people of Saorstát Éireann in 1937 consider that the offence created by Victorian statute should no longer be in force?"' The mere fact of an evolution in interpretation will always lead to some uncertainty, but this is not a bad thing as long as it is circumscribed within reasonably clear confines. Also, the underlying acceptance of *stare decisis* helps conformity. The enforcing of value judgments that were constitutionalised can be legitimate even if the particular circumstances of the case could not have been precisely envisaged at the time of the adoption of the Constitution.

Whatever may happen in future in regard to amending the Constitution, we will never reach a stage where the executive and legislature can always be assured, before the courts have examined legislation, that it will be constitutional. There is no reason, however, why this uncertainty should induce paralysis in difficult areas such as that relating to property rights. There has been an undue reluctance to propose legislation on which there is some doubt as to constitutionality. In this regard, greater use of the procedures set out in article 26 should be contemplated. Under this article the President, in his absolute discretion and having consulted the Council of State, may refer a bill to the Supreme Court to establish its constitutionality before it becomes law. The fact that references to the Supreme Court are comparatively rare is because governments have been excessively hesitant in proposing legislation on which there may be a doubt as to constitutionality. Whilst recognising that the President may on occasion properly conclude that it would be inappropriate to refer legislation on which there is a constitutional doubt (on the grounds that it would be better to test its constitutionality through ordinary litigation than in the more abstract conditions of a reference), there are many other instances where making a reference would resolve uncertainties in an entirely desirable way. It would be likely in his consideration that account would be taken by the President of the views of the Attorney General expressed in the Council of State, and the Government could thus propose legislation in this context.

An additional and increasingly important dimension to the concept of judicial review, and to relations between the Government and the judiciary, has been added by Ireland's accession to the European Communities.

In the first instance, this has meant a superimposition of Community law, with the Court of Justice in Luxembourg as the final arbiter of what is compatible with the Treaties. Irish courts may now, for example, refer matters having a European dimension to the Court of Justice[17] for a preliminary ruling. Individuals may take issues of European law to court in a number of areas also. The Court of Justice has therefore the ultimate role in determining the validity and interpretation of Community law—which is either directly or indirectly applicable in Ireland—and that role is comparable to that of the Supreme Court in regard to purely domestic legislation. Having regard to the supremacy of Community law, the constitutional implications of our joining the European Communities are considerable. The functions of the European Court of Justice, and the possible future implications for the Irish Constitution of the teleological approach that it has adopted, has caused some to entertain excessive fears. It has been suggested for example that at some future time a ruling of the European Court could override the Constitution in matters of public morality. I have always considered such speculation as unfounded. The competence of the Court is clearly defined by the Treaties establishing the European Community, and at no time has it attempted to venture into the sensitive areas that are being referred to. In other aspects of human rights, involving

Community law, the Court of Justice adds another element to the protection afforded nationally.

The Court of Justice has ruled, in a series of important judgments, that rules for the protection of fundamental rights are part of Community law in that Community legislation is invalid if it infringes these rights. In reaching this conclusion the Court of Justice went beyond the words of the Community Treaties, which say nothing about fundamental rights. However, the Court has said that in identifying the fundamental rights to be protected, it will look at two main sources: the European Convention on Fundamental Rights, and the constitutional laws of member-states of the Community. This approach was wise, and statesmanlike. It largely resolved the fear that had been felt by some lawyers about what would happen if a Community measure was in conflict with a fundamental rights rule in a national constitution. The Court of Justice said, in effect, that there is no need to apply national law (which would be contrary to the principle of the primacy of Community law), because Community law itself provides equivalent protection.

More important for my subject, the Court's use of the European Convention and of national constitutional law enables it to develop rules of fundamental rights *without* laying itself open to the criticism that it is inventing fundamental rights without an objective basis for doing so. Using the European Convention and national constitutional laws makes it possible to synthesise a common Community body of standards or principles from existing legal rules. If, as at least one Community lawyer believes,[18] the Community rules on fundamental rights apply to national measures in the sphere of Community law as well as to measures taken by the Community institutions, the Court has created a firm foundation for a common body of fundamental rights principles for the peoples of Europe.

The second manner in which accession to the Community has influenced the role of judicial review is where Irish courts are asked to arbitrate upon the compatibility of European obligations with the provisions of the Constitution, as was the case, for example, with the challenge to the constitutionality of the ratification procedures for the Single European Act. Here, in very controversial majority judgments, the Supreme Court ruled that, on the one hand, the amendments to the original Treaties included in title II of the Single European Act were covered by the 1972 amendment, adapting the Constitution to allow accession to the Communities, whereas on the other hand, the provisions of title III, which were viewed in all other member-states as no more than codification of an existing practice of foreign policy co-ordination, required ratification by referendum. The court considered that the relevant provisions in title III represented a surrender of sovereignty and exceeded the normal power to conclude international agreements that the Constitution delegated to the Government in article 29.4.2.

This conclusion required an extreme interpretation of article 29.4.2, which, on first reading, gives the Government full powers to 'adopt any organ, instrument, or method of procedure used or adopted for the like purpose by the members of any group or league of nations with which the State is or becomes associated for the purpose of international co-operation in matters of common concern.' Basically, what the court ruling has done is to considerably circumscribe the extent to which the Government can, even with the approval of the Dáil, ratify international agreements. The results of the majority judgment are so far-reaching that consideration may have to be given at some future time to a further amendment of the Constitution in order to restore to the Government the powers that previously it was generally believed to enjoy.

The reference in article 29 to article 28 (which says that the exercise of the executive power is subject to the provisions of the Constitution) does not seem to me to carry the automatic consequence that any surrender of sovereignty, however limited and controlled by an effective right of veto for the state in the international forum concerned, must be subject to ratification by referendum. Whatever the merits of the judgment in the particular case of the Single European Act, the judicial interpretation of those particular provisions of the Constitution could create serious difficulties for the conduct of our foreign policy in the future, and place Ireland at a considerable disadvantage relative to its international interlocutors in a wide range of international negotiations.

In an increasingly interdependent world, the notion of sovereignty and how best to protect it, and indeed of how far it can usefully be said to exist, is evolving rapidly. Almost any meaningful and worthwhile international co-operation in order to influence the world in which we live necessarily means surrender of sovereignty in the definition now applied. A more realistic approach to sovereignty would surely recognise that the ability to so influence the world in which we live through certain international co-operation agreements can be an enhancement of sovereignty rather than the converse. It would neither be realistic nor appropriate to suggest that such agreements must all be subject to ratification by referendum.

We in Ireland can take legitimate pride in the integrity, independence and erudition of our judiciary. From the foundation of the state, they have made a substantial contribution to national life, and in significant measure have been enabled to do so under the Constitution. But the primary responsibility for government remains with the elected representatives of the people, who must not seek to use the courts to sort out the more intractable social and economic issues facing the nation. There has been a tendency to require more from the courts than should be the case in directing the development of the values of our society. It has been the case that the human rights that have been protected by the courts through the judicial review mechanism have been generally political and civil in nature rather than social and economic. By social and economic I mean rights of the kind recognised by the Universal Declaration of Human Rights and the International Covenant on Economic, Social and Cultural Rights: the right to food, clothing, housing, education, and so on. At a time when issues relating to institutional capacity to implement socio-economic rights concerning, for example, taxation may become more and more relevant, it is very important that boundaries of authority be well defined. They are not well defined at present.

The Supreme Court has effectively faced the challenge of elaborating and protecting human rights in a changing world, notwithstanding some deficiencies in the clarity of the text of the Constitution. That it will be faced with further challenges in the future is beyond question. A serious debate as to how it can best face these challenges has begun, and not before time.

NOTES

1. John Kelly, 'The Constitution: Law and Manifesto', in *Administration*, vol. 35 (1988), 209.
2. Ronan Keane, 'The Constitution and Public Administration: Accountability and the Public Service, Administrative Law and Planning Law', op. cit., 144.
3. *Vivian Grey*, book 1, chapter 7.
4. Address at dedication of National Cemetery at Gettysburg, 19 November 1863.
5. 5 US 368, 1 Granch 137, 2.L.Ed.60, 1803.
6. Michael Forde, *Constitutional Law in Ireland*, Cork and Dublin: Mercier Press 1987, 55.
7. *State (Woods)* v. *Attorney General*, [1969] IR 385, 398-9 (Supreme Court).
8. See, for example, *United States* v. *Steffens*, 100 US 82, 96, 1879.
9. See Michael Perry, *The Constitution, the Courts and Human Rights: an Inquiry Into the Legitimacy of Constitutional Policymaking by the Judiciary*, New Haven: Yale University Press 1982.
10. *Ryan* v. *Attorney General*, [1965] IR 294.
11. Gerard Hogan, 'Constitution Interpretation', in *Administration*, vol. 35 (1988), 178.
12. *McGee* v. *Attorney General*, [1974] IR 274.
13. *State (Healy)* v. *Donoghue*, [1976] IR 325.
14. Article 40.3.
15. Patrick Lynch and James Meehan (eds.), *Essays in Memory of Alexis Fitzgerald*, Dublin: Incorporated Law Society of Ireland 1987, 105-17.
16. *Norris* v. *Attorney General*, [1984] IR 36, 96.
17. Article 177 of the Treaty of Rome.
18. Temple Lang, 'The Duties of National Courts under the Constitutional Law of the European Community' (1987 Lasok lecture, Exeter), 18 ff.

MR JUSTICE BRIAN WALSH

14. The Constitution: a View From the Bench

Brian Walsh was called to the Bar in 1941 and to the Inner Bar in 1954. He was appointed a judge of the High Court in 1959 and of the Supreme Court in 1961, and has been the Senior Ordinary Judge of the Supreme Court since 1969. He served as president of the Law Reform Commission from 1975 to 1985 and chairman of the Committee on Court Practice and Procedure from 1962 to 1988. He is a judge of the European Court of Human Rights since 1980, and is president of the International Association of Judges.

IN case the title of this paper should leave anyone under the impression that the courts stand outside the Constitution, I hasten to state that they do not. On the contrary, they are very much part of it.

Article 6 of the Constitution reads as follows:

> 1. All powers of government, legislative, executive and judicial, derive, under God, from the people, whose right it is to designate the rulers of the State and, in final appeal, to decide all questions of national policy, according to the requirements of the common good.
> 2. These powers of government are exercisable only by or on the authority of the organs of State established by this Constitution.

This separation of powers, as it is called, is the cornerstone of the system of government set up by the Constitution. As the legislative, executive and judicial powers of government are all exercised under and on behalf of the state, the interest of the state, as such, is always involved. But this division of power does not give paramountcy in all circumstances to any one of the organs exercising the powers of government over the other.

Thus the power conferred upon the courts by the Constitution is one that makes the judiciary a co-ordinate of government. But there is one great difference between the judicial power, on the one hand, and the executive and the legislative powers, on the other hand. The executive power and the legislative power can initiate matters. They can propose new laws and pass new laws and can do the many other acts for governing the country that the Constitution authorises them to do. On the other hand the judicial power has no power of initiative and therefore cannot function unless called upon to do so by parties to a law suit. It is the Oireachtas that enacts laws that make general provision to cover the various aspects of the social and economic life of the country. But because these laws can give rise to disputes, which the courts are called upon to determine, the application and interpretation of the legislation in the particular rather than the general instances fall within the judicial sphere of government. Access to the courts is the foremost political right of the citizen and is one guaranteed to the citizen by the Constitution. Therefore it can be said that it is in the courts that the citizen primarily feels the cutting edge of the law, rather than in the Oireachtas.

Respect for the law is one of the principles essential to the effective and equitable operation of democratic government. It is binding both on the governed and upon those who govern. The administration of justice is committed to courts established by law under the Constitution. While one often uses the phrase 'justice under the law', it is clear from decisions in several constitutional cases that in the event of conflict, justice must prevail over the law. The Preamble to the Constitution refers specifically to justice as being essential to the assurance of the dignity and freedom of the individual, and to the attainment of true social order. To secure that great interest, the Constitution has provided that justice will be administered by judges appointed under the Constitution, which assures them of independence and freedom from prejudicial pressures and from forces both inside and outside the other organs of government. In consequence, the executive branch of government is not answerable for the decisions of the courts nor for the conduct of litigation.

It has sometimes been suggested that because judges are not elected by popular vote, as are the members of the other two branches of government, they should have less power than is conferred upon them by the Constitution. The fact that they are not required to be elected is a feature, and an essential feature, conducive to the performance of their basic task, namely, the impartial administration of justice. Furthermore, save where provided by law in special and limited cases, the Constitution prescribes that justice must be administered in public. An essential characteristic of the judicial power is that it cannot be delegated. Yet as the judicial power controls neither the purse nor the sword, it must depend upon the other organs of government exclusively to apply the sanction of the law.

There is another essential difference between the judicial power of government and the legislative and executive organs of government. The judges must decide the cases brought before them. The courts cannot avoid judging: a judge is not permitted to abstain from deciding the controversy that is brought to him. However, it does not follow that the judges have a complete and unfettered freedom. They have not. They are not at large to decide according to their personal predilections. This limitation upon their freedom may be found in the Constitution itself, and in the laws; in precedent, in tradition, and even in judicial technique itself. The courts do not strike down statutes because they think they are unwise: that is for the citizens to do at the ballot box. Judges cannot dispense justice according to considerations of individual expediency.

More than any other organ of the state, the courts must operate with fastidious regard for known procedures. Each party before them is entitled to be legally represented and to present full arguments both as to the law and the facts. Witnesses can be compelled to testify to their knowledge of the relevant facts, and privilege from testifying may be permitted only by the court's authority. The power to compel the attendance of witnesses and the production of evidence is an inherent part of the judicial power of government of the state and is the ultimate safeguard of justice in the state.

Theoretically, law is not essential to the administration of justice. Justice in disputes could be achieved by the courts deciding individual issues on their merits and in accordance with what were seen to be the dictates of justice in that particular case. However, in practice, the merits of deciding most issues in accordance with generally applicable and known public rules are great. Furthermore, the judicial power of interpretation and the application of judicial discretion and of equity can do much to mitigate injustice.

The obligation of justice is not, of course, exclusively reserved to the courts. Both the executive and the legislative organs of government are also expected to act in accordance with the dictates of justice. But in the last analysis, under our constitutional provisions, and particularly article 40 of the Constitution, the ultimate decision as to whether or not there has been an injustice rests with the courts. The supremacy of the judicial power in this field is guaranteed by the Constitution itself.

In this country there are three types of law that the judges are called upon to interpret and to apply. They are, firstly, the common law and equity, which are essentially law that has been made by judicial decisions and as such can, in proper cases, be unmade by the judges; secondly, the statute law, that is, laws enacted by the Oireachtas or by earlier parliaments that had the power to make laws for this country; and, thirdly and most importantly, the Constitution, which is superior to all other types of national law, public as well as private. The Constitution as the basic law of the state and of the government of the state controls the statute law and the common law, to the extent that where either of these conflict with the Constitution they are unenforceable and void. In the case of any such conflict arising, the courts must apply the superior of these laws, namely the Constitution. Thus what is known as judicial review is the power of the courts to hold unconstitutional, and therefore unenforceable, any law, whether statute law or common law, or any official action based upon such law, found to be in conflict with the Constitution.

It is, perhaps, not generally appreciated that except for the exclusive jurisdiction conferred by the Constitution on the High Court and the Supreme Court with regard to the validity of laws enacted by the Oireachtas (that is to say, since the coming into force of the Constitution on 29 December 1937), any court set up under the Constitution, whether it be the District Court, the Circuit Court, or the Court of Criminal Appeal, in addition to the High Court and Supreme Court, may entertain the assertion of any constitutional right or the challenge to the constitutionality of any law or regulation, or to the constitutionality of any activity such as, for example, arrest and the search of dwellings, etc. In practice this does not often happen, because most constitutional challenges are initially raised in the High Court. However, it is important to remember that the judges of all the courts I have mentioned are judges appointed under the Constitution and are the judges to whom the administration of justice is committed by the Constitution.

Judges therefore see the Constitution as the highest law of the state. It is a law that embraces both social and political objectives, and is one that gives force of law to certain moral concepts. Therefore it is inevitable that many of the cases that come before the courts will mirror many of the social, economic, philosophical and political debates that engage our people. All such questions can ultimately be cast in the form of cases to come before the courts in an attempt to secure the resolution of them by our courts. Such suits are not necessarily confined to the activities of governmental agencies but may also involve the scrutiny of the activities of other public bodies, and even private bodies and persons. By virtue of the provisions of the Constitution, the courts have already been called upon to adjudicate in matters as diverse as contraception, censorship of books, trade union membership, personal liberty, inviolability of one's dwelling, discrimination on the grounds of religion, the income tax code so far as it concerned married women, the basis of the rateable valuation of land, the control of rents, the disqualification of persons from practising their professions, the liability of the state for the activities of its servants and agents, sex discrimination in the composition of juries, and many other subjects.

These are not matters that are in all cases expressly touched upon in the Constitution itself. The Constitution cannot and does not endeavour to go into such detail, because the Constitution is not intended to be a detailed legal code. It is a law that lays down general principles according to which both current and future problems can be addressed by the courts.

The Supreme Court is the ultimate interpreter of the law. It is also the ultimate interpreter of the Constitution, although not the exclusive interpreter. In addition to the other courts already mentioned, the executive branch of government and the legislative branch of government, in the performance of their assigned constitutional and legal duties, must initially interpret the Constitution and the laws. But the other organs of government do not have a primary responsibility for the resolution of constitutional problems, and in the result, the primacy of the judicial branch of government in this area is emphasised.

Because the judiciary is the institution for the ultimate protection of constitutional and legal rights, it is essential to ensure that the judiciary can provide an effective remedy against the infringement of those rights. Contrary to the outlook of those philosophers who have argued that there can be no right unless there is also a remedy provided, our courts have said that whenever there is a constitutional right the very existence of that right provides its own remedy, and gives the courts power to take the measures necessary to give effect to the vindication or the defence of that constitutional right. It is well established in our case law that procedural deficiencies will not leave a constitutional right without protection and enforcement where necessary.

However, the fact that the judges are sometimes called upon to face and to decide some of the important social, political, economic and philosophical issues thrown up by our times does not mean that the courts are charged with making social, political, economic or philosophical decisions for the government of the country. To the extent to which that function is an executive or legislative function, it is the function of the elected representatives of the people. When such issues arise before the courts, for the most part they arise within the framework of concrete cases, and the judges are charged with the task of deciding according to the Constitution, the law, and the relevant facts.

The Constitution does not take the form of a list of specifics. There are some specifics in the Constitution; but constitutional protection is afforded also to very many rights which, though unspecified, have been recognised by the courts as having the full backing of constitutional protection.

There are very few cases where the constitutional answers are clear all one way or the other, particularly when they arise out of conflicts between the individual and the organs of the state. Ultimately the courts must resolve these conflicts of competing interests. Such conflicts are inescapable. They can relate to freedom of speech, religious freedom, and threats to public order or public morality, to name but a few, in situations where considerations of administrative convenience or expediency may appear to infringe them. In this way important aspects of the most fundamental issues confronting a democracy can end up ultimately in the courts for judicial determination. Frequently these issues may be ones upon which society is consciously or unconsciously deeply divided and which may arouse the deepest emotions. Their resolution by the courts may, in one way or another, influence, and even determine, the future course of history. By explaining what the Constitution means in the context of a particular problem, the courts can shape what the Constitution means in the future.

It is quite clear that the Constitution did not confer upon the Oireachtas an unfettered power to legislate. Yet the courts, when dealing with a question of the validity of an Act of the Oireachtas, extend to such legislation the presumption of constitutionality, because the Constitution itself directs the Oireachtas to pass no unconstitutional legislation. But it is a cardinal principle of statutory construction to save rather than to destroy. Therefore if any statute is capable of being given a construction that is not inconsistent with the provisions of the Constitution, the courts will presume that that is the construction intended by the legislators. This will displace any other possible interpretation. The fact that the Oireachtas may occasionally enact some legislation that is found to be unconstitutional does not, of course, mean that the Oireachtas intended to act contrary to the Constitution. Therefore when a challenge is mounted it is left to the courts finally to determine the matter. There is no appeal whatsoever from the decision of the Supreme Court, which, under the Constitution, is the court of final appeal. It can only effectively be set aside by recourse to the people in a referendum. But what might be termed 'judicial parsimony' plays its part. If a case can be decided on non-constitutional ground, the courts will do so.

In reality the total number of constitutional cases that come before the courts is comparatively small, but because of their very nature and for the great effect they may have, they attract much publicity. It is probably true that the availability of judicial review is itself a deterring element in the minds of those who, by their activities, or laws, may be tempted to go outside the constitutional restraints.

The courts are themselves also constrained by the Constitution to do nothing that runs counter to the Constitution or to the law, because every judge, upon assuming office, must take an oath to uphold the Constitution and the laws. This oath not merely constrains their own judicial activities but also obliges them to constrain all others who infringe the Constitution. The courts have no higher duties to perform than those that involve upholding the rights guaranteed by the Constitution as rights of substance that cannot be set at nought or circumvented, and to ensure that no person or body can with impunity do so.

The courts see the Constitution as a contemporary fundamental law that speaks in the present tense. As a document it speaks from 1937, but as law it speaks from today. It will therefore be interpreted and applied on the basis of what the text means in our times. It will not be interpreted on the basis of having a static meaning determined fifty years ago, but on the basis that it lays down broad governing principles that can cope with current problems. It is therefore seen as a law that is not concerned with what has been, but with what may be.

This approach has been most clearly demonstrated in the many judicial decisions dealing with the fundamental rights guaranteed by the Constitution. It is important to note that these rights are not *conferred* by the Constitution. They are acknowledged as pre-existing natural rights, inherent in man because he is man. What the Constitution does is to guarantee their protection and vindication. It has been acknowledged in the Universal Declaration of Human Rights and in the European Convention on Human Rights and Fundamental

Freedoms that man, by virtue of the very fact that he is man, has inherent rights. This had been already recognised by the Constitution of Ireland more than a decade before these international instruments came into existence.

Our Constitution is, by judicial interpretation, capable of far greater flexibility than international conventions for the protection of human rights. Unlike international conventions, our Constitution—like that of the United States—enables the courts to discern and protect unspecified rights that may claim constitutional protection and vindication. Because international conventions are international treaties, they do not lend themselves to being the protectors of rights to which the parties to those treaties did not agree. Therefore they do not allow for perceiving and protecting unspecified rights.

Those who often urge that we should adopt the European Convention on Human Rights do not fully appreciate that it is far less capable of development than our own Constitution. The Court of Justice of the European Communities at Luxembourg has on a number of occasions stated that it will respect the fundamental rights guaranteed by the constitutions of the member-states of the Communities and that it will also respect the provisions of the European Convention on Human Rights. However, no attempt has ever been made in Luxembourg to reconcile all of these instruments, or even to ascertain if they are reconcilable in all respects. It is idle to speak of adopting norms established through international instruments. The national constitution of every state reflects the political and social philosophy and the culture of the people of that state. These, naturally, can vary to a greater or lesser extent from state to state.

While the fundamental rights provisions of the Constitution give rise to most debate, they occupy only five of the fifty articles of the Constitution. The other articles are also of very great importance. They concern the organisation of the state and its political institutions, and deal with the political objectives of the state. In these articles the people, when enacting the Constitution, determined the political organisation of the state and the machinery by which they wished to be governed. They thus set certain substantive and procedural limitations on the governing power. Some of these articles also have been the subject of court cases. The subject matter of these provisions could give rise to the most delicate political problems. Yet because of the care with which these matters are dealt with in the Constitution, there has been very little litigation concerning them. It is because they are concerned with laying down the rules for the organisation and structure of the state that they lend themselves to more detailed provisions in the Constitution than do the articles on fundamental rights, because the latter are not the creations of the Constitution. In the fifty years since the enactment of the Constitution there have been only two cases dealing with the question of Dáil constituency boundaries, and only three cases dealing with the exercise of the ballot.

There have been many cases dealing with the exercise of the judicial power itself. It is perhaps not surprising that the courts have been always vigilant to restrain any attempt to usurp their functions. All matters that fall within the judicial power of government in the state remain exclusively in the hands of the judicial organ of government. This sensitivity on the part of the courts does not reflect professional jealousy, but rather the realisation that the Constitution commits to the judges the ultimate guardianship of the Constitution itself, and the vindication of all the rights that it guarantees or that it confers. To allow that function to be encroached upon would be to fail to discharge the duty imposed by the Constitution upon the judges to ensure that the provisions of the Constitution that give legitimacy to government are upheld, and to maintain the citizen's moral rights against the state and others.

It is significant that, apart from the President of Ireland, the only persons who are obliged by the Constitution to take an oath to uphold and defend it are the judges. This they do, in the words of their oath of office, 'without fear or favour, affection or ill-will towards any man . . .'

PROFESSOR BRIAN FARRELL

15. De Valera's Constitution and Ours

DE VALERA devised his constitution at a dangerous time for democracies. Fifty year on, the effort to maintain reasonably free and reasonably effective government remains difficult and dangerous. Over the half-century, his constitution has become our constitution. In the course of this series we have examined what de Valera intended and achieved, and have reviewed some of the ways in which we have developed his constitution. At the end, we might ask how well suited is Bunreacht na hÉireann to the circumstances, needs and aspirations of Irish society in the eighties.

The 1930s witnessed serious challenges to the whole idea of liberal-democratic society. In the euphoria that followed the end of the First World War there was a flurry of constitution-making. The defeat of old, absolutist empires, the emergence of new nation-states, the proclaimed commitment of the victors to self-determination—all contributed to an air of optimism. The prospects for constitutional engineering seemed endless. Within a decade, they were destroyed.

Across the face of Europe the constitutional rule-books and the values they enshrined were discarded. New ideologies offered different models of government and proposed some collective ideal as superior to the liberal-democratic emphasis on individual rights. Whether dressed in socialist theory in the Soviet Union or fascist rhetoric in Germany and Italy, authoritarianism became the dominant mode of government in small and great states alike.

Contemporaries in the 1930s could scarcely guess how far the tide of officially sponsored illiberality would sweep what was still known as the civilised world. Incidentally, that western world was as yet blind to the contradictions implicit in, and the injustices perpetrated by, its own rampant colonial imperialism. The idea that the cognitive traps so cleverly manipulated by Stalin and Hitler might become literal death-traps for millions was unthinkable.[1] The Gulag was unknown; the final solution had not yet been implemented. But enough was known and had been implemented to illustrate the fragility of civil society and expose the inadequacy of paper constitutions as real safeguards.

Modern constitutionalism, as Professor Nicholas Canny indicates in the first essay, was still a relatively new political system. During the nineteenth century it had gradually expanded. Its apparent material success in the United States, Britain and France was reinforced by their military victory in the Great War. But the effort to emulate their performance was now challenged by alternative philosophies. The established democracies themselves were shaken. As the depression deepened and lengthened there were doubts about the capacity of these constitutional states to provide for the needs of their peoples; soon the emphasis might shift from questions of their effectiveness to questions of their legitimacy.[2] Even for long-established and powerful states it was not a time for unnecessary constitutional experimentation. It was still less opportune for a newly established nation-state that had emerged from a civil war, with a disputed border, an undeveloped economy and an uncertain future.[3]

But de Valera was not deterred. Re-writing the Irish constitution was bound to stir up suspicions of his motives, and it did. It was likely to raise new issues of potential difficulty, and it did. Most noticeably, perhaps, de Valera's efforts to devise a suitable constitutional formula to cover the complex character of Irish church-state relations—so carefully analysed by Dr Dermot Keogh in an earlier essay—illustrate the delicacy required in devising a new fundamental law. Moreover, the fact that de Valera retained so much of the existing machinery of government seemed to justify the kind of critical complaint quoted by Professor Basil Chubb at the beginning of his essay, that de Valera 'spent his time drafting a document for which there is no demand.'

Political opponents, of course, are always ready with accusations. In the case of de Valera the charges often spilled beyond the ordinary tactics and conventions of adversarial politics. There was a personal, passionate, bitter note of criticism. De Valera was the lost leader; the man they held responsible for the Civil War; a self-centred and malign 'all-controlling shepherd with well-directed dogs'.[4] The mere fact that the text presented in 1937 was his was enough to condemn it in the eyes of such dedicated partisan opponents.

It is easier for us to take a more detached view and arrive at a more balanced judgment. A starting-point, as Professor Ronan Fanning suggested, is the recognition that 'the dynamic that impelled him . . . had less to do with inaugurating a brave new world than with bringing an old and—from de Valera's perspective—desperately unhappy world to a close.' He wanted to dismantle the Treaty settlement of 1921.

Certainly he was consistent in seeking to replace the Irish Free State Constitution with what he called 'an Irish Constitution from top to bottom'.[5] He had rejected the 1922 Constitution as soon as it was published; he had promised a new one in his inaugural address to Fianna Fáil.[6] As soon as he came to power in 1932 he applied his mind to the issue. A fortnight after the government was formed, the Attorney General wrote to Alfred O'Rahilly that constitutional questions 'have now reached a stage when they must be dealt with as matters of practical politics . . . In the course of discussion with the President [de Valera] we agreed that it is vital that we should have the help of men who have been considering these matters and have . . . expert knowledge of them.'[7]

This letter is worth noting for a number of points. It reinforces Dr Dermot Keogh's thesis that de Valera maintained important contacts with well-informed Catholics who 'were wholly free of the stridency associated with' conventional characterisations of mid-1930s Irish Catholicism. Secondly, it supports Gearóid Ó Tuathaigh's argument that there were pressing practical political reasons for symbolic constitutional change. There was an unreconciled IRA, and an even larger body of sympathisers grouped around Sinn Féin, who denied the legitimacy of the Irish Free State and its institutions. De

Valera was determined either to capture them for constitutional politics or, as Professor Ronan Fanning suggests, condemn them unambiguously as traitors. Thirdly, the letter illustrates that, far from being a personal obsession on the part of de Valera, the case for a new constitutional basis for the state was accepted by a wider circle.

That circle included his cabinet colleagues. Their compliance, and de Valera's method of policy-making, deserve some comment. It has been suggested with some delicacy that 'de Valera never burdened his fellow ministers with the task of making a government decision on the matter until it was too late.'[8] Professor Ronan Fanning has argued that their assumed 'acquiescence in his wishes well illustrates his predominance over his ministers.' All of this hints at a broader critique of de Valera as a dictatorial leader who simply 'looked into his heart' and led from the front without consultation.[9]

Yet the truth was that Fianna Fáil, as a party, was committed to a new constitution; the ministers as a cabinet were willing to trust de Valera to produce a text broadly in line with their thinking. And, finally, the text was made available both to government and Dáil for amendment before being put to the people in a referendum. Moreover, in the process of drafting—both in relation to suggestions made by the small group of officials directly involved and in the complex negotiation to produce article 44—de Valera showed a degree of subtlety, pragmatism and patience far removed from the image of a self-centred and dictatorial leader.

At the same time, he valued the freedom and flexibility made possible in confidential discussions with a limited and loyal group of assistants. This enabled him to prepare a detailed text without risk of unnecessary internal cabinet dissension or dangerous external leakage of his intentions. Always critical of the way in which the Provisional Government had negotiated the content of the draft Irish Free State Constitution with the British government, he was determined to preserve his constitution from interference by London.

Simultaneously, this new fundamental law had to recognise political realities yet acknowledge still-unfulfilled aspirations; had to provide a stable, secure and certain framework but allow for change; had to accommodate new institutions and preserve existing organs of government. It was a challenge that required high political skills, and the finished constitution is a remarkable monument to de Valera's consummate ability. It has also exposed its author to the charge of being ambitious, ambiguous, hypocritical and insensitive.

Contemporary political opponents—perhaps mesmerised by their own concentration on his political charisma—were quick to seize on the innovations as evidence of a sinister threat. In particular they found it difficult to imagine that the man they knew as President de Valera (since he was president of the Executive Council and had been president of Dáil Éireann)[10] would lightly relinquish such a prestigious title. Assuming that de Valera was proposing to become President of Ireland, his opponents claimed to read an outlandish prospect of authoritarian power into the office. Nearly three of the seven days devoted to the committee stage discussions of the draft constitution concentrated on a detailed scrutiny of articles 12, 13 and 14. The flavour of the discussion is well represented in the opening remarks of Patrick McGilligan moving the first of forty-five amendments put down on the Presidency:

> In analysing this Constitution, I prefer always to take this test: what could a man, ambitious of power, do, who had succeeded to this office and who, at the end of its term of years, had a subservient Government about to face the people with a certainty of being defeated?... Constitutions are founded on the principle that men go bad when in power and have got to be coerced and prevented, as much as possible, from going bad.[11]

Not for the first time, the mistrust of his political opponents led them to misunderstand his proposals and misjudge their effects. The truth is, as Dr Michael Gallagher has demonstrated, that the Presidency is a largely ceremonial office, and 'a President who tries to step too far beyond his ceremonial role will meet with resistance in high places.'

The charge of ambiguity was inevitable given the chequered history of the early Irish state. Contemporaries applied the term broadly to question whether de Valera had truly converted to democratic politics. Later critics are more prone to point specifically to the provisions of articles 2 and 3 as evidence of an unresolved ambiguity in de Valera's ideas, although these occupied little time in the Dáil debate. Article 2 was not even debated either at committee or recommittal stage, and the two-column discussion on article 3 revolved around the distinction between a moral claim and the *de facto* position of the state. Later generations were more sensitive to Unionist charges that behind the ambiguity lay a territorial claim. In this volume Mr Justice Barrington has persuasively argued that in the context of the Constitution as a whole and the provision of article 29 in particular there is an implicit acceptance that national unity requires consent. On the other hand many citizens might feel the all-party committee on the Constitution established in 1966 was correct when it proposed to replace article 3 with an explicit recognition of that principle of consent in the form:

> 1. The Irish nation hereby proclaims its firm will that its territory be re-united in harmony and brotherly affection between all Irishmen.
> 2. The laws enacted by the Parliament established by this Constitution shall, until the achievement of the nation's unity shall otherwise require, have the like area and extent of application as the laws of the Parliament which existed prior to the adoption of this Constitution. Provision may be made by law to give extra-territorial effect to such laws.[12]

The charge of hypocrisy was explicitly raised in the Dáil by Frank McDermot when he attacked the provision of article 8 naming Irish as 'the first official language'.[13] Subsequently it has been applied on the other side of that argument in light of the failure of successive administrations to provide the necessary resources to convert an aspirational constitutional text into reality.

The fourth charge made against de Valera in his constitution-making was that of insensitivity. It was applied particularly to the provisions regarding women, and largely made outside rather than inside the Dáil. It obviously touched a tender spot, and de Valera raised the matter himself in his long opening speech at the second stage. Naturally he denied the charge: 'I myself was not conscious at any time of having deserved all those terrible things that I am told I am where women's rights are concerned.'[14] Loyally, Mrs Concannon spoke up in favour of the chief's gloss.[15] But, as Dr Yvonne Scannell has documented in her paper, the Constitution as drafted, passed, and implemented for decades relegated women to a life of 'domesticity and powerlessness'. It is only when the terms of the Constitution regarding women are removed from their immediate context, stripped of their implicit prejudices and subjected to a clinical examination that its positive, protective guarantees become apparent.[16]

Indeed, the potential of the Constitution as an instrument to protect and extend citizens' rights has yet to be fully realised. De Valera had built in the mechanism for change in the provisions for formal amendment and for judicial review. He could scarcely have envisaged how adventurously Irish courts might come to relish that role. As Professor James Casey has suggested, when de Valera said that determining the constitutionality of laws would be one of the Surpreme Court's principal functions he probably meant 'most symbolically significant functions' rather than 'most frequently exercised functions'.

In fact, it is mainly through judicial review that de Valera's document is becoming our Constitution. It is not just a historical description of the institutions of government as established but a living organism that can grow to protect the lives, liberties and interests of citizens through changing times. The legal contributors to this volume in particular explored some of these developments.

In the process, they touched on some contentious issues. Dr Yvonne Scannell, for instance, concluded that ironically, 'the Constitution, though rooted in a patronising and stereotyped view of womanhood, may yet justify the claim that it is truly ours.'

Mr Justice Ronan Keane, in a comprehensive review of property in the Constitution and the courts, noted in relation to current controversies involving planning issues that 'it is simply not the case that legislation that restricts the owner's use of his property without compensation is necessarily unconstitutional... If existing legislation is tilting the balance unfairly in favour of the private speculator and against the public interest, then it should be perfectly possible for the legislature to design a scheme that further delimits the property rights of the people concerned, in the interests of the common good.'

Professor John Kelly noted on the same point that 'the matter is still undecided, and promises, when an appropriate case squarely arises, to give us perhaps the legally most revolutionary case of the century.' A former Attorney General, he also made the point that 'the methods adopted by the courts [in interpreting the Constitution] are not all above criticism.' That theme was taken up even more trenchantly by another former Attorney General, European Commissioner Peter Sutherland. He stressed the risk of unnecessary conflicts arising between the various organs of the state, and, pointing to the Crotty case, warned that 'there may be serious differences within the judiciary itself, resulting in majority decisions moving from one position to another.'

A suitably magisterial yet intimate survey of the philosophy, principles and practice of judicial review is presented in the penultimate essay by Mr Justice Brian Walsh, recognised as one of the most innovative and influential interpreters of the Constitution. This view from the bench, coming from such an experienced source, rounds out the discussion of the process which, above all, has been instrumental in converting de Valera's historic text into our living constitution. Certainly, judicial review has been far more central in the process than formal amendments.

But in considering the evolution of the Irish constitutional state over the last half-century, it is wrong to concentrate exclusively on the issue of judicial review. No doubt its vigorous, if late, development is in marked contrast to the complacent inertia or even careless regression so evident in other areas. The readiness to extend constitutional protection to rights not enumerated in the text has not been matched by any similar willingness by the legislature. Indeed, the courts have often been forced to intervene to fill a vacuum left yawning by the failure of those constitutionally responsible for law-making to fulfil their role. Nor have constitutional referenda stimulated the houses of the Oireachtas to provide the consequential framework of laws, regulations and services so evident in such explicit expressions of the popular will. Much of the blame for these omissions can be traced to the failure to correct the imbalance of power between the executive and legislative arms of the state.

In theory, there is a separation of powers and a responsibility on the government to be answerable and responsible to the expressed wishes of elected deputies. In practice, there is a fusion of functions in a cabinet that usually dominates the Dáil, determines its agenda, and effectively dictates its decisions. That concentration of power flies in the face of a basic purpose of modern constitutionalism: to define, divide and confine the power of those in charge of public affairs. It is difficult to see how such a programme could be achieved and maintained without adequate public information on how the state does its business.

But in modern Ireland, precisely as the state has taken on an ever-expanding role there has been no attempt to reform an indefensible situation. In Professor Basil Chubb's sombre words, 'the stark fact is that the people can play only a very limited part in government.' Democratic constitutionalism was intended to provide for a more open and accessible governmental system. Instead we have tolerated a cabinet system cocooned in a shroud of executive secrecy that makes it impenetrable to outsiders.[17]

What little is known has given rise to a popular (and undoubtedly distorted) notion that an entrenched bureaucracy provides what John Healy has termed 'the permanent government of Ireland' and casts the ministers in the role of public, but ultimately powerless, performers in the shadow-theatre of parliamentary politics. A more measured observation of the situation might exchange an analytical metaphor and suggest that the apex of power in the political-administrative arch where policy is made has become a log-jam, exhibiting the characteristic chaos of government overload.[18] One attempted solution to the problems thus identified has been to invoke the 'social partners' to assist in the formulation and implementation of broad public policy—almost as, in critical situations, an army presence is deployed in aid of the civil power. More thought and attention might be devoted to devising institutional reforms that would engage a wider body of citizens more directly in the decisions that affect their lives. Only the Government itself can effectively undertake such reforms, and to do this, as Basil Chubb has noted, 'is to saddle itself with more effective controls and better-informed critics and to commit itself to a more give-and-take, consensus-seeking process of policy-making.'

But constitutional government was not created to provide an easy way of exercising authority. It was not designed for a passive population of deferential subjects. It was never to be accepted as a frozen model, fixed forever in some remote Jeffersonian idyll that could complacently ignore the black slavery that helped to sustain it. On the contrary, it was a revolutionary experiment to provide not merely representation but participation. At the heart of constitutional-democratic government lies an active concept of consensus: that as far as possible, citizens should be consulted and their views accommodated in the formulation and execution of public policy. It carries with it its own built-in dynamic: to engage an ever larger number of people in the process of self-government.

Initially that central thrust of constitutionalism was translated into practical programmes to extend the franchise: reducing property qualifications, removing sex discrimination and lowering age barriers that limited the right to vote. The next stage must be to involve this extended electorate in more regular, frequent, active and effective participation. That task is not simply a matter for the political parties. It will require a major reform of the interlocking executive, legislative, judicial and administrative systems established under the Constitution.

I started by suggesting that the 1930s, when de Valera shaped his constitution, were a dangerous decade for democracy. The 1980s are equally, but differently, dangerous. What happens when the nurturing of consensus is ignored has been, and is, amply and tragically exemplified in Northern

Ireland. Within our own state there is a palpabale drift towards ungovernability. It is demonstrated in the naked pursuit of special interests, the casualness towards the rules of law, the apathetic indifference towards the general good. It leaves no room for complacency.

In a radio broadcast to mark the first anniversary of the Constitution, Éamon de Valera said:

> As faith without good works is dead, so must we expect our Constitution to be if we are content to leave it merely as an idle statement of principles in which we profess belief but have not the will to put into practice . . . To realise that the common good is in the long run the good of each individual requires a high standard of intelligence in a community unless a long tradition has made such wisdom to be the rule amongst us. We are too young as a state for such intuitive wisdom to be the rule amongst us.[19]

Fifty years on, it becomes less convincing to plead the state's immaturity as an excuse for inadequate performance. The task of manufacturing a living constitution is perennial, a process that is never complete. We have scarcely begun that work on de Valera's Constitution. But if it is to be accomplished it will require that contemporary Irish people, and their leaders, should be no less courageous, no less subtle, no less determined than the man who gave us 'our' Constitution.

NOTES

1. The notion of cognitive traps becoming death-traps is derived from a comment about the dangers of nationalism as an ideology by Karl Deutsch, 'Nation and World', in I. de Sola Pool (ed.), *Contemporary Political Science: Towards Empirical Theory*, New York: McGraw-Hill 1967.
2. On problems of effectiveness and legitimacy see Seymour M. Lipset, *Political Man: the Social Bases of Politics*, London: Heinemann 1960, chapter 2. These issues are discussed in an Irish context in Richard Rose, *Governing Without Consensus: an Irish Perspective*, Boston: Beacon Press 1971, chapter 1.
3. On the problems involved in creating a viable Irish state see Brian Farrell, *The Founding of Dáil Éireann: Parliament and Nation Building*, Dublin: Gill and Macmillan 1971.
4. Richard Mulcahy, quoted in Maryann Gialanella Valiulis, '"The Man They Could Never Forgive", the View of the Opposition: Éamon de

Valera and the Civil War', in J. P. O'Carroll and John A. Murphy (eds.), *De Valera and his Times*,Cork: Cork University Press 1983, 99.

5. Speech at Ennis, Co. Clare, 29 June 1935, quoted in Dónal O'Sullivan, *The Irish Free State and its Senate*, London: Faber and Faber 1940, 457.
6. See the section 'Proposed Policy' in the expanded text of the La Scala address, 16 May 1926, in Maurice Moynihan (ed.), *Speeches and Statements by Éamon de Valera, 1917-1973*, Dublin: Gill and Macmillan 1980, 136-7.
7. Conor Maguire to Alfred O'Rahilly, 23 March 1932, in unpublished O'Rahilly correspondence. O'Rahilly appears to have forwarded a copy of his own draft of the Irish Free State Constitution. For further discussion see Brian Farrell, 'The Drafting of the Irish Free State Constitution, III', in *Irish Jurist* (new series), vol. 6 (1971), 1.
8. Dermot Keogh, 'The Constitutional Revolution: an Analysis of the Making of the Constitution', in *Administration*, 35 (1987), 7.
9. For a further discussion of de Valera's leadership style see Brian Farrell, 'De Valera: Unique Dictator or Charismatic Chairman', in O'Carroll and Murphy, *De Valera and his Times*.
10. Initially the head of government under the Dáil Constitution of 1919 was termed 'Príomh-Aire' or 'President of the Ministry'. This was amended to 'President of the Republic' at a private session of the Dáil on 23 August 1921; see the debate in *Private Sessions of Second Dáil*, Dublin: Stationery Office n.d. 54-6.
11. *Dáil Debates*, vol. 67, col. 1008, 25 May 1937.
12. *Report of the Committee on the Constitution*, Dublin: Stationery Office 1967 (Pr. 9817), 5-6.
13. *Dáil Debates*, vol. 67, col. 986, 25 May 1937.
14. *Dáil Debates*, vol. 67, col. 64, 11 May 1937.
15. *Dáil Debates*, vol. 67, col. 241-7, 12 May 1937.
16. For a discussion of this view see Brian Walsh, 'The Constitution and Constitutional Rights', in *Administration*, vol. 35, 98.
17. A recent short summary is Brian Farrell, 'The Irish Cabinet System: More British Than the British Themselves', in J. Blondel and F. Müller-Rommel (eds.), *Cabinets in Western Europe*, London: Macmillan (forthcoming).
18. The political-administrative arch model developed by Peter Self is discussed in Basil Chubb, *Government and Politics of Ireland*, London: Longman 1982, 176-7. On government overload in Ireland see Basil Chubb, 'Prospects for Democratic Politics in Ireland', in H. Penniman and B. Farrell (eds.), *Ireland at the Polls, 1981, 1982, and 1987: a Study of Four General Elections*, Durham (North Carolina): Duke University Press 1987. See also T. J. Barrington, 'Whatever Happened to Irish Government?' in F. Litton (ed.), *Unequal Achievement: the Irish Experience, 1957-1982*, Dublin: Institute of Public Administration 1982, and Brian Farrell, 'Politics and Change', in K. Kennedy (ed.), *Ireland in Transition: Economic and Social Change Since 1960*, Cork: Mercier Press 1986.
19. Moynihan, *Speeches and Statements by Éamon de Valera*, 364.